Message Control

COMMUNICATION, MEDIA, AND POLITICS

Series Editor
Robert E. Denton, Jr., Virginia Tech

This series features a range of work dealing with the role and function of communication in the realm of politics, broadly defined. Including general academic books and texts for use in graduate and advanced undergraduate courses, the series encompasses humanistic, critical, historical, and empirical studies in political communication in the United States. Primary subject areas include campaigns and elections, media, and political institutions. *Communication, Media, and Politics* books will be of interest to students, teachers, and scholars of political communication from the disciplines of communication, rhetorical studies, political science, journalism, and political sociology.

Recent Titles in the Series

Message Control

How News Is Made on the Presidential Campaign Trail

Elizabeth A. Skewes

ROWMAN & LITTLEFIELD PUBLISHERS, INC.
Lanham • Boulder • New York • Toronto • Plymouth, UK

ROWMAN & LITTLEFIELD PUBLISHERS, INC.

Published in the United States of America
by Rowman & Littlefield Publishers, Inc.
A wholly owned subsidiary of The Rowman & Littlefield Publishing Group, Inc.
4501 Forbes Boulevard, Suite 200, Lanham, Maryland 20706
www.rowmanlittlefield.com

Estover Road, Plymouth PL6 7PY, United Kingdom

British Library Cataloguing in Publication Information Available

Library of Congress Cataloging-in-Publication Data
Skewes, Elizabeth A., 1957–
  Message control : how news is made on the presidential campaign trail /
Elizabeth A. Skewes.
    p. cm. — (Communication, media, and politics)
  Includes bibliographical references and index.
  ISBN-13: 978-0-7425-5461-0 (cloth : alk. paper)
  ISBN-10: 0-7425-5461-9 (cloth : alk. paper)
  ISBN-13: 978-0-7425-5462-7 (pbk. : alk. paper)
  ISBN-10: 0-7425-5462-7 (pbk. : alk. paper)
  1. Presidents—United States—Election. 2. Political campaigns—United
States. 3. Communication in politics—United States. 4. Mass media—Political
aspects—United States. I. Title.
JK528.S57 2007
324.7'30973—dc22

                                                                                    2006101222

Printed in the United States of America

♾™ The paper used in this publication meets the minimum requirements of
American National Standard for Information Sciences—Permanence of Paper
for Printed Library Materials, ANSI/NISO Z39.48-1992.

To the reporters

Contents

Acknowledgments

This project took two election cycles and several years to complete, and it would not have been possible without the encouragement, support, and sage advice provided to me by a number of colleagues and friends. I owe many people debts of gratitude; among them are these.

The journalists who took time out of their schedules to talk to me and who made room for me on the press planes—Dan Balz, Richard Benedetto, Geoff Boucher, Edwin Chen, Toby Eckert, Don Frederick, James Gerstenzang, Cragg Hines, David Jackson, Martin Kasindorf, Bill Lambrecht, Jill Lawrence, Charles Lewis, Carl Leubsdorf, David Lightman, Patty Reinert, Ann Scales, and Scott Shepard.

Mike McCurry, Dan Pfeiffer, Patrick Ruffini, and Tracey Schmitt, who graciously gave of their time for interviews during and after the 2000 and 2004 elections.

Dr. Pamela J. Shoemaker, the John Ben Snow professor at Syracuse University, who was my adviser and mentor through my graduate work and through the early stages of this project, and who has been a kind and generous friend ever since.

Dr. Jan Whitt, an associate professor at the University of Colorado at Boulder, who prodded me when I was slow to get the proposal for this book together, who listened when I needed to talk through problems I was having with the manuscript (even though she's a much bigger fan of William Faulkner than she is of presidential politics), and who brought her very keen editor's eye to an early draft of the book.

Dr. Patrick Lee Plaisance, an assistant professor at Colorado State University and a colleague and coconspirator since our days at Syracuse, who helped me negotiate some of the rougher patches of this project very early on, and who, along with his wife, Atisaya Vimuktanon, helped me rework the title over sushi one night.

Brenda Hadenfeldt, Bess Vanrenen, Jehanne Schweitzer, and Melissa Ollila at Rowman & Littlefield Publishing Group, who have been understanding when I've run behind schedule, who have answered my many questions, and who have gently guided me through the process of getting the book published.

Drs. Bob Reimers and Theresa Nicklas, who first got me thinking that an academic career was a possibility and who have encouraged me at every step along the way.

Andy Mazur, who has been a thoughtful and generous friend, even when deadlines kept me from visiting, or sometimes from even returning phone calls.

Dr. Pete and Ellen Gigliotti, and their sons, Nick and Mike—I don't have the words to tell you all how much you mean to me. Thanks for the midnight pickup at Harrisburg's airport, for helping me keep things in perspective, for knowing when to push me, and for your belief in me.

1

Media Coverage of Modern Campaigns

Friday, October 8, started out slowly for the 75 journalists traveling with John Kerry in 2004. While the 15 pool members staying at the Westin Hotel with Kerry and the campaign staff had an 11:45 a.m. call time, the rest of the media, who were lodged at a Radisson nearby, didn't have to be in the lobby until 5:30 p.m. The campaign, which was focused on that night's second debate with George W. Bush, wasn't planning any events, so the traveling press corps had a rare opportunity to catch up on background research, plan ahead for future stories, and perhaps even do a load of laundry. It was the last real break the press corps would have until the Kerry campaign settled in Santa Fe, New Mexico, to spend a day or so getting ready for the final debate.

When the call came at 5:30, the members of the traveling press corps lined up in the hotel lobby for a bus ride to Washington University in St. Louis, where they were lined up once again for a security sweep before heading into the university's field house, which was serving as the press filing center for the night. Inside the filing center were nearly 1,500 credentialed media—reporters, photographers, camera crews, bloggers, and others—who came to St. Louis to cover the story. But they could have saved themselves the trouble and the airfare. Despite the close proximity to the debate stage, the journalists covering the debate in St. Louis never got there. With the exception of a very small pool, the media covering the debates were sequestered in the field house, which was filled with about 50 televisions that provided the debate on a closed-circuit feed from the Commission on Presidential Debates. Since the CPD was following its own rules on the debate, there were no split-screen shots in the feed, so unlike those watching at home, the journalists didn't have the opportunity to see the reactions of Bush to Kerry's statements or the reactions of Kerry to the statements made by Bush.

What they did get in the course of the 90-minute debate was a series of 17 press releases—12 from the Bush campaign and five from the Kerry campaign. The first, at 8:25 p.m., was a "breaking debate fact" from the Bush campaign responding to Kerry's answer on his first question in the town hall–style debate. The second, seven minutes later, also came from the Bush camp and was a response to Kerry's second answer. The Kerry campaign fired its first paper volley at 8:36, titled "Bush vs. Reality," and kept the releases coming for the next half hour. Bush's staff kept the copy machines going until nearly 9:20 p.m., about 10 minutes before the end of the debate. That's also when campaign managers and candidate spokespeople started to show up in "spin alley," each flanked by a young volunteer holding a sign with the spinner's name—McAuliffe, Hughes, Cahill, Devenish. And it's when the traveling press started packing up to head out to the press buses that would take them to the 10 p.m. rally that Kerry was holding at the St. Louis Convention Center. At the rally, photographers jockeyed for a few good shots, and a handful of reporters took notes. Many pulled out their BlackBerries or laptops looking for the early poll results naming a debate winner. An hour or so later, the journalists were back on the press buses, heading back to the hotel for some sleep before a 6 a.m. baggage call and a 7:15 departure for a flight to Ohio.

The debate stops typically provide a break in an otherwise grueling schedule for the candidates and the press corps. In fact, in the last days before Election Day 2000, the reporters traveling with Al Gore were sometimes flying overnight from the West Coast to events back east, starting another day of work without a shower or the chance to change their clothes. But the hallmarks of campaign travel—waking up in one city and spending the day at speeches or rallies or other events in four or five different places, having to check a press schedule just to know where you are at any given moment, hearing the same speech for days or weeks to the point that you can lip sync it with the candidate, and struggling to find something new to write about despite the lack of news coming from the candidate—are present no matter whether the day is long or short and whether it's January in New Hampshire or October in Florida.

So why did nearly 500 reporters, photographers, and camera crews crowd into the basement of WMUR studios in Manchester, New Hampshire, on January 26, 2000, to watch on a bank of televisions the debates going on upstairs between the Republican and Democratic candidates for president? And why did they spend the next week trailing the candidates around the state, site of the nation's first primary election?

Why did nearly 15,000 media people—reporters, photographers, technicians, and support staff—show up at the national political conventions, which most called "merely coronations" for the two major party candidates?

And at up to $1,500 a day, why did close to 200 journalists travel cross-country with George W. Bush, Dick Cheney, Al Gore, Joe Lieberman, John Kerry, and John Edwards as they stumped for the White House after the conventions and through Election Day in both 2000 and 2004?

In part, the answer can be found in the news values that guide the industry, particularly the values of prominence—which holds that the actions of powerful people are important because powerful people can affect the public—impact, and timeliness (Shoemaker & Reese, 1996). In part, it is because the news net, as defined by Gaye Tuchman (1978), traditionally includes government institutions—especially the presidency—which reinforces the idea that anything that happens involving the presidency, including the quest for it, is inherently newsworthy. In part, the newsworthiness of the campaign is established by the very presence of reporters from the wire services, the major television networks, and the top newspapers in the nation, who frequently set the agenda for each other, other media organizations, and the public (Reese & Danielian, 1991; Shoemaker & Reese, 1996). And in part, at least in the eyes of some of those who cover elections, they go out on the trail with the candidates because despite the lack of breaking news, the campaign itself is a distinctly American narrative. As Dan Balz, a reporter for the *Washington Post*, said,

> I still think that campaigns count. I think that they make a difference. I think that even those that are not great campaigns tell us something about who we are as a people and where the country is. I think campaigns are a wonderful snapshot as the country evolves and changes.—Dan Balz, July 1999

This book looks closely at how reporters construct that narrative—at the processes and practices of journalism, as well as the beliefs of the people who do the job—to better understand the nature of presidential campaign coverage. It is a study of the reporters who travel with the candidates and the effects of that travel on their relationships with the candidates, their editors, and their colleagues on the press planes. Ultimately, this book is an attempt to better understand the nature and content of contemporary campaign coverage and the forces that shape it.

AN OVERVIEW OF CAMPAIGN 2000

In the end, the election came down to Florida. With its 25 electoral votes and a margin of victory that was less than one half of one percent, the Sunshine State became the key to George W. Bush's eventual victory and the focus of an electoral contest that was finally decided by the U.S.

Supreme Court 36 days after voters went to the polls. And while those 36 days of court battles and ballot counts will be what most people remember about the 2000 presidential election, the campaigning that went on before November 7, 2000, had its own highlights and low points.

Long before the first caucus in Iowa on January 24, 2000, or the first primary in New Hampshire on February 1, 2000, the election contest was well under way. Both of the eventual major party nominees—Republican George W. Bush and Democrat Al Gore—had launched their nomination bids in June 1999. Going into the early primary battles, Bush was the Republican front-runner and was well ahead of any of his challengers in fundraising, with $67 million in contributions compared to just under $14 million for his closest rival, John McCain. Gore was in a tighter fiscal contest with his closest challenger, Bill Bradley. Both Democrats had raised more than $27 million, with Gore roughly $600,000 ahead of Bradley. And both Bush and Gore were well ahead in Gallup polls taken in early January—Bush led McCain by a 45-point margin, and Gore had a 29-point lead over Bradley (Newport, 2000).

The early primaries provided a few surprises. McCain took the New Hampshire primary and also defeated Bush in the Michigan and Arizona primaries on February 22, 2000. And while Bradley didn't beat Gore in any of those early primaries, he did collect enough votes to stay in the race. But the March 7 "Super Tuesday" primaries changed all of that. Gore and Bush both pulled well ahead of their challengers in the primary races in delegate-rich states including California, Georgia, New York, and Ohio. Two days later, on March 9, Bradley withdrew from the presidential race, and McCain suspended his campaign, never to reenter the race. And even though the primary contests would continue through early June, within a few weeks after March 7, Bush and Gore had amassed enough delegates to win their parties' nominations.

While the primary season didn't result in any major political upsets, with the possible exception of McCain's New Hampshire victory, it was significant in the contest between Bush and Gore. Bush went into the primary season with a 15 percentage point lead over Gore in head-to-head polls conducted by the Gallup Organization (Moore, 2000). Coming out of the primary season, however, Bush's lead had narrowed to roughly 6 percent over Gore. And although Bush widened his lead over Gore following the Republican National Convention—held from July 31 to August 3, 2000, in Philadelphia—by the end of the Democratic National Convention in Los Angeles, held from August 14 to 17, 2000, the race was dead even, and Gore managed to pull ahead slightly through August and early September (Moore, 2000).

While the summer Olympics pulled public attention from the presidential campaign in late September, the election took center stage once again in early to mid-October with a series of three presidential debates: October 3 in Boston, Massachusetts; October 11 in Winston-Salem, North Carolina; and October 17 in St. Louis, Missouri. "While Gore was perceived as the 'winner' in the first and third debates by those who viewed the debates live, the net effect of all three debates was that Bush moved into the lead for the first time since the [Republican] convention" (Moore, 2000, p. 2).

Going into the final weeks of the campaign, the election was too close to call, although most journalists on the press planes saw it "trending" toward Bush. And in the final days of the campaign, the reporters traveling with Republican vice presidential nominee Dick Cheney were speculating that, for the first time since 1888, the popular vote would go to one candidate while the electoral vote, and the presidency, went to the other. They were right . . . and wrong. The reporters on Cheney's press plane thought that Gore would win the presidency while Bush would win the popular vote. In the end, it was Gore who took the popular vote, beating Bush by 540,000 votes—about one half of one percent of the total votes cast in an election that, despite the closeness in the polls, saw a turnout rate of only 55.6 percent among eligible voters (Althaus, 2005). But it was Bush who took the White House after a too-close-to-call battle in Florida on election night and a 36-day fight over whether and how to recount Florida's ballots. The postelection contest, which wound its way through the Florida and federal courts, ultimately was decided by the United States Supreme Court in a 5–4 vote on Tuesday, December 12. Gore conceded the election to Bush at 9 p.m. the next day.

A BRIEF SUMMARY OF CAMPAIGN 2004

The 2004 election cycle got its official start when, on May 31, 2002, Howard Dean became the first Democrat to form a presidential exploratory committee. During the preprimary and primary seasons, the main story was the race in the Democratic Party. The Republicans, of course, had their presumptive nominee in incumbent President George W. Bush—although 30 other people also filed, including Millie Howard, a 66-year-old medical receptionist from Ohio running in her fourth presidential race, and Tom Laughlin, an actor from California best known for the "Billy Jack" series of movies he produced in the 1970s. But not one of the candidates who filed against Bush was a big name in the Republican Party, and the only story coming out of the Republican campaign that seemed to matter was the considerable size of Bush's campaign war chest—which stood at nearly $132 million before the primary season began (Edsall & Cohen, 2004).

On the Democratic side, however, there was a contest. According to Politics1.com, 73 people, including John Kerry, either filed to run for the presidency or, in the case of candidates who got a lot of buzz but did not file (like Hillary Clinton), were "hopefuls" or "possibles." Of these, there were 10 who generated any significant news coverage: John Kerry, the eventual nominee; John Edwards, who eventually became Kerry's running mate; former Illinois Sen. Carol Moseley Braun; Ret. Gen. Wesley Clark; former Vermont Gov. Howard Dean; Florida Sen. Bob Graham; Missouri Rep. Richard Gephardt; Ohio Rep. Dennis Kucinich, who stayed in the race even after Kerry locked up the nomination; Connecticut Sen. Joseph Lieberman, who was Al Gore's running mate in 2000; and Rev. Al Sharpton. It was Dean, however, who garnered a lot of early media coverage, largely because he used the Internet to generate a lot of grassroots support and money. In fact, by the time Dean suspended his candidacy—after a third-place finish behind Kerry and Edwards in Iowa on January 19, a second-place finish behind Kerry in New Hampshire on January 27, and a third-place finish behind Kerry and Edwards in Wisconsin, which he said was his "do-or-die" state, on February 17—he had raised a record high $50.3 million, and much of that from donations he received via the Internet.

Still, it was Kerry who captured the primary votes, starting with his win over Dean and Edwards in Iowa, and he racked up a steady string of victories in late January and throughout February in New Hampshire, Arizona, Delaware, Missouri, New Mexico, North Dakota, Michigan, Washington, Nevada, Wisconsin, Hawaii, Idaho, and Utah. In the process, Kerry collected 518 of the 2,162 delegates he'd need to secure the Democratic nomination. Then came March 2, or Super Tuesday, where primaries or caucuses were held in 10 states, including delegate-rich California and New York. Kerry won victories in every state except Vermont, which was won by Dean, and added another 785 delegates to his count, bringing his total to 1,303. After Super Tuesday, John Edwards bowed out of the race, leaving Kerry as the presumptive nominee—something that the Democratic National Committee acknowledged in mid-March when it touted Kerry as its candidate.

Bush, who filed his papers to run for reelection on May 16, 2003, had been running ahead of Kerry by one to two percentage points in the polls since the start of the primary season. When Kerry essentially secured the nomination, he got a bounce and started running ahead of Bush by about the same margins, according to weekly poll results posted by Rasmussen Reports (2004). And while Kerry and Bush swapped the lead throughout the race, the poll numbers remained tight leading up to Election Day on November 2, 2004, with a *Washington Post* poll showing Bush up by just one point—49 percent to Kerry's 48 percent—on the day before the election (Charting the Campaign, 2004).

The campaign itself was marked more by the influence of outside 527 groups—named for the section of the tax code that made them possible—

than by the tactics of the campaigns themselves. On the Democratic side, MoveOn.org helped create and cultivate the Dean candidacy, then shifted its resources to Kerry when Dean suspended his campaign. On the Republican side, Swift Boat Veterans for Truth, which protested ads produced by the Kerry campaign in early June, came out with a controversial—and highly covered—set of ads questioning Kerry's service in Vietnam in early August. The ad campaign, which launched on August 4, went unanswered by Kerry until August 19, when he finally gave a speech denouncing the ads. The fact that the media repeatedly played the Swift Boat ads and wrote about them gave the relatively small ad buy a lot more reach. The media—CBS's *60 Minutes* in particular—also became a story in the campaign when Dan Rather went on air with a story, complete with copies of documents, charging that Bush had shirked his duty in the National Guard. Within hours, bloggers were challenging the authenticity of the documents and, after initially defending the story, within two weeks, CBS said it could no longer stand by the veracity of the memos it had received.

The fall presidential debates—on September 30 at the University of Miami, on October 8 at Washington University in St. Louis, and on October 13 at Arizona State University—were considered wins for Kerry, particularly the first debate. But polls showed little movement in the race for the White House. And in the end, it was Ohio in the spotlight, where long lines at the election precincts led to allegations of vote fraud and a slow count. It was another race that was too close to call, until Kerry, in the early hours of Wednesday, November 3, realized that even with the provisional and absentee ballots that were yet to be counted, he would lose the state to Bush. He conceded the election in a speech later that morning. The race did generate greater voter interest, with 59.6 percent of eligible voters turning out, but turnout was spurred in some states by the presence of referenda on gay marriage. In fact, in those states—Arkansas, Georgia, Kentucky, Michigan, Mississippi, Montana, North Dakota, Ohio, Oklahoma, Oregon, and Utah—about 2.4 percent of the increase in voter turnout could be attributed to the gay marriage issue rather than the presidential race (Althaus, 2005).

HOW CONTEMPORARY CAMPAIGN COVERAGE DEVELOPED

Campaign coverage as we know it today is a relatively modern invention. As recently as 1968, when Richard Nixon defeated Hubert Humphrey, media coverage of the campaigns tended to simply follow the candidates and what they were saying. But the success of Theodore White's *The Making of the President* books on the campaigns and Joe McGinniss's *The $elling of the President* about Nixon's 1968 campaign changed not only the style of campaign reporting, but the tone of it as well.

> Most . . . adopted White's magic formula: present politics in novelistic terms, as the struggle of great personalities, with generous helpings of colorful detail to sugar the political analysis. . . . By 1972 most editors were sending off their men with rabid pep talks about the importance of sniffing out inside dope, getting background into the story, finding out what makes the campaign tick, and generally going beyond the old style of campaign reporting. (Crouse, 1973, pp. 34–35)

At the same time that the media were turning up the heat on the candidates, and looking at the things they weren't saying as much as at what they were saying, the role of the media in the political process was changing as well.

Although television was in use during the 1952 and 1956 election years, it wasn't until the 1960 debate between John Kennedy and Richard Nixon that candidates and campaign managers had a real inkling about the power the medium could wield. It has been argued that Kennedy's confidence on air during those debates—especially contrasted with Nixon's image as someone who was dark, nervous, and uncertain—helped swing a close election to Kennedy (Witcover, 1977). However, whether the debates actually gave Kennedy the victory in 1960 is less important than the perception by those who ran the campaigns that the media—and television in particular—were essential to candidate image building. And as the role of the political parties in the nominating process has waned, protecting the candidate's image and campaigning through the media have become central features of presidential politics.

While the 1960 campaign may have provided candidates and campaign managers with a notion about the potential power of the press, it was a combination of reforms within the political parties—particularly the Democratic Party reforms that were in place for the 1972 election—and the increasing use of the primary election by individual states as a means of selecting delegates that gave the media the powerful role that they now have in the nomination process (Witcover, 1977; Blendon, et al., 1998; Busch, 2000; Hagen & Mayer, 2000). Most of these reform efforts, which began with the Progressive Era in the late 1800s and early 1900s, were aimed at making the nomination process more democratic (Sundquist, 1983). Florida, perhaps the most critical state in the 2000 presidential contest, figured heavily in the weakening of the party system by enacting legislation in 1901 that allowed national convention delegates to be selected by direct election (Witcover, 1977). The move for direct election of delegates grew through the Progressive Era, with 26 states allowing selection by primaries in 1916. The popularity of primary elections among legislators waned somewhat in the 1930s and early 1940s. However, the primary election again became popular with presidential candidates in the late 1940s when they were used by Republican Thomas Dewey in 1944 and 1948, and then by Democrat Estes Kefauver in 1952, to prove their viability as contenders for their respective party nominations (Witcover, 1977).

Though the candidates were seeking momentum from the primary elections, most states were still using other methods to select their convention delegates, and party bosses still had the power to broker a nomination. That was the case in 1968 when Bobby Kennedy didn't announce his candidacy until March of the election year, and Hubert Humphrey, who became the Democratic Party nominee after Kennedy's assassination that June, hadn't run in a single presidential primary. Humphrey's selection was the result of deals made by party bosses, who screened the candidates and found the one they thought best represented the party's ideology and who they believed had the best chance of winning a general election (Fiedler, 1992). But Humphrey's failure to win the White House and the perception among Democrats that the closed-door selection process was conducted by people out of step with the general public led to calls for reform. And four years later, when former U.S. Sen. George McGovern of South Dakota became the Democratic nominee, the party reform guidelines hammered out by the McGovern-Fraser Commission between 1968 and 1972 had so reduced the influence of party bosses that McGovern came to the convention with only a string of primary victories. Those victories, however, gave him enough momentum to win the nomination, despite the backroom objections of longtime party leaders.

Among the guidelines adopted by the McGovern-Fraser Commission were rules that forbade proxy voting by delegates and the ex officio designation of delegates, that required public notice of all meetings regarding delegate selection, and that mandated that the delegate selection be conducted within the calendar year preceding the election. The new rules proved to be both complicated and difficult to put in place, and "many states decided that the easiest way to comply—and thus avoid a challenge to their delegations at the next convention—was to hold a primary" (Hagen & Mayer, 2000, pp. 10–11). In other states, party officials moved to a primary election because they wanted to separate the candidate selection process from other party business so that issue activists who might take a keen interest in the presidential nominee would be less likely to show up for party caucuses and meetings (Hagen & Mayer, 2000). Although it took two election cycles for the full impact of the commission's work to be felt, the early signs of the change were evident in 1972 when the number of states holding Democratic primaries jumped from 17 to 23, and the number of those holding Republican primaries went from 16 to 22 (Hagen &

Mayer, 2000). By 1980 a majority of states were holding Democratic and Republican primaries, and in the 2000 election season, 40 states held Democratic primaries and 43 held Republican primaries. And over time, the selection rules in both parties have been modified to require delegates to be committed—at least on the first ballot—to nominate the candidate they were elected to represent at the convention (Eskenazi, 2000).

More recently, the role of the parties has been weakened—and that of the media strengthened—by the front loading of the primary calendar. Each state, in an effort to draw the attention of the candidates and the press, has been gradually moving forward the date of its primary in an attempt to have an impact on the nomination process. In the early 1960s, even as more states began looking at primary elections as a method of delegate selection, the primary calendar itself was leisurely. Most primaries—and especially those in large states like California—were held in late spring or early summer. The slower pace gave candidates time to build a base of support, both in voters and in contributions, and gave the parties several viable candidates to review throughout the spring and going into the conventions. In the 2000 election, however, more than 70 percent of the delegate count in both parties had been decided by March 14—only seven weeks after the first primary in New Hampshire on February 1 (Eskenazi, 2000). Candidates who don't do well in the Iowa caucuses or in one of the first few primaries generally don't survive even to the Super Tuesday primaries. "Not only are they written off by the press, which deprives them of extensive 'free media' coverage; they are also unable to raise enough money to conduct the kind of campaign that might reverse their downward momentum" (Hagen & Mayer, 2000, p. 40).

And the front loading of the primary schedule puts more emphasis on the delegate selection in Iowa and New Hampshire—two states that are not largely representative of the United States as a whole—and results in media attention for the Iowa caucuses and the New Hampshire primary that far outstrips the importance of either state in the general election. While Iowa does play a role in narrowing the field of candidates, a win in the Iowa caucuses has not been a sure path to the party nomination, nor has finishing third been a real blow. In the 1988 primary season, for instance, George Bush lost to both Bob Dole and Pat Robertson in the Iowa caucuses but went on to win the New Hampshire primary a week later and ultimately the White House. Four years later, Bill Clinton trailed in the Iowa caucuses behind Tom Harkin, Paul Tsongas, and uncommitted delegates. Clinton also went on to win his party's nomination and the presidency.

While New Hampshire has a better track record than Iowa at choosing party nominees, it does no better than several other states. Of the 14 Republican primaries held since 1952, New Hampshire has picked the eventual nominee 11 times, and out of the Democratic primaries it has selected the eventual nominee eight times. States such as California, Illinois, Nebraska, Oregon, Pennsylvania, and Wisconsin have similar records (Buell, 2000). And although no candidate who has finished third in New Hampshire has gone on to win his party's presidential nomination, success in New Hampshire is important more for the momentum it generates than for the delegates it provides. In fact, the New Hampshire primary generally gets about 10 times the amount of coverage of any subsequent primary election, and in 1996, the network news had 6.31 stories for each delegate selected in New Hampshire compared to 2.96 for each Iowa delegate and less than one story for each delegate selected from any other state in the nation (Buell, 2000).

A MEDIATED VIEW OF POLITICS

For the vast majority of citizens, their knowledge about the candidates and the campaigns—much like what they know about most of the world outside of their immediate environments—relies on the stories they read or see in the mass media. Walter Lippmann, a columnist for the *Herald Tribune*, noted this in his 1922 book, *Public Opinion*. Lippmann said the mass media helped people make sense of the world around them, which was otherwise too complex (Lippmann, 1997). Lippmann wrote that the media help shape the "pictures in our heads," and his perspective spurred some contemporary media studies that examine how the media shape the public's attention and knowledge. Since Lippmann's time, and especially with the decline of political parties in voters' lives during the 1970s and 1980s, "the electorate's information about political issues has become more dependent on what the news media cover during campaigns and the way the issues are covered" (Blendon et al., 1998, p. 121; see also Davis, 1992, and Patterson, 1994).

Today's political campaigns, and particularly the 2000 and 2004 presidential campaigns, have to operate in an increasingly complex media environment (Norris et al., 1999). Communications staff members working on political campaigns have to attend to the daily news needs of television, radio, and newspaper reporters. But the media picture is broader than that since it now also includes nontraditional media such as *The Daily Show* and talk shows on radio and television. In addition, the growing contingent of reporters working for Internet sites or bloggers who may not be affiliated with a major news organization are becoming a significant force in political news. In the 2004 campaign, for instance, it was bloggers who challenged the veracity of memos used in Dan Rather's report on *60 Minutes* about George W. Bush's National

Guard service, which led to CBS eventually saying it could not authenticate the memos in question. And while that story might have eventually found its way into the mainstream media without bloggers leading the way, Toby Eckert, Washington news editor for Copley News Service who covered the 2000 and 2004 campaigns, said the story moved faster because of the blogs.

> You have to be mindful of the competition, which nowadays includes blogs, but we also have to fulfill our mission and our role, which is to present the most balanced and in-depth view of something that we can. We can't get wrapped up in who's first. That sort of thing matters to reporters and editors, but I'm not sure it matters to readers. Blogs are popular, but the number of people who actually read blogs is much smaller than the number who read newspapers or tune in to television.—Toby Eckert, July 2006

The impact of blogs and the Internet is limited on the campaign trail itself. While the campaign staffs and traveling journalists may peruse what's being written on the Web, they are more likely to take their immediate cues from the campaign strategists and other reporters covering the campaign with them. While the number of journalists who make up the traveling press corps is relatively small—numbering up to 200 or so for the major party presidential and vice presidential candidates by the week before Election Day—the numbers at any one event can swell. Both the Republican and Democratic parties issued nearly 15,000 press credentials for their national conventions, and roughly 1,500 journalists were credentialed for the fall presidential debates.

The result was a plethora of campaign news, including some Internet websites, such as Project Vote Smart and Politics1.com, that were designed to provide wall-to-wall campaign coverage. And at every event, the candidates played to the media's need for something to cover, although usually it was little more than a photo opportunity. For example, on September 15, 2000, after landing at the regional airport in Clearwater, Florida, Al Gore and his wife, Tipper, stepped onto the "air stairs" that had been wheeled up to Air Force II, stood arm in arm, and waved to those gathered at the bottom of the stairs. But the "throng" at the bottom wasn't filled with supporters. Instead, it was a dozen or so camera people, most of them from the local media, and roughly the same number of Secret Service agents assigned to protect the vice president. The event was played out solely for the benefit of local press.

In fact, once the candidates get past the New Hampshire primary, where voters expect—and get—town hall meetings and face time with the candidates, the campaign becomes increasingly media focused. And by the time of the Super Tuesday primary in early March, the campaigns in 2000 and

2004 had shifted into little more than a series of events aimed at getting the news coverage that would put the candidate's name in front of the electorate. The courting of the press in 2000 went as far as George Bush's playing host to the reporters on his press plane by cruising through the cabin with beverages, joking with reporters, and, on occasion, even hugging them (Mnookin, 2000a). In 2004, pool reports from the Kerry press corps note that the candidate made several trips to the press section of the plane throughout the campaign season to celebrate a birthday or two, but not to talk about issues. Candidates play to the press because they understand the role that the media play in their success or failure.

> The media's role today in helping to establish the election agenda is different from what it was in the past. Once upon a time, the press occasionally played an important part in the nomination of presidential candidates. Now its function is always a key one. The news media do not entirely determine who will win the nomination, but no candidate can succeed without the press. The road to the nomination now runs through the newsrooms. (Patterson, 1994, p. 33)

But the media's coverage of the candidates, despite the candidates' attempts to court the press, is not always favorable. In fact, Patterson (1994; see also Patterson & McClure, 1976; Sabato, 1991; Dautrich & Hartley, 1999; McChesney, 2004) says that coverage focuses on public opinion polls, campaign strategies, and stories about the candidates that put too much emphasis on the negative aspects of their characters. An evaluation of coverage of the 1992 campaign, for instance, found only 40 percent of the references to either Bill Clinton or George Bush were positive, whereas 75 percent of the references to either John Kennedy or Richard Nixon during the 1960 campaign were positive (Patterson, 1994). And campaign advertising—a primary source of information for many voters—also is increasingly negative in tone (Ansolabehere & Iyengar, 1995).

A study of preprimary coverage of the 2000 election conducted by the Project for Excellence in Journalism (2000) found little evidence of "negative" coverage in terms of bias toward a candidate—either Republican or Democratic—but found that reporters generally focused their stories on issues that impacted the candidates or political parties rather than voters. Roughly 80 percent of the early campaign coverage discussed tactics of the candidates and parties, fundraising by the campaigns, and internal organizational problems. Only 13 percent of the stories were about the candidates' ideas, their honesty, or what they had done for their constituents in previous elected offices that they had held.

In terms of story topics, more than half of those written or aired prior to the Iowa caucuses and the New Hampshire primary were about political polls, campaign tactics, candidate advertisements, and fundraising

(Project for Excellence in Journalism, 2000). The Project study—a content analysis of 430 stories published in five major newspapers or aired on nine television news programs on five networks—concluded that reporting in the early part of the election season was dominated by stories about the tactics and strategies of the campaigns. And of the stories analyzed, only 7 percent examined the candidates' ideas or core values. Moreover, the Project study says that campaign coverage, as Patterson (1994) noted of the coverage in earlier campaigns,

> paints a picture not of a contest of ideas between men but of a massive chess game of calculation and calibration in which little seems spontaneous or genuine. And occasionally, the camera turns to the audience for a shot of its reaction. . . . What's more, the focus on so-called inside baseball is hardly new, and the political press has vowed in years past to seek better ways of connecting with voters, and making the campaign more relevant. Apparently, even in the early days of the campaign, the press has had difficulty keeping sight of that goal. (Project for Excellence in Journalism, 2000, p. 4)

Journalists themselves recognize the problems with news coverage of political campaigns. Responding to a 2004 survey by the Committee of Concerned Journalists, 42 percent of the reporters polled gave the season's campaign journalism a grade of C, while 3 percent gave it an A, 27 percent a B, 22 percent a D, and 5 percent an F (Committee of Concerned Journalists, 2004). The journalists who responded to the study said that news coverage was too superficial, and "by large majorities they feel the news media has become sidetracked by trivial issues, has been too reactive and has focused too much on the inside baseball that doesn't really matter to voters," the study's authors wrote (Committee of Concerned Journalists, 2004, p. 1).

THE EFFECTS OF A MEDIATED POLITICAL WORLD

The content and tone of political coverage in the mass media are important because, as many scholars argue, they are contributing to an increasingly alienated electorate and turnout that hovers at only half of the eligible voters. This is true for England, where turnout dropped by 12 percent in that nation's most recent election, from 71 percent in 1997 to 59 percent in 2001 (Voters, 2001). With an electoral system that has increasingly adapted the campaign styles and tactics that are used in elections in the United States, British voters are, in the words of Home Secretary David Blunkett, "switched off [to] politics, they are disenchanted with representative democracy, young people in particular don't see it as being relevant to their lives" (Voters, 2001). In fact, turnout in national elections is falling throughout Western Europe (King, 2001a), and the dramatic drop in the United Kingdom in 2001 is due largely to a perception by the voters—fed in part by the media's coverage of the election—that the candidates "are dealing in slogans and soundbites" (King, 2001b).

Voter turnout in elections in the United States did rise slightly for the 2000 presidential election, but even then it was only 55.6 percent among eligible voters (Althaus, 2005). In an election when the contest between George W. Bush and Al Gore was too close for the pollsters to call—both before and after the ballots were cast—the turnout was up only three points from the 1996 election when Bill Clinton easily defeated Bob Dole. Since 1960, when television started to play a major role in campaigns by bringing the debate between Kennedy and Nixon into our homes, voter turnout in presidential elections steadily declined from close to 70 percent of eligible voters down to just over 50 percent in the 1996 contest (Mc-Chesney, 2004). Several studies have shown that a person's attitudes about politics (Robinson, 1974; Becker & Whitney, 1980), as well as his or her political knowledge (Clarke & Fredin, 1978; Becker & Whitney, 1980), are decreased by the person's increased reliance on the mass media—especially television. One reason for this is that television is a passive medium that has caused political activism to give way to merely watching the political scene (Volgy & Schwarz, 1984; Patterson, 1993; Patterson, 1994; Comstock & Scharrer, 1999).

While most people don't rely on any single medium for political information (Blendon et al., 1998), researchers studying the differences between newspaper and television users found that in the 1992 election, people who used newspapers more than television for campaign information were more likely to know about the differences between political parties on the campaign issues; television users, however, could still distinguish between the candidates on issues (Chaffee, Zhao, & Leshner, 1994). Using data from the 1992 National Election Study, Simon (1996) found that newspaper use, particularly, was positively correlated with voter turnout, although the relationship was a low-level one. He concluded that newspaper use is more likely to be related to thinking about the campaign than other media, to increased political knowledge, and to the ability to discriminate between issues (Simon, 1996). However, Simon notes,

> The findings of this study come against a backdrop of nearly 200 daily newspapers ceasing publication since 1972, a steady decrease in readership as a percentage of population, and a 30-year trend toward increased reliance on television as a primary news source. (1996, p. 32)

Although those who do pay attention to the news are more likely to actively process the political information that they see or read (Graber, 1988), most people have little interest in politics and pay attention—when they do pay attention—out of a sense of civic duty. Graber (1988) says that the media are important in information processing, but that the media's focus on stories that voters do not find useful leads to a ritualistic and passive use of the media, especially television, for political news (Comstock & Scharrer, 1999). People may be exposed to a lot of political news in an election year, but their lack of attention to it results in little information processing. Ansolabehere and Iyengar (1995, p. 102) report that for most people watching television "takes less concentration than eating a bowl of cereal," and Soley (1992, p. 109) says that the 30-second ads that have marked most recent political campaigns have "denuded U.S. politics of grassroots citizen involvement." Relying on the media for political information—and the vast majority of Americans get their information about the national elections solely from the mass media—also is related to voter disgust and a lack of participation in elections (Cappella & Jamieson, 1997).

Additional research shows that voters who rely on television for political information, especially compared to those who seek out information in newspapers, are more likely to make decisions based on image and are more susceptible to alienation from the political process (McLeod, Glynn, & McDonald, 1983).

> The voters begin each campaign without a firm opinion about the candidates, but after months of news that tells them over and over again that their choices are no good, they believe it. . . . News coverage has become a barrier between the candidates and the voters rather than a bridge connecting them. (Patterson, 1994, pp. 24–25)

In the 2000 election season, increasing numbers of Americans began avoiding news coverage of the campaign. A Pew Research Center survey of citizens conducted in the early fall of 1999 showed that while 53 percent of Americans reported paying at least "some attention" to the campaign in July 1999, the number had dropped to 46 percent by September (Kohut, 1999). The same study showed that despite the fact that the campaign had been in the news for nearly a year, and despite the fact that the leading Democratic candidate was the sitting vice president and the leading Republican candidate was a governor and the son of a recent former president, about half of those surveyed couldn't name a Democrat running for the presidency and 37 percent couldn't name a Republican (Kohut, 1999). And voters uniformly believed that the press was too intrusive and played too great a role in the presidential nomination process. They also told the Pew researchers that news editors paid more attention to the desires and opinions of pundits and political insiders than they did to readers or viewers (Kohut, 1999).

In the face of these studies and others showing that the public is getting turned off to politics partly because of the media's coverage of campaigns, and in light of public opinion polls showing that Americans want more discussion of political issues and less of political personalities and peccadilloes, the unanswered question is, why does political coverage look the way it does? That is, what are the factors that shape the content of political campaign coverage? And why does the content, which is concentrated on poll numbers and candidates' strategies for winning (Patterson, 1993), provide so little of the information that voters say they want?

Perhaps it is because of an adversarial—or at least skeptical—outlook that many reporters bring to the job. Candidates struggle to stay "on message," talking on any given day about the issue that they think will most resonate with voters. But the national political reporters try to pull them off message, asking questions about topics the candidates are trying to avoid or that focus on campaign strategies. This gap between what the candidates want to say and what the reporters want to write about has led to reduced access to the candidates, even when they're traveling on the same plane. In four days of traveling with the Dick Cheney campaign, the vice presidential candidate held press conferences for the local media at nearly every campaign stop. The national press corps did get invited to one of the local availabilities, but had to wait to ask questions until the regional reporters were done. And when they finally did get to ask a few questions, which were noticeably tougher in tone, the press conference was quickly shut down.

Cheney also talked to the national press once in an off-the-record chat on the campaign plane, but the conversation came just before a Fox News reporter broke the story about George W. Bush's driving under the influence arrest in Maine in the 1970s. When reporters on the Cheney plane then wanted a quote from Cheney about the DUI arrest, Cheney wasn't available. The reporters grumbled that Cheney was hiding in the front of the plane to avoid the press, and another brick was added to a wall that keeps journalists and candidates at a distance from each other.

2

The Big Picture

In an October 16, 2004, e-mail pool report to the rest of the traveling press corps, David Halbfinger from the *New York Times* and Jake Schlesinger from the *Wall Street Journal* reported on some interviews that Democratic nominee John Kerry was doing at a pumpkin patch in Xenia, Ohio, via satellite for local media outlets in Cincinnati, Ohio; Pittsburgh, Pennsylvania; Milwaukee, Wisconsin; and Albuquerque, New Mexico. Before they summarized the interviews, though, they led—as any good journalist would—with the most important element: "NO NEWS. no color."

The pool report then briefly describes the scene:

> weird gimmick from one station that presents kerry with voters' questions then asks him to respond to the voter by name, while looking at the reporter, not at the camera. "so I have to call you Mary?" JK said to the male TV reporter, who concurred. . . . entirely standard fare. i have tape if you are suicidal. sorry so messy, no time.

The following day, *Newsday*'s Tom Frank started his pool report with the same declaration: "No news." He then described Kerry's visit to a local deli in Columbus, Ohio.

> Owner Diane Warren said she learned about the visit 20 minutes earlier when her daughter Rachel, who was working at the deli, called her on her cell phone while she was at the grocery store to say JK advance staff had just come in to set up a visit. She seems a little overwhelmed. She wore an "Ohio for Kerry" button.
>
> JK entered with Peggy Kerry, who snapped photos on a disposable camera whose exterior looked like the stars and stripes.

JK greeted workers and patrons, shaking hands, saying "Thank you for
coming here. . . . How you all doing? . . . Thank you so much."

The deli has a seating area with small coffee tables on one side, a market
area on the other that sells gourmet food, homemade bread, etc., and a long
refrigerated display case of salads and pastas. JK went to the display, ordered
cole slaw, potato salad, Szechuan noodles and an egg salad sandwich on
whole wheat with lettuce, tomatoes and Swiss cheese (cq). He ordered from
Ashley Sullivan, who is 20. (Later, after touring the deli, he added four
brownies with no nuts.)

Total bill: $29.70. Warren offered to pay. JK refused and stuffed a $10 bill
for a tip in the plastic container on the refrigerated counter. Ashley said it
wasn't the biggest tip she had gotten and that it's shared with the staff.

Frank's pool report describes Kerry's tour of the food prep kitchen and
some interactions with other patrons in the deli, and a two-minute stop at
the Parsley Patch Wellness Center, where Kerry purchased throat lozenges
and vitamins.

Another pool report sent out later in the month, on October 20, 2004,
filled in the rest of the traveling press on Kerry's evening in a Holiday Inn
in Boardman, Ohio, with some of his campaign staff watching Game 7 of
the American League Championship pitting the Boston Red Sox against
the New York Yankees (Boston won by a 10–3 score). The pool report describes what Kerry was wearing (a blue shirt, khakis, and a Boston Red
Sox hat), where he was sitting, and how he was joking with the press pool
and his staffers. But it started, much like other pool reports, with the quick
summary: "Good color—no news."

Press pools, which are sometimes necessary and sometimes simply con-
venient, are just one way that news is shaped by campaign and journalistic practices. There are others—editors at home who want a story that's different from the competition, but not too different; deadlines that come
several times a day, but can cause an event early in the day to drop off the
news agenda by late in the day; and the 24-hour news cycle that has the
opposite effect of making every small step and misstep news—often before
reporters have a chance to put the step or misstep in perspective. All of
these factors, and others, help determine what information gets to voters.
The problem, as other scholars have noted in numerous studies, is that the
information coming out of campaign coverage often does little to serve
voters (Patterson, 1994; Cappella & Jamieson, 1997; McChesney, 2004).

JOURNALISTS' VIEWS OF THE ROLE OF THE MEDIA

In July 1999, Carl Leubsdorf, Washington bureau chief for the *Dallas Morning News*, and the other members of his political staff were already immersed in election coverage. With then-Texas Governor George W. Bush be-

ing recognized as the leading candidate for the Republican nomination—and certainly the best funded contender—they knew they'd have to be even more aggressive and more comprehensive in their coverage of the 2000 campaign. But even early on, most of the paper's coverage was focusing on profiles of the candidates—especially of Bush.

> We want to look at Bush in totality, but in different parts. So we've got some people who are looking into his background. And the day that the *LA Times* came out with their National Guard story, we had one that was virtually done, and ours also came out that same Sunday. We wrote a story about some of the personal stuff he would face in November, including one saying that he drank a lot at a certain point. My view is that you have to write these things. You don't write them in a "gotcha" way. You write them in a straight way. The voters will decide whether they're important or not.—Carl Leubsdorf, July 1999

Leubsdorf said that the profile pieces on Bush were important early on because voters need to get a sense of who the candidates are. Besides, he said, Bush "doesn't have many stands on issues yet."

With more than 15 months to go before Election Day, the Dallas newspaper—along with a handful of other national newspapers—was leading the way in terms of campaign coverage. Television stations were giving sporadic coverage to the leading candidates, but the *Dallas Morning News* was one of the newspapers that already had a political staff assembled to cover the election. And the reporters and editors were deciding what voters would find out about the candidates. So while—as Leubsdorf suggested—the voters might decide what information in the paper was important to them, they were making the decision from an already limited menu that had been determined by journalists.

The Dallas newspaper was not the only one that was already spending a fair amount of time and space covering the campaign that summer. Both the *New York Times* and the *Washington Post* were running lengthy, multipart profiles of Bush and Al Gore—the candidates who, early on, looked to be the likely nominees of their respective political parties. Dan Balz, a *Washington Post* political reporter, said the *Post* was already "knee deep" in its coverage of Campaign 2000 by July 1999. And looking ahead to the coverage that would come for the rest of 1999 and most of 2000, Balz was optimistic that the *Post* would have a good blend of stories about the candidates and their stands on issues, as well as the behind-the-scenes coverage of the campaigns and the polls to let voters know how the race was shaping up. His optimism, however, was tempered by the reality of recent campaign coverage, which he said has been shaped by the values of television:

> The celebritization, if that is a word, of coverage in general tends to wash away debate and discussion about issues. And I think that we're

all affected by that. And you can kind of fight against that in some small ways and try to balance your coverage, but . . . it's just a lot easier and the ratings are a lot better if you get people to talk about, you know, is Al Gore boring or how much money has George Bush raised, than it is to talk about what they think about the role of faith-based institutions in trying to alleviate poverty or move people from welfare to work. And every news organization will say we've covered that, and that's right, but we tend to sort of quickly go back to the other story. And I think over time that that has an effect on the way people approach campaigns.—Dan Balz, July 1999

The problem is multifold, but it starts with a disconnect between the calendar that the major mainstream media outlets use when they consider campaign coverage and the calendar that most citizens use when they start thinking about politics. Much like the front loading of the primary calendar, the presidential campaign season seems to get an earlier start in each new cycle. Coverage of the 2004 presidential campaign, for instance, got started as early as December 14, 2000—the day after Gore conceded the election to Bush—with stories in the *Chicago Sun-Times* that speculated about the impact of the controversial outcome on Bush's reelection bid. And the summer of 2006 saw lengthy cover stories in magazines ranging from *Time* to *Esquire* that profiled some of the early contenders for the 2008 election, such as Hillary Clinton and John McCain. Adam Clymer of the *New York Times* said that the problem with the early coverage is that they are driven by the competitive pressures on media outlets—the need to have the best profile first—"and we're left with the dilemma of how to say it all again, in a different voice, in the fall of the election year itself" (Clymer, 2001, p. 783). Toby Eckert of Copley News Service said the early coverage really doesn't reach many voters:

> We kind of gear up for this long before people are paying attention, and we write a lot of stories before people are paying attention. That can have a negative impact because when you want to come back to it closer to the election, your editor says, "Well, we've already done that." But 90 percent of the people didn't read it back then. With the papers that I write for, people are going to be tuning in and out of politics, and they won't really tune in until the last month or so. Personally, I think the campaign season runs too long.—Toby Eckert, July 2006

Some editors argue that even if voters aren't paying attention a year or two before the election, when the in-depth analyses and profiles are appearing, those stories are available closer to the election on the paper's archived Internet site. So a voter who wants, in September 2008, to read the in-depth candidate profiles that started running as early as the summer of 2006 can simply call them up. And the highly motivated voter will likely do so. But the highly motivated voter typically is someone who has strong feelings about the election, is more likely to be a strong partisan, and may, as a result, have made up his or her mind about which candidate to vote for very early in the campaign cycle. For those voters, reading about the candidates becomes something that confirms or solidifies their choices. For the undecided voter or the person trying to decide whether to vote, the motivation to pay attention to politics is minimal. The active attention processes required to seek out stories from archives—and in some cases to pay a small fee for that access—simply aren't present (Petty, Priester, & Briñol, 2002; Doppelt & Shearer, 1999).

And the voters are largely disengaged, as evidenced by years of academic research (Robinson, 1974; Clarke & Fredin, 1978; Becker & Whitney, 1980; Simon, 1996) and by voter turnout that has dropped almost steadily since 1960. More to the point, public affection for the major political parties and for the candidates that they nominate has dropped significantly since 1960 as the role of the media in the election process has grown and as the media have increased their attention to strategy and personality (Robinson, 1981).

> Correspondents and editors now feel a great need to explain policy statements in terms of campaign strategy, and a greater freedom to expose the blemishes of each prospective incumbent. . . . Obviously, *nobody expects or wants the press to flack for the candidates*, or to let the incumbent president garden his roses into re-election. We should not be at all surprised—or displeased—to find the media covering front-runners and incumbents with considerable and growing suspicion. Under the unstated, contemporary rules of the free press, that's the way it is—and, perhaps, should be. . . . If the press insists that we have to face the reality of our democratic leadership, warts and all, that's understandable. But then we also have to face the reality of our passive democratic electorate in a media system geared to covering the dark side of the major candidates. (Robinson, 1981, pp. 185–186)

As Robinson notes, the focus on strategy has come at a cost. Voter turnout has withered in national elections, and Robinson and others put the blame—at least in part—on news coverage that creates distaste for politics and politicians. The emphasis on strategy also turns the candidates into performers at the center of a drama, which is helpful for journalists who are trying to find a good narrative for the story but which puts voters in the role of being merely passive spectators (Jamieson, 1993; Patterson, 1994). More recent election coverage has been marked by the same tendency to cover the candidates warts and all, but it also has been marked by a greater freedom on the part of reporters to "lead readers to evident, but slightly controversial conclusions" (Guttenplan, 1992a, p. 4).

Reporters like Adam Clymer of the *New York Times*, who became news himself on September 4, 2000, when Bush called Clymer "a major league asshole" in a side comment to running mate Dick Cheney before a speech, argue that the digging into candidates' backgrounds and the focus on electoral motivations behind candidates' actions have improved political coverage.

> I think of a story my colleague Rick Berke wrote about the way Bush and Gore ran their campaigns and handled their staffs. You may remember: Gore designed his own campaign logo and Bush didn't know what a logo was. That story gave us insight into Bush's future style in office, and to what Gore's might have been. (Clymer, 2001, pp. 779–780)

In his examination of media content on elections from 1948 through 1996, Roderick Hart identifies several functions that the media serve in an election, including a "disciplinary function" to monitor the candidates and what they say, and an interpretive role, which he says is part of the "exploratory function" of the press (Hart, 2000). The public, he argues, can quickly find out the facts about what happened on any given day. And while people do turn to television and newspapers for those facts, they could get the facts from headlines and news briefs. The public will spend time with the media because they want something more than a factual recitation. "Instead, they want to know *what it means* that something happened. . . . The press operates as it does for a reason: because the world refuses to interpret itself" (Hart, 2000, pp. 97–98). But this interpretive function of the media can sometimes put reporters at odds with the candidates, who typically have a policy orientation. Hart's study looks at the functions of the media from a macro perspective, but the functions that he identifies at a broad level have their counterparts at the individual level with the members of the press corps.

For the journalists covering a political campaign, the roles that they play sometimes seem to be in conflict. On the one hand, they want to inform voters about the candidates and the issues that could turn the election. Doing this sometimes means delving into the candidate's personal background as part of a profile or simply to assess the candidate's trustworthiness or even his mettle to hold office. Political writers believe that voters want information about a candidate's trustworthiness, and that they prize this information above stories about the candidate's speeches and stands on issues—especially when it comes to making their choices in the voting booth (Fiedler, 1992). And the scrutiny that the candidates must go through as a result of press disclosures about their characters helps ready them for office because "the candidate who emerges from the test of white-hot [media] heat will be cleaner and stronger for it, like fired and tempered steel" (Fiedler, 1992, p. 558).

The notion that some of the character coverage is depressing voter turnout and turning off the electorate (Robinson, 1981; Simon, 1996; Doppelt & Shearer, 1999) may raise questions among political writers and editors as they plan their news coverage, but it doesn't result in fundamental changes in news content because most journalists don't believe that low voter turnout is a problem for them to solve. And even if they recognize—in the emphasis on character—a disconnect between what gets covered and what voters say they want, journalists still see character as a critical element in political coverage. Carl Leubsdorf, the *Dallas Morning News* Washington bureau chief, sums it up like this:

> When the Donna Rice thing came out [in May 1987], people wrote it, partly because [Hart] was so blatant about it. But we all wrote it. You know, character does matter. My view is when things come up, you write them if they are justified to be written based on your standards. But it's not up to us to decide what the public view of it will be, and if the public decides it doesn't matter, that's fine.
> *Question: But doesn't that kind of coverage contribute to an overall sense of people just turning off to politics?*
> Yeah, I think it does. I think a lot of people hate it.
> *Question: So are you doing a disservice to the voters?*
> Well, the question is what you base your news judgments on. We have certain standards, and we ought to keep our standards. We can't determine news play by whether fewer or more people vote. I'm not sure it's our job to do that.—Carl Leubsdorf, July 1999

Leubsdorf's view is echoed by others who cover politics. Among the journalists interviewed for this study, most said that encouraging political participation in elections is beyond the scope of journalistic duty. A few added that while some newspapers are beginning to recognize some role in responding to voters—mostly through the civic journalism movement—the choice not to vote can be an active form of civic participation, rather than simply a decision made based on apathy. Don Frederick, a political editor for the *Los Angeles Times*, said in July 1999 that people are "sending a message" to their political leaders by not voting. Cragg Hines, a *Houston Chronicle* political columnist and former Washington bureau chief, and Bill Lambrecht, a Washington correspondent and now bureau chief for the *St. Louis Post-Dispatch*—a paper that advocates civic journalism—hold similar views:

> I think we have to provide, as best we can, a full picture of what is going on in the campaign leading up to an election. And if people act on that, that's fine. If editors want to editorialize about people voting more, that's fine. But as to taking the potential voter by the hand to the

election booth, I'm not sure that's my job. And I think that's the view of a lot of reporters, even though it's not terribly PC [politically correct] to say so.—Cragg Hines, July 1999

People not voting—a lot of that has to do with a feeling of helplessness at the process. Just because people don't vote, it doesn't mean they're not interested, and it doesn't mean they're not paying attention. I think it's a conscious decision not to vote—a choice. . . . In the debate over civic journalism, the ardent proponents believe that the role of the newspaper is to foster more of an engagement in the process among people. The other part sees themselves in a role in which they sort through all sorts of information and tell readers what is important. What happens after that is out of their control.—Bill Lambrecht, July 1999

Lambrecht himself admits to falling in the latter camp—seeing the role of campaign journalism to be informative and to distill the myriad number of events that occur down to the snippets of news that might help readers as they make their election decisions, including whether to vote at all. It's a view that has a rich tradition among reporters. Jack Germond, a political reporter for more than 40 years, writes that reporters who do push a cause—even the cause of political participation—lack "a certain purity of purpose" that should be the hallmark of campaign journalism (Germond, 1999, p. 258). In his memoirs of his days on the campaign trail, he writes,

It turns out I have not made the world safe for democracy. But I have always argued that newspapers should not have any civic purpose beyond telling readers what is happening. If the political system is rotting away, as seems to be the case, it is our job to report it but not to make the repairs. (Germond, 1999, p. 258)

Frederick of the *Los Angeles Times* argues that the job of the journalist is to provide political coverage that is comprehensive and "as interesting as we can make it." Beyond that, he said, it's up to each citizen to decide how and whether to participate in the election.

We do things like letting people know that the voting [registration] books will close in 30 days in California. We make sure that we run little graphics that say this is the last day to register. But as we're doing our job, is it a major factor trying to get people to vote? No. I don't feel it's my responsibility to become an advocate for increasing voter participation.—Don Frederick, July 1999

Those who are advocates of civic journalism—and even some reporters who cringe at that moniker but support a more civic-minded role for political reporting—argue journalists do have a role in voter participation.

They say that those who hold the "it's not my job" view end up substituting a journalist's judgment, which is often refracted through a somewhat cynical lens, for that of the voters in determining what is important. It shows up, writes Adam Clymer, in news coverage that goes beyond a healthy skepticism "a few steps too far into cynicism, thinking candidates never mean what they say and so the strategy and tactics are always the story, rather than the speech and its argument and whether it makes any sense" (2001, p. 780). The cynicism of the media is then transferred through the coverage to the electorate, which results in greater alienation among the public to politics. Civic journalism advocates also agree that while the media should not actively advocate for a political candidate, except on the editorial pages, participation can be encouraged. Campaigns and candidates need to be covered in ways that make the issues relevant and that move the tone to one that is less cynical and negative. Increasingly, argue Bill Kovach and Tom Rosenstiel, the press is ignoring what citizens need in their election coverage.

> Policy and ideas are ignored or presented as sport, or couched in the context of how a certain policy position is calculated to gain someone power over a rival. Even the practice of reporters interviewing voters in political campaigns, reporters admit, is a vanishing art. . . . Citizens have become an abstraction, something that the press talks about but not to. (Kovach & Rosenstiel, 2001a, p. 27)

Some scholars, including Jay Rosen (1999), point out that as political campaigns became more media savvy and—especially with the waning role of the political parties in the nomination—had to rely on the media more, the candidates orchestrated more events for the press. The media responded by looking more closely at the contest and the political maneuvering by the candidates, resulting in the "inside baseball" coverage that focuses on the process of getting elected and that appeals more to the candidates and their staffs than it does to the average citizen (Glasser, 1999; Rosen, 1999; Kovach & Rosenstiel, 2001a). Writing about the 1988 campaign, Joan Didion said that the journalists covering the election spoke in a language unique to Washington, D.C., leaving the vast majority of Americans as outsiders merely watching a contest between rivals. Journalists, Didion writes, "speak of a candidate's performance, by which they usually mean his skill at circumventing questions, not as citizens but as professional insiders, attuned to signals pitched beyond the range of normal hearing" (1988, p. 19).

Rosen argues for coverage in a pitch that appeals to the readers, not the sources, and cites examples of election coverage from the *Charlotte Observer* or the *Orange County Register*, both of which poll readers and run reader focus groups to find out about the issues that matter to them. They then try to cover those issues in the context of the campaign, as evidence that political journalism can be meaningful to voters (Rosen, 1999). David Broder, a political writer and columnist for the *Washington Post*, has long been an advocate of putting voters at the center of election coverage, although he and his colleagues at the *Post* don't call it civic journalism. To them, it's just good journalism. Broder, in a 1991 lecture in Riverside, California, cited the then-widespread dissatisfaction among voters with politicians and the political process and said that while the media were not fully to blame for it, the "disillusionment about the heart of politics—the election process—is something in which we play a part" (cited in Rosen, 1991, p. 41). Broder argued then that campaign reporters needed to distance themselves from the candidates and campaigns and spend more time talking to voters and nonvoters.

At a speech at Colby College in Maine, Broder elaborated on his argument that voters need more of a voice in campaign coverage. Coming off of the lessons of the 1984 and 1988 campaigns, Broder said that the media "have to redefine our role and our mission in the coverage of campaigns. We have to become activists on behalf of the process" (1990, p. 4). He told the Colby College audience that the media need to pay more attention to campaign advertising, since they are "the most important speeches that candidates give in any campaign" (Broder, p. 4), and that journalists need to turn the focus of election campaigns back to issues that concern voters.

> For far too long, all of us in political journalism have accepted the notion that the campaign is whatever the candidates choose to talk about. They run the campaign. They make the speeches. They decide what's on the agenda. Our job in journalism, it is just to report on what they are saying or doing.
>
> Well, there are problems. First of all, there are fewer and fewer speeches in political campaigns in part because we in the press have gotten out of the habit of reporting speeches even when they are made. And there is less and less said about the subjects that people really care about. … I think we ought to start each election cycle as reporters, in the precincts with the voters themselves. Talking to them face-to-face, finding out what is on their mind, we then ought, to the extent possible, let their concerns set our agenda, influence the questions that we take to the candidates in the press conferences, and help determine how we use the space in our newspaper and the air time on our broadcasts. (Broder, 1990, p. 5).

Broder's colleague at the *Post*, Dan Balz, holds a similar view, saying that the press today has to compete with a lot of other constraints on their readers' time, so making a story more readily relevant to the reader is especially important in contemporary campaign reporting.

> We've got to be more creative about it than we have in the past because we have readers who won't spend more than 20 minutes with the paper,

even if they're regular readers, and we've got to get to them. So it comes back to your question, how do you provide people with what they need to be good citizens? And on that, I don't know that the media collectively have done a terribly good job. There's a great line, which is that none of us, including journalists, can sort of stand on the sidelines as citizens and watch democracy kind of fall apart. And I think that's true. I mean, I know that we can't shape our coverage day to day on whether we think this is going to make it more likely voters will vote or less likely, but you have to step back from that and say to what extent has the media contributed to a decline of interest in politics.—Dan Balz, July 1999

USA Today's Richard Benedetto, much like David Broder, argues that the key to invigorating voter interest in an election is involving real citizens in the debate. While that's often difficult to do from within the confines of the traveling press corps, it's an essential element to understanding the key issues and to understanding how the candidates are resonating with the electorate. Even at rallies and speeches, reporters often can learn more from the citizens who turn out than from the speech, Benedetto said.

We'll go out and cover the candidates from day to day, and we'll talk about what's being said on the campaign trail and then frame it in terms of what Bush said today and what Kerry said today and how they differ. But at the same time, we should be talking to the people. Naturally you've got a crowd that's partisan there, but they've still got something to say. . . . Near the end of the campaign, I was in rural Ohio, Zanesville, I think. Bush came on the stage, and there was a woman in the back waving a Bush-Cheney sign. As Bush finished his speech, I asked her, "Tell me why you like the Bush-Cheney ticket." She said, "See this cell phone? I'm waiting for a phone call at any minute that I've become a grandma. Bush and Cheney are for life, and I'm with them." Now that tells you something. That says the pro-life people are out there and they're going to vote. You can draw some conclusions from that.—Richard Benedetto, July 2006

While most journalists acknowledge that campaign coverage can be improved, and that making voters (and nonvoters) more prominent in stories can shift the focus from strategy to issues, they stop short of endorsing civic journalism models. Seasoned political reporters, they say, can bring a critical eye to the campaign trail and can sometimes spot a story that others might miss.

There are some in the world of civic journalism who want to markedly restrict what the readers get about the engagement between the candidates. They want to change the focus from what the candidates say and do, and why, to what readers think they want to hear. But for the most part, I think that in the initial coverage—and perhaps all the way through—it falls on the political reporter, who I think best serves the reader through experience, to set the stage. . . . There should be a blend of experienced journalists telling the voters what happened and filtering campaign information to the voters, and plugged-in voters telling candidates and telling journalists what they want to hear.—Bill Lambrecht, July 1999

At most newspapers, the plans for coverage of the 2000 and 2004 presidential campaigns called for extended, multipart profiles of the major candidates, comparison pieces that would put the major candidates "on the record" on specific issues, and stories from the campaign trail that would include reaction from the voters at the various stump speeches to the candidates. The journalists who were planning the campaign coverage were hoping for a delicate balance of stories that would provide them with information about the candidates, but more importantly would provide them with insights about the people running for office without striking too cynical a tone. Some, like Leubsdorf and Lambrecht, were more pragmatic and argued that stories needed to be more appealing to the reader—in content and in tone—in order to have an audience for their work and that of their colleagues. The impact of news coverage on the political process wasn't their concern. Others, like Balz, saw the need for the same kind of coverage—calling it "just good journalism"—but they recognized that the media do play some role in the process. Their coverage for the elections, they hoped, would meet the needs of voters without going to the extremes of polling readers for story ideas. Those, they thought, should come from the journalists who were out there with the candidates and the campaigns. But at a minimum they hoped their coverage would do no harm.

SETTING THE MEDIA'S AGENDA

The concept of agenda setting, as postulated by Bernard Cohen (1963), holds that while the media do not play a large role in shaping people's attitudes and opinions, they have been "stunningly successful in telling [their] readers what to think *about*" (p. 13). In the political sphere, Maxwell McCombs and Donald Shaw first put agenda setting to the test in a 1968 study of voters in North Carolina. The authors compared the issues that were played most often in the content of local media in the Chapel Hill area to the responses from people living in that region to a survey question about the most important problem facing the country (McCombs & Shaw, 1972; McCombs, 1994). The authors found a high degree of correlation between what the media covered and what the public thought was important, providing strong evidence of the impact of the media on the public's sense about what the issues of the day really were. The McCombs and Shaw study was especially important in that it caused scholars to reexamine their thinking about the findings by Paul Lazarsfeld and his colleagues that the media had only limited effects on the electorate (Baran & Davis, 1995; Lowery & DeFleur, 1995).

The initial agenda-setting research found that the media had the ability to shape what people thought was important—something that in and of itself is a powerful effect. As E. E. Schattschneider wrote, "He who determines what politics is about runs the country, because the definition of alternatives is the choice of conflicts, and the choice of conflicts allocates power" (1975, p. 66). Thus, issues such as AIDS (Rogers, Dearing, & Chang, 1991) or the war on drugs (Reese & Danielian, 1991) became important to the public because of the media attention that was paid to those issues. But the agenda-setting function hasn't been limited to just a handful of issues. A 1973 study of issues across the 1960s showed a high correlation between the agendas of the media and the public (Funkhouser, 1973). And a replication of the Chapel Hill study by Shaw and McCombs (1977) found that not only was the media's agenda highly correlated to the public's agenda, but that increased exposure to campaign coverage can result in a greater degree of agenda setting. By helping to set the public's agenda for the issues most critical to the nation, the media play an important policy-making role in society.

The ability of the media to set an agenda has since been extended beyond Cohen's concept of telling us what to think about. Indeed, more recent research has begun to examine a second level of agenda setting through which the media not only shape public opinion about what is important, but they also shape the public's view of how to evaluate those issues or, in the case of campaign coverage, the candidates (Robinson & Sheehan, 1983; McCombs & Bell, 1996). Since 1968, the positive evaluations of the candidates for president have lagged behind the negative ones (McCombs & Bell, 1996), and many media critics place the blame for this squarely on the negative tone of campaign coverage (Robinson & Sheehan, 1983; Sabato, 1991; Patterson, 1994). Putting the concept of second-level agenda setting to the test, one researcher found strong correlations between voters' images of the candidates and the attributes of the candidates highlighted in newspaper coverage and political advertising in a mayoral election in Texas (Bryan, 1997, as cited in Lopez-Escobar et al., 1998). And a study of voters in a mayoral election in Taipei in 1994 reported similar findings—that news coverage of the candidates also shaped the voters' perceptions of the candidate attributes that were most important (King, 1997).

The findings over the years of the media's impact on the public's agenda began to beg a new question—who sets the media's agenda? The answer has come in a number of studies that have looked at the role of public relations practitioners, the president and other U.S. government officials, political pundits and "spin doctors," the wire services, and other news media outlets. Turk (1986), for instance, provides evidence that public information officers working for a variety of government agencies were relatively successful in getting stories placed in the news media in Louisiana. Slightly more than half of the releases or tips that the public information officers provided to the press were picked up on, although many were included in part of a larger story (Turk, 1986), which lessened the ability of the public information officers to control the message. The study also showed that the public information officers were most successful when they produced news releases that were simply informative, rather than ones that made an attempt to be persuasive (Turk, 1986).

Rather than reaching out to the press, the pundits and members of think tanks that Lawrence Soley (1992) writes about are successful in shaping news content because they are in the Rolodexes of the reporters—particularly the reporters who work in and cover Washington, D.C. Soley argues that these reporters, who also are part of the Washington "power elite," seek out the think tank analysts because they carry the tag of "expert" and because they often travel in some of the same circles as the elite reporters. In fact, Soley points out,

> Prestige reporters are also part of Washington's revolving door, which moves elite members from one part of the elite network to the other. Reporters become think tank analysts, government officials, or professors, government officials become think tank analysts, professors and reporters, and think tank analysts become reporters, professors and government officials. (Soley, 1992, p. 143)

Essentially, it's an insider's game in Washington, and the system is designed to keep it that way. Thus, the analysts and those in power have an edge in determining what journalists write about and how they frame their stories. Surprisingly, one study of the ability of the president to set the media agenda through his State of the Union address found that the media had a greater impact on the president's agenda as outlined in his speech than the speech did on the subsequent media agenda (Gilberg et al., 1980). The study was confined to only one State of the Union address—the January 1978 speech by President Jimmy Carter—so it's difficult to determine if the findings would hold up over time and across presidents.

But even if the members of the press don't always pay attention to the president, they do pay attention to each other. A number of studies have examined the tendency for one news outlet to pick up on a story or a story angle that another news outlet has—a phenomenon called intermedia agenda setting. It happens with the wire services, as demonstrated by the earlier gatekeeping studies that showed that the stories selected from the wire services by newspaper wire editors were proportionate to the stories on those topics that appear on the wires (White, 1950; Snider, 1967; Bleske, 1991). And the trend held in a broader study of wire editors in Ohio who participated in a news selection experiment (Whitney & Becker, 1982). Editors were given sets of cards that had the lead paragraphs of stories on them. One group was given cards that were evenly spread out among seven topic areas, while the other was given a sample that was heavier in some topics—particularly political and international news—than it was in other topics. Whitney and Becker found that the editors given the unbalanced set of cards chose more political and international stories, thereby using the flow of information from the wires as a cue about the relative importance of the topics.

But intermedia agenda setting goes well beyond picking up on subtle cues that come from the wires. Walk into any newspaper newsroom around 6 p.m. and you'll find someone monitoring the evening news on television to make sure that anything the local television station has tonight will also be in tomorrow morning's paper. Likewise, the television station monitors the local newspaper and pays close attention to any broadcast competition it may have. On the campaign trail, reporters routinely check their own organization's website, as well as the stories running on the wires and in their competition. And they all read the *New York Times*. Getting to the baggage call room a little late for a member of the press traveling with any of the candidates for the White House typically means a fruitless search for a copy of the *Times*. Most mornings on the campaign trail, it's the first paper to disappear from the pressroom and any hotel newsstand.

The stories that run in the *New York Times* influence what other media outlets carry in their own columns and programs. A study of national news coverage of the drug issue in the mid-1980s found that *Times* coverage of cocaine use in the late winter and early spring of 1986 was quickly followed by stories in the other New York newspapers (Reese & Danielian, 1991). And coverage of the cocaine problem surfaced in the next few months in both the *Washington Post* and the *Los Angeles Times*. The authors concluded that the pattern of news coverage in the print media

> suggests that the *Times* laid the groundwork for the story, which gathered strength when the *Post* picked up the story and expanded it with a heavy

focus on the Len Bias death. With two elite papers running with the story, *The Los Angeles Times* was obliged to join in. (Reese & Danielian, 1991, p. 247)

They found a similar intermedia agenda-setting effect for the broadcast networks—particularly with CBS and NBC. And while the broadcast media tended to pay the greatest attention to the *New York Times*, the networks followed the other elite print media as well (Reese & Danielian, 1991).

Other researchers have found that newspapers, in particular, tend to set the agenda for other media more than the reverse (Atwater, Fico, & Pizante, 1987), and the flow of influence in the print media tends to go from the larger newspapers to the smaller ones. Agenda setting also occurs between nonnews communication and the news (Lopez-Escobar et al., 1998). In a study of intermedia agenda setting in Spain, the authors found that political advertising influenced the agendas of both the issues covered (first level) and attributes of the candidates deemed important (second level) for newspapers and television. In United States elections, newspapers, and television have increasingly been led in their coverage by political advertising under the guise of "ad watches" geared toward ferreting out the truth or falsity of an advertisement's claims (Jamieson & Campbell, 1992; Cappella & Jamieson, 1997). News organizations also are responding more and more to what's turning up in nontraditional venues—the Gennifer Flowers story that first showed up in a tabloid newspaper during the 1992 election, for instance, or the increasing number of stories and rumors that now get reported on the Internet during an election cycle. Martin Kasindorf, a political reporter for *USA Today*, said the Internet has created some unique challenges for mainstream journalists.

> There was one day during the Wisconsin primary, it was subfreezing weather, and [Matt] Drudge had a report that Kerry had had an affair with a young woman who had been dispatched to Africa to get her out of the way. It was something we had to check out, even though it originated with Drudge. You sort of have to follow the crowd. If mainstream news organizations are working on it, then you work on it. But you don't want to be the only one writing about something that got started on a blog.—Martin Kasindorf, July 2006

Herbert Gans (1979) argued that there are several causes of intermedia agenda setting. A story appearing in another paper—particularly an elite newspaper—has already been viewed as being newsworthy, so it eliminates the need for an editor to judge the story on his or her own. Moreover, in the case of stories that pick up on trends—like homelessness or AIDS—the fact that the issue has been covered by another major newspaper helps establish its appeal to readers. In addition, intermedia agenda setting provides reporters and editors with a measure of comfort, letting them be more certain that they haven't missed anything important (Reese & Danielian, 1991). Media outlets do have reputations—the *New York Times* for international news, the *Washington Post* for national news and political coverage—but it is the *Times* that is most widely recognized as the newspaper that the rest of the media pay attention to. In fact, Gans (1979) argued that "if the *Times* did not exist, it would probably have to be invented" (p. 181).

OUTSIDE FORCES THAT SHAPE THE NEWS

But just as the reporters on the campaign trail read the *New York Times* (and increasingly *USA Today*, which often is delivered to the hotel room door free of charge), so do their editors, their publishers, and their sources. Thus, the agenda-setting impact of newspapers like the *Times* can affect the content of other news organizations at any one of a number of gates in the gatekeeping process. Shoemaker and Reese (1996) identify five levels of influence on media content, starting with the individual reporter and moving outward—in increasingly larger circles or layers—to the routines of news production, the news organization, the institutions outside of the newsroom (including government), and the predominant ideology of the culture in which the news is produced.

Much of what occurs in campaign coverage occurs at the ideological level, as press coverage of political campaigns helps keep the front-runners in front and pays little attention to candidates who don't have significant resources and political backing. Bagdikian (1997), in writing about media ownership and the power of advertising, says that the desire of advertisers to reach mass audiences erodes the level of political coverage and increases the costs for candidates who want to run for national office. Bagdikian (1997) points out that as ownership of the media has become increasingly concentrated in the hands of only a few elites, the sense of obligation to inform the public about policies, rather than products, has all but disappeared. The needs of an informed citizenry, he argues, take a back seat to merchandising, which "has made American elected office the prize of rich men and women or candidates backed by rich men and women" (p. 189). Some scholars have even argued that media content is designed to keep citizens uninformed and less inclined to vote. Moscovici (1991) calls it a "spiral of apathy" (p. 299):

> In order to function well, a democracy depends not on the participation but on the ignorance and indifference of a large number of voters. These, limiting the influence and expression of some layers of society, ensure the stability and

cohesion of political life. Like the spiral of silence, the spiral of apathy thus al-lows the ruling elites to rule legitimately. (pp. 298–299)

The ideological battles, which often are fought by the two major politi-cal parties, have allowed upper-income whites to capture the power among both Republicans and Democrats, leaving lower-income citizens to fend for themselves when it comes to concerns that affect their daily lives. With nowhere to turn in the political system, these Americans are becoming alienated from politics (Templeton, 1966). Disproportionately, these citizens are nonwhite manual workers, less educated, and in the lower rungs of socioeconomic status (Templeton, 1966). For the ruling elites, the voluntary disenfranchisement of these groups is what keeps power in their hands. To help accomplish this, they turn to the media. As noted earlier, several media effects studies have shown that increased re-liance on the media for political information is related to increased dis-trust and cynicism (Robinson, 1974) and to voter disgust and a lack of par-ticipation (Cappella & Jamieson, 1997).

For those in power, this isn't a problem. And any appearance of a bat-tle for the presidency is really a battle of essentially like-minded people, keeping at bay any real threat to the status quo. The interlocking social and cultural connections between media owners, elite reporters, politi-cians, and corporate leaders result in those in the media adopting the ide-ology of the power elite (Soley, 1992; Bagdikian, 1997). These relation-ships, over time, reinforce the commitment of the media to the dominant political order (Gitlin, 1980). The interaction between reporters and sources creates a high level of trust between them and further solidifies a common view. As Gitlin (1980) writes,

> Once hired and assigned, reporters customarily form strong bonds with the sources (especially in Washington) on whom they depend for stories. They absorb the worldviews of the powerful. They may also contest them. . . . But even when there are conflicts of policy between reporters and sources, or re-porters and editors, or editors and publishers, these conflicts are played out within a field of terms and premises which does not overstep the hegemonic boundary. (p. 263)

In the realm of electoral politics and campaign coverage, the "conven-tional wisdom" of those in power is played out through common news frames applied to political reporting, including the emphasis on conflict and personality, the focus on specific events, and the framing of the cam-paign as a game (Patterson, 1994; Cappella & Jamieson, 1997). Patterson (1994) and others have amply documented the media's reliance on poll numbers and campaign finances as a source for stories. In the 1980 presi-dential election, for example, polls alone made up 15 percent of the cov-erage (Stovall & Solomon, 1984). This focus on the "horse race" aspect of the election, according to Arianna Huffington, perpetuates the status quo because "the establishment candidates are much more likely to get the early money and then use the hypothetical match-ups (in polls) to get more money" (Rivlin, 1999).

The "establishment candidates"—Republicans and Democrats who have name recognition and fundraising ability, and typically have held a seat in Congress or as a state governor—also have the ability to influence the news agenda. In recent elections, the campaign communications staffs have become increasingly savvy at shaping news coverage by keeping the candidates "on message" (Norris et al., 1999). Campaigns accomplish this by loading the press up with news releases, written rebuttals to statements by other candidates, position papers, and staged events with a stump speech. Campaign press managers are on hand at every event to provide reporters with their interpretation of an event or of something occurring in an opponent's campaign. They also limit access to the candidate—especially in press conferences or other "on the record" question-and-answer sessions—in order to avoid letting the press pull a candidate off the message of the day.

At one point early in the 2000 election, Al Gore was giving one-on-one interviews to a handful of reporters from the national press shortly after the announcement that Joe Lieberman, a devoutly religious Jew, would be the Democratic Party's vice presidential nominee. But the interviews were short—no more than five minutes, said one reporter who interviewed Gore that day and was traveling with the Gore campaign in the fall. The reporter, who was speaking off the record, said he wanted to ask Gore about an open letter from the Anti-Defamation League suggesting that Lieberman should be less public about his religion. Gore, however, wanted to talk about Lieberman's character and moral fiber. "The first answer Gore gave me was the sound bite for the day," the reporter said. "Then I asked a totally different question, but I got the exact same answer. That happened five or six times." By that time, his five minutes was up. "They dollop him out, but that brings out an attitude with us that we are not going to let them [the campaign managers] use us. That sets up a struggle between us and the campaign."

The campaign staffs also control access to the candidates, deciding who will be in the press pool for events that cannot accommodate the full traveling press corps. The decisions are sometimes made strategically, particularly when the race is tight in certain states, and sometimes made to punish a reporter or news organization that has stepped out of line with a question or story—at least in the eyes of the candidate and his staff. For the journalists on the campaign trail access is a major issue, and better access can result in better coverage. At an Election Day lunch at the *Concord Monitor* in February 2000, the *Washington Post*'s Dan Balz said

John McCain got better treatment from the press during his 2000 presidential bid because of the access he granted to members of the press. The press pool, when McCain needed to use one, rotated so that every major newspaper (and many smaller ones) following McCain got to be a part of the pool at some point. He also was "a quote machine who could be turned on at three in the morning" if needed (Wolper & Mitchell, 2000, p. 21), which is invaluable for reporters who need something—anything—for the next edition.

NEWS VALUES AND NEWS ORGANIZATIONS

Part of the pressure on the campaign trail comes from the fact that publishers and editors at the news organizations back home want a solid return on the resources they invest to put a reporter out on the road. Campaign coverage is costly. In late January when the candidates were campaigning heavily in New Hampshire prior to the first primary election, a seat on the candidate buses cost $80 to $100 a day. By fall, however, when the campaigns are national in scope and the candidates fly across the country several times a week in their quest to win over the undecided voters, the costs to news organizations for each reporter, photographer, or producer they have on the road runs $5,000 a week or more. Early in the election season, news organizations have to decide which candidates will be covered full-time, which may be covered only occasionally, and which ones to ignore. But the investment of newsroom staff and resources means that some candidates will get more coverage than others. Reporters are being paid to find stories, not to simply be around a candidate in case news happens, and news organizations are in the business of running those stories. So news from the campaign trail becomes defined early on by the allocation of resources—especially a traveling reporter—to the various candidates.

One effect of this allocation of scarce resources is that the reporters and editors who provide campaign coverage find themselves involved in a delicate negotiation as they assess the newsworthiness of events. The impact of individual reporters and editors on the process is undeniable, but Tuchman (1978) argues that in their work they are guided by routines that also impact on the "reality" that we see in the media: "News is located, gathered, and disseminated by professionals working in organizations. Thus it is inevitably a product of newsworkers drawing upon institutional processes and conforming to institutional practices" (Tuchman, 1978, p. 4). But Tuchman identifies some of the strategies that journalists use to help manage the flow of news, including the development of beats and the categorization of stories into categories—hard news, soft news, spot news, developing news, and continuing news. By and large, the news of the day can be folded into one of these categories, and at daily editorial meetings those who decide what will be aired or published try for a balance between these categories of stories.

But even the break-out story—the one that draws on all the resources of the newsroom and in the Hollywood version of journalism would end up with someone running down to the basement yelling, "Stop the presses!"—has a typification that helps reporters and editors manage it. Tuchman (1978) calls this the "what-a-story" (p. 59) and says that journalists rely on past experience in those special situations as a guide for handling the "what-a-story." In her study, the staff of the newspaper she was observing scrambled at President Lyndon Johnson's March 1968 announcement that he would not seek reelection.

> It would be impossible to describe the amount of revision accomplished in a remarkably brief time as reporters summoned by telephone, volunteering editors, and mounds of wire service copy poured into the newsroom. But the comments of editors and reporters are significant. Lifting their heads to answer telephones, bark orders, and then clarify them, the editors periodically announced, "*What* a story! . . . The story of the century. . . . What a night, what a night! . . . Who would have believed it? . . . There's been nothing like it since Coolidge said, 'I will not run.'" (Tuchman, 1978, p. 61)

Tuchman notes that the editors' reference to the Coolidge story served to provide some guidance about how to handle Johnson's announcement by invoking a similar "what-a-story." In the 2000 election, the fact that Election Day didn't result in a clear winner was a "what-a-story" that persisted through December 13, the day Gore conceded to Bush, after a U.S. Supreme Court decision to stop manual vote recounts in Florida. The *60 Minutes* piece on Bush's National Guard service may well have been the "what-a-story" in 2004, but given the media's role at the center of that story, it was, in some ways, a more difficult story for journalists to cover. Of course, the defining characteristic of a "what-a-story" is that it flies in the face of journalistic conventional wisdom. It's a story that's not only unexpected, it's almost unimaginable.

Most news from the campaign trail doesn't fit that category. Campaigns are highly scripted, with schedules that are carefully planned to get the candidate into key states and onto the nightly news with the campaign's message. Even given standard news values, the news that the campaign tries to push may not make the grade. Walter Cronkite, a former CBS news anchor once dubbed "the most trusted newsman in America," said that news, by its very nature, focuses on conflict, controversy, and the unusual. Cronkite's description, while succinct, doesn't capture everything that manages to capture the media's attention. The timeliness, proximity, and impact of an event, along with the prominence of the players in the story, can influence whether it makes it past editors and producers to reach the news audience (White, 1950; Bleske, 1991; Shoemaker, 1997; Comstock & Scharrer, 1999; Rich, 2000). Newsroom norms also determine what gets media attention. For instance, the media practice of providing both (or several) sides to the story means that some people will end up getting media attention simply so they can serve as sources to provide a counterpoint to others who are in the news because of an event (Tuchman, 1973). Likewise, the classification of stories as "hard news," "soft news," and "breaking news" will affect the attention that each gets. Breaking news, for instance, is a story that commands the entire staff's attention. It's the JFK Jr. plane crash in 1999, or the 2000 election night fiasco in Florida, or even the tightness of the 2004 election battle and the possibility that the Ohio vote would result in another post–Election Day legal battle. Because covering breaking news commands much of a newsroom's resources, it dominates the airtime of a broadcast or space in a newspaper. Hard news is often expected, so the space it will take is generally planned for, but it still commands more attention from reporters and editors in getting the details, nuances, and opposing viewpoints in place. Soft news— the profiles and features that can run at virtually any time—are typically less resource intensive. However, in recent years soft news has been the focus of attention for more news executives since there are greater profits to be made from a news mix that places more emphasis on soft news.

But the key underlying factor that drives most news choices—that causes those in the media to stand up and take note of a story or event— is a story's deviance (Shoemaker, 1984; Shoemaker, Chang, & Brendlinger, 1987; Shoemaker & Reese, 1996). In an attempt to make the news more exciting, more interesting, and more appealing—in short, to better capture the public's attention—news often puts the emphasis on events or people that are very different from the social norm. However, while a story may focus on someone or some event that is different, it will give more attention within the story to normal points of view. More time and space (and thus attention) will be given to comments by official spokespeople than will be given to those protesting a government position on an issue. Groups that are deviant will get coverage, but they will be treated less favorably, and the media may question their legitimacy. So while deviant events do get covered, they are covered in a way "calculated to underscore their deviance" (Shoemaker & Reese, 1996, p. 225).

Several scholars argue that there is a larger reason for this awkward dance of covering that which is different, but doing it in a way that confirms its very deviance. They say that media, which are owned by major corporations and have much at stake in the current socioeconomic system, are agents of the status quo (Gilbert, 1986; Herman & Chomsky,

1988; Bagdikian, 1997). And the concentration of media ownership in fewer and fewer hands, combined with the influence of news norms and routines, means that despite thousands of media outlets, the news that the average person gets is very homogenized. The "McNuggets" of information that are broadcast on NBC are very similar to those on ABC or CBS. And while the *New York Times* or the *Washington Post* might have more in-depth coverage than the nightly news, their news agenda won't be all that different.

TRAVELING WITH THE PACK

The final presidential debate—the one focused on domestic policy and held on October 13, 2004, at Arizona State University—was nearing its end. With a question or two to go, John Kerry's press staffer started rounding up the reporters in the traveling press and getting them onto the three buses that would take them to the postdebate rally at Tempe Beach Park. On the way to the rally, several reporters started reviewing the candidates' performances. The focus was on how Kerry and Bush came across—their style and posture and level of confidence. The consensus, at least among the reporters on the second press bus, was that Kerry won the battle of poise. "He was looking at the camera. He was presidential. Bush wasn't," concluded one reporter in the small group that included Jill Zuckerman of the *Chicago Tribune* and David Halbfinger of the *New York Times*. That analysis showed up the next day in the *Times*'s story, in which Kerry was described as "sounding confident," and a Kerry campaign consultant was quoted as saying that Kerry "appeared more presidential than the president himself" (Bumiller & Halbfinger, 2004). News coverage in other papers, *USA Today* and the *Washington Post* among them, also noted the style differences between the two candidates. And while it's very possible that how the candidates carried themselves would have been a key element of news coverage no matter what, there is little debate about the fact that pack journalism—a prevalent feature on the campaign trail—increases the sameness of the news from one outlet to another.

For those covering candidates during the primary season who are more likely to win the nomination, or covering the nominees in the fall, pack journalism is a way of life. Unlike John McCain, who provided an unusual amount of access for members of the press early in the 2000 primary season, Al Gore and George W. Bush kept media members off their own buses in New Hampshire and on separate press buses that followed the candidate from town to town. On a short trip, a reporter from one of the more elite news outlets might be invited onto the main Gore or Bush bus, but generally the travel time between stops was used by the candidates to rest or to make calls to prospective donors. For the press corps, this means long hours spent on buses or in planes—often with access only to a few campaign staff members and each other—as they go from one place to the next. And depending on where that next stop is, there may not be enough room to accommodate all of the members of the press.

For instance, on the Monday before the 2000 New Hampshire primary, reporters covering Gore spent their day on the buses going from one diner to another—in Nashua, Tilton, Concord, and Manchester—as Gore traveled the I-93 corridor meeting voters. However, the diners were too small to allow all of the press to go in as well, so each stop was "pooled," with one video camera, one still camera, and one reporter allowed into the diner. Those journalists then shared their footage, pictures, and notes with the rest of the press corps. The effect of the pack was twofold. First, it resulted in only one "view" of the news, with the *New York Times* reporter and the Fox camera operator generally serving as the filter for the morning's stops. Second, it created ill will among the press covering Gore that day. Left literally standing out in the cold (reporters and photographers were corralled into a corner of the parking lot by campaign staffers holding a yellow rope barrier) with only photo opportunities of the vice president entering and leaving diners, reporters struggled to find a news angle for their coverage. And most of the campaigning that follows the New Hampshire primary, which is noted for its extraordinary opportunities for both voters and the press to talk to the candidates, takes the format of the press pool or photo op. The result is that news from the campaign—especially after New Hampshire—becomes increasingly homogenized. Everyone has the same story because only a handful of journalists have access to the candidates, and their notes become the notes for the entire press corps.

Still, the influence of the members of the press corps on each other goes beyond the pool arrangements and the time spent in close quarters. The reporters reading the *New York Times* at the John Kerry rally in Elyria, Ohio, on a sunny Saturday afternoon in early October 2004 weren't simply trying to catch up on world events—they were making sure that they hadn't missed something that the *Times* reporters had seen. In makeshift press filing centers, reporters who aren't writing on a tight deadline spend the larger blocks of "down time" on e-mail or calling up sites from other news organizations to see what their press colleagues are up to. And at home, their editors are doing the same thing, and then dashing off hurried messages to their field reporters with tips they've picked up off the Internet. For reporters on the campaign trail, the e-mails from the home office sometimes bring an additional level of pressure since the story from the speech or rally isn't what the editors want, and the confines of the press pack make it difficult to come up with something else.

If you've got editors who don't think that basic political coverage is important, then you're banging your head against a wall. I think they're looking for the hottest story they can find. I think there's a thing running through our business today, especially with the 24-hour news cycle, there's this feeling that dribbles all the way down to the local level that every story has to have some pizzazz to it in order to make it into print. So then you become caught up in a battle of how can I make it not boring, maybe to the point where you're distorting the story, because you have to sell the story to your editor.—Richard Benedetto, July 2006

For the reporter in the field, the editor at home can exert a fair amount of pressure to tell a story in a certain way. Benedetto said that oftentimes editors "are telling reporters what to go out and find" based on what they've just seen on CNN and on preconceived notions about what the story should be. But there are other constraints as well. Deadlines, for instance, can affect the threshold for an event to become news. Campaigns try to plan events for early enough in the day that they can make the evening news, and they typically allow filing time in order for reporters—especially those from television outlets—to meet routine deadlines. But events that occur after a deadline—Kerry's 10 p.m. airport rally in New Mexico, for example—aren't unusual enough to warrant a rewrite and won't, for the national press corps, be newsworthy the next day. The members of the traveling press still attend the late night rallies and "nonnews" events, but typically pay only passing attention, just in case something newsworthy occurs. "The main advantage of being on the Kerry plane is that there's a chance news might happen," said one reporter as he waited for the second debate in St. Louis, Missouri, to start. But the reality of the campaign trail is a lot of waiting, he said.

BREAKING FROM THE PACK

While a journalist's ideas about what constitutes "real news" is influenced by campaign managers and editors and the rest of the press pack, his or her notions about news also are shaped by his or her own experiences. The result is that the news coming from the campaign on any given day may also be affected by who is covering the candidate. "Reporters bring their own expertise to bear—their environment, their heredity, their biases. If you have all males on the campaign, there won't be any questions about abortion rights. If you have no people of color, you may not get a question about reaction to the beating of Mr. Byrd in Jasper," said Ann Scales, an African American reporter for the *Boston Globe* who covered the Gore campaign in 2000. Scales readily admitted that her experiences in life are factors that sometimes shape the questions she asks and the stories she writes.

And increasingly new reporters come to the newsroom with lists of what makes something newsworthy already drilled into their heads as a result of the news writing classes they've taken in college. In 1971, only 23 percent of reporters with college degrees had journalism degrees, and only 58 percent of reporters had college degrees (Johnstone, Slawski & Bowman, 1976). By 2002, however, nearly 36 percent of journalists with college degrees had studied journalism, and 89 percent of reporters had college degrees (Weaver et al., 2007). Thus, the news definitions taught in college classrooms were becoming an increasingly greater influence on the news than when Breed first studied newsroom socialization. Breed (1955) said that over time, reporters develop a sense of what news is through experience and under the guidance of more senior reporters and editors. Breed suggested that this learning occurs because younger journalists both respect the senior reporters and editors and see, on some level, that adapting to the conventional view of news will ultimately lead to better beats and more status for themselves in the newsroom. But as more and more journalists now come to the newsroom with college degrees in the field, the impact of newsroom socialization is being layered upon the earlier socialization that occurs in the college classroom. And, as noted earlier, while the textbook definitions of news vary from one book to another, the essential elements of conflict, controversy, timeliness, proximity, and the unusual are common to most lists (Mencher, 1997; Rich, 2000).

Still, reporters on the road don't consult a list of news values to determine what's news. Like the courts with pornography, journalists say they know it when they see it. Don Frederick of the *Los Angeles Times* says that what influences political reporting at his newspaper is less what the candidates may say than what the reporters think readers should know. "We try not to be driven by what the candidates say. We look, as well, at what they're not saying. We give our readers what we think people need to know about the candidate to be an informed participant." Frederick isn't the only one to see the "journalist as expert" in defining news. Bill Lambrecht of the *St. Louis Post-Dispatch* says, "Reporters become skilled over the years in determining what is noise from what is not. . . . It's a blend of experienced journalists filtering campaign information to voters and plugged-in voters telling candidates and journalists what they want to read and hear." Berkowitz (1990) says that news workers routinely use their own instincts to determine what news is, and Fishman (1997), in a study of local news reporters, found that journalists follow their beat structures rather than specific news values in determining what's newsworthy and what isn't.

As one of the first "gates" in the gatekeeping process (Shoemaker, 1991), reporters shape news content. They do this not only by making choices about what the news story is, but also about how to present it. In choosing one element for the lead over another, they are putting greater emphasis on that element. In choosing to ask about strategies and poll results rather than issues, they are framing the campaign as a game (Patterson, 1994). "There are always, throughout the election, a lot of stories on polls and horse race aspects. Political writers are kind of like sports writers—they're covering the game. Political reporters are more comfortable covering the politics than covering the policies," said Martin Kasindorf of *USA Today*.

Communications research shows that the media can affect our attitudes and opinions about people and issues by framing them in certain language and by priming us to consider some aspects over others in our evaluations of candidates. Frames, according to Entman (1993), are the narratives that people use to make sense of situations. The frames are important in news reporting because they ease the news production process and help provide a structure for the news that audiences can better understand (Gans, 1979). For readers and viewers, frames are understood by assessing social cues, particularly cues from the media. This is necessary because we simply don't have direct access to all of the situations that occur in a day, so we rely on mediated representations of what occurs in Congress or on the campaign trail to fill the gaps of our own experience. Because we turn to the media for these stories, our frames and expectations are shaped by the media's narratives; thus the media provide the context and the criteria that people use to evaluate issues and candidates (Shaw, D. R., 2001). Over time, these frames are adapted by people and become part of their own schema for interpreting and understanding public issues. And while people do not "slavishly follow the framing of issues presented in the mass media," they do use the media frames to "actively filter, sort, and reorganize information in personally meaningful ways" (Neuman, Just, & Crigler, 1992, pp. 76–77).

In covering national politics, the frames are often ones that cast the candidates and the election process in a negative light (Patterson, 1994; Cappella & Jamieson, 1997). This is particularly true of television coverage, which reaches a broader audience than newspapers, magazines, or radio, and which is associated with lower levels of political knowledge and greater levels of political alienation (Clarke & Fredin, 1978; Becker & Whitney, 1980; Chaffee, Zhao, & Leshner, 1994; Pinkleton, Austin, & Fortman, 1998). Thus, the frames and traits that the media use in reporting on political campaigns "make salient the self-interest of those actions, invite negative character attributions, cue stock stories about 'politics as usual,' and reinforce cynicism" (Cappella & Jamieson, 1997, p. 60)—even among those who may not be attending closely to news coverage of the campaigns.

3

The Reporter's Role

With less than a week to go before the November 7, 2000, election, David Lightman, a veteran reporter with the *Hartford Courant* in Hartford, Connecticut, found himself standing outside the South Ocean Grill in Palm Beach, Florida, waiting for a press bus and a two-hour bus ride to Port St. Lucie, Florida, for a Bush-Cheney rally. Lightman was on his second day with the vice presidential campaign of Dick Cheney. He was originally scheduled to travel with George W. Bush, but he was "bumped" at the last minute to make room for reporters from the media in swing states. Campaign officials, he explained, "knew they weren't going to take Connecticut, so they bumped me." Lightman was one of several reporters who got bumped from the Bush plane in that final week as the campaign staff readjusted seating to make room for reporters from media outlets in swing states—states where the race between Bush and Al Gore was close and where the extra news coverage might make a difference in the outcome.

Being bumped to Cheney's plane meant several things for Lightman and the *Hartford Courant*. First, it meant more cost to the *Courant*, since the cost for a seat was a simple matter of dividing the number of available press seats by the number of journalists sitting in them. It also meant less pressure on Lightman to produce a fresh story every day, since the news from the vice presidential candidates often is folded into someone else's story or a political roundup column. And it meant less prominent play for Lightman's daily stories because, unless the vice presidential candidates are saying something very different from the presidential candidates, it's the "primaries"—in the case of the 2000 election, Bush and Gore—who are the newsmakers in the final days of the election season. In fact, if Joe Lieberman, the Democratic vice presidential candidate, had been from somewhere other than Connecticut, Lightman might well have stayed home rather than taking the bump to Cheney's plane.

"The only reason I'm here is we have to be fair because we're doing so much on Lieberman," Lightman said. "We were looking for an excuse to cover Cheney more, and the schedule gave us a hook—the fact that he and Lieberman are both in Florida on the same days. I had hoped to be with Bush. I've been doing this since 1980 and I've never been bumped before. But Connecticut is gone. It's Gore's state. They only wanted people [on the Bush plane] who serve the governor's needs."

So, on Wednesday, November 1, 2000, Lightman and nine other journalists from newspapers, television, and the wire services found themselves waiting outside the South Ocean Grill, a small diner where Cheney had just stumped for votes and signed autographs among a group of Republican volunteers over coffee and breakfast, for a bus that would take them north on Route 1 to the Thomas J. White Stadium in Port St. Lucie, where the New York Mets hold their spring training. The rest of the day would take Lightman and the rest of the press corps across the state to a second rally in Punta Gorda, Florida, and a press filing room at the local Holiday Inn, then to a third rally at the Weeki Wachee Springs theme park in Spring Hill, Florida, and finally to Nashville, Tennessee, at 9:30 p.m. for "RON"—or "rest overnight"—at the Opryland Hotel at the end of a 14-hour day. Lightman's story the next morning, which was coauthored with Liz Halloran, was a page-one piece that examined the styles of the two vice presidential candidates as they "crisscrossed Florida Wednesday in search of its 25 electoral votes" (Lightman & Halloran, 2000, p. A1). The analysis and context carry the top of the story, with the first quote from a candidate—in this case, Lieberman, who's being quoted from an appearance on *Today*—coming in the seventh paragraph.

THE CHANGING ROLES OF THE JOURNALIST

Journalists bring to their profession differing views of the roles they should play as reporters. Johnstone, Slawski, and Bowman (1972, 1976) identified two roles—the neutral observer and the participant journalist. The former see their role as simply to transmit the events they see to the public. They value speed of communication, accuracy, and objectivity, and believe that reporters should remain uninvolved in the stories that they cover. For them, the journalist is an "impartial transmission link dispensing information to the public" (Johnstone et al., 1976, p. 114). Those who advocate a participant role acknowledge that journalists can't be completely objective—even by choosing what goes in the lead versus what goes in the fourth paragraph they are using some subjectivity—therefore the duty of the reporter is to seek out stories and take some responsibility for them. For participant reporters, the characteristics that are highly valued are investigation, analysis, and interpretation. The participant journalist takes "personal responsibility for the information he seeks to transmit, and his relation to news sources is more circumscribed: sources provide leads but the reporter must sift through them for the real story" (Johnstone et al., 1976, p. 115). Although the two roles seem incompatible, Johnstone et al. (1972, 1976) found that most reporters straddled both worlds. While they tended to have a stronger belief in one of the two roles—older, less educated journalists favored a neutral role, while younger, college-educated reporters favored a participant role—the values associated with each role were shared by most journalists.

Janowitz (1975) notes that there has been a shift over time in the roles that journalists believe they serve in society. He said the gatekeeper role (the neutral journalist of Johnstone et al.) sought scientific objectivity as a goal for providing verifiable information for the public. In this model,

> the journalist sought to apply the canons of the scientific method and enhance his effective performance. The model was reinforced in part by the increased prestige of the academic social researcher, and it assumed that, through the application of intellectually based techniques, objective, and valid results could be obtained. The gatekeeper orientation emphasized the search for objectivity and the sharp separation of reporting fact from disseminating opinion. (Janowitz, 1975, p. 618)

Over time, however, journalists began to question the neutral role and began seeing their function as being social critics and interpreters. The model changed from one of detachment to one of involvement, and the advocate journalist (or participant journalist in the language of Johnstone et al.) strives for fairness and social justice. Culbertson (1983) identified a third role—an activist one—in his study of journalists. The newspeople in this role "endorse the use of news columns to tell people how they can right society's wrongs. Such a journalist takes change agents and reformers . . . as role models" (Culbertson, 1983, p. 18).

Later work by Weaver and Wilhoit (1996) further refined the concept of role conceptions. In their survey of working journalists, the authors identified four different role conceptions held by reporters—a disseminator role, an interpretive role, an adversarial role, and a "populist mobilizer" role. The disseminator role was similar to the neutral observer identified by Johnstone et al. (1972, 1976). The journalists who identified with the disseminator role were those who thought their primary duty was to get information to the public as quickly as possible. Those who advocated an interpretive function were similar to Johnstone et al.'s participants—they thought it was important to investigate stories and provide their readers with analysis of complex issues. Weaver and Wilhoit (1996) added a third and fourth role to the mix, however. The adversarial role is one that puts journalists at odds with their sources and encourages a skeptical, perhaps even cynical view of those in power—especially those in government. The populist mobilizer role, which can be seen in attempts at civic journalism, holds that journalists need to help develop public interest, set the public agenda, and provide a forum for ordinary citizens to express their opinions. In the 1996 Weaver and Wilhoit study, journalists again straddled multiple roles, but the authors found that the interpretive role was the most common (62 percent), followed by the disseminator role (51 percent), the adversarial role (17 percent), and finally the populist mobilizer role (6 percent). In the most recent update of that study, the interpretive role emerged as the most strongly endorsed role, with 63 percent of journalists rating it as important (Weaver et al., 2007). The disseminator role was endorsed by only 16 percent in the most recent study, while the adversarial role was deemed important by 19 percent of journalists, and the populist mobilizer role was rated highly by 10 percent. Still, as in past studies, most journalists held multiple role conceptions, with heavy overlap between the interpretive, adversarial, and disseminator functions. The authors concluded that "journalists have their priorities in terms of role conceptions, but these priorities are not exclusive. Not only do they recognize the existence or necessity of other journalistic roles; they accord those roles substantial importance" (Weaver et al., 2007, p. 146).

CHANGING CONTEXTS FOR CAMPAIGN JOURNALISTS

As a young reporter covering John F. Kennedy's primary campaign in 1960, Jules Witcover writes that he was able to walk alongside the candidate as Kennedy stumped for votes in communities across the country, and frequently got to join Kennedy for a drink and a long chat about the day's events (1977). In his memoir, Jack Germond (1999) writes about spending a three-hour flight in 1968 from Omaha, Nebraska, to Washington, D.C., talking about children living in poverty with Robert Kennedy, who was starting his run for the presidency. Scott Shepard of Cox Newspapers traveled with the Hubert Humphrey campaign in 1968 and talked about getting invited, along with a handful of other reporters, to go out to dinner with the candidate when the campaign stopped for the day. But, as Witcover points out, the world of campaign reporting has changed since the 1960s.

Presidential campaigns have become marathon exercises in complex logistics, and except for the longest long shots in the early primaries, presidential candidates are often remote and inaccessible to the traveling press attempting to take their measure for the American voters. (Witcover, 1977, p. 4)

The changes are myriad. More news outlets and a 24-hour news cycle have made the media more omnipresent, and the waning political party system has made the media more important. But changes also have occurred with the campaigns, which have increasingly turned to political strategists to set the tone and the agenda for the election and to costly national advertising campaigns to reach voters. And the electorate has changed. Declining voter turnout is evidence of less interest in politics and elections, candidate character and electability have become new standards for vote choice, and there's a long-held belief that the public doesn't really want the "nuts-and-bolts" news about government and elected officials, said John Salant, a Washington, D.C., correspondent for the Syracuse, New York, newspaper (Stepp, 1992). Finally, the press corps itself has changed, according to some who have been a part of it for decades. Witcover (1977) writes that a generation of political reporters who came of age during the Vietnam War and Watergate are holding candidates to a higher set of standards than their predecessors. They're also more likely to inject their own perceptions—typically ones colored by a strong sense of cynicism—into their stories, said *USA Today* reporter Richard Benedetto, who has covered national politics since the 1980 presidential election.

In the late 1960s, the reporters were of a different generation. Many of them were still of the World War II generation. They basically kept their personal opinions about politics to themselves. They had no axes to grind. They weren't advocates of anything. And they liked politicians as a group. They also had a good feel for their communities and they knew that without taking a poll. . . . A lot of journalists now come in with a set of attitudes about politics. They've got more formal education, and they came into the business thinking they were going to change the world in some way.—Richard Benedetto, July 2006

But even reporters like Benedetto, who advocate a more traditional role for the media as news disseminators, are increasingly using what they observe and their own insights to provide what they believe to be more meaningful news coverage. In some cases, these are the stories that editors are looking for—partly because they provide more detail and analysis than the nightly news can in the limited space it has, and partly because they believe it serves a public good. Benedetto said that while covering what the candidates are saying and doing is an important function for campaign reporters, it's not the sole function. It's also his job, he said, to pay attention to the reactions of the crowds at rallies and to size up the electoral health of a candidate using what he sees from the confines of the press bus. At the 2004 debate in Arizona, for example, Benedetto got a sense of the Bush and Kerry campaigns from the postdebate rallies.

> Bush went to a baseball park. I was never so amazed. There were 55,000 seats that were filled. When I looked around the crowd, I saw that they were from all walks of life—young and old—but they were all hugely supportive of Bush. Kerry had about 8,000 people at his rally, mostly young kids. That told me two things: that Bush had more broad-based support, and that the Republicans were highly organized. I wrote about it, but that's a column kind of thing or an analysis. You use your observations to draw some conclusions.—Richard Benedetto, July 2006

In fact, according to a study by Project for Excellence in Journalism, only 14 percent of the stories reported in the final weeks of the 2004 campaign relied on news dissemination as the primary goal. The majority of the stories were focused on internal campaign strategies (55 percent), with the rest divided among stories about policy stances (13 percent), candidate fitness (7 percent), and other topics (11 percent) (Project for Excellence in Journalism, 2004b). Interpretation, mostly through the lens of political strategy, also was the hallmark of 79 percent of the stories about the presidential debates (Project for Excellence in Journalism, 2004b). Benedetto and his colleague at *USA Today*, Martin Kasindorf, both said that the media have an obligation to report what the candidates are saying on any given day, but they—like most reporters—straddle the world between strict dissemination of news and providing some interpretation of events, what they call context. Kasindorf, who was covering the Kerry campaign in 2004, said that the candidates' messages do get covered every day, but

> there's increasing context being put into these stories comparing and contrasting the candidates. . . . Things are said for political reasons, policies are laid out for political reasons, and you always have to ask about that. How is it going to go over? And how to gauge what the likely benefit would be to the campaign. And you always got a Republican comment on it and what mileage they got out of it.—Martin Kasindorf, July 2006

Benedetto added that the emphasis on strategy and the political impact is driven by editors who "don't want to hear just what the candidate says today" and by the fact that only small changes are made in the candidate's stump speech from one day to the next. The sameness of the speeches leaves reporters looking for what's different, which may be the strategy or may be the handful of protesters in the back of the crowd. But all of that pushes political reporting into a more interpretive role, with the events of the day sometimes serving simply as backdrop for a broader story. That was often the case for Ann Scales, who as the White House reporter for the *Boston Globe* ended up covering Al Gore's campaign in 2000.

Traveling with a handful of other reporters from the Iowa caucuses to New Hampshire in late January for the primary election there on February 1, 2000, Scales was just at the start of a long campaign season. The cramped flight—dubbed the "Barbie plane" because it had maybe 50 seats and not enough room for all the reporters' equipment—and the long hours meant Scales was already exhausted when she landed in New Hampshire. Still, sitting in the basement of WMUR studios in Manchester, with about 500 other reporters who were covering the Republican and Democratic debates on January 26, Scales was listening for something that might resonate with her readers. Like most of the other journalists there, she was talking to the campaign press directors and political analysts who—even as the candidates were still debating upstairs—were putting their own spin on the debate, calling the winners and interpreting what it all meant. And while Scales and the other reporters there weren't completely buying what the pundits were saying, they were listening for the nuggets that would help them provide context for the debates so they could make sense of the process for their readers. Scales said that making sense of the political debate, especially when it involves reading the political tea leaves, is an important part of her job.

> You can't just report the event. Our job as political reporters is, oftentimes, picking up the nuances. For instance, the president said a week ago that tax cuts were off the table. Now he's saying after Social Security and Medicare have been shored up, he will consider it. You try to pick up on that difference and let people know that that change means something, because they drop these hints all the time, and you don't always know what they mean, but they really are significant. And part of our jobs—we're kind of the eyes and ears of the public—so we have to watch out for that.—Ann Scales, July 1999

For many reporters, part of the emphasis on the interpretive role is driven by their perceptions of their readers' interests, wants, and needs. Political journalists recognize that their interest in the campaign far outstrips that of most readers, so they have to interpret the nuances and seemingly small developments to provide the reader—who likely isn't following the story as closely—with the bigger meaning. Carl Leubsdorf of the *Dallas Morning News* said this often means putting the story in a context, such as the story his paper ran when Lamar Alexander announced his candidacy for the 2000 Republican nomination:

> In the past we've just done the straight kind of stories. But one of the editors said that's not very interesting. I said, well, if we make them

miniprofiles, if we tell the reader something about them, and say, for instance, two days after the 1996 election Lamar Alexander was back in Des Moines campaigning once again, you know, and discuss how he's been running ever since, that's more interesting than the traditional kind of a story. See, we try to make it interesting.—Carl Leubsdorf, July 1999

Even in Washington, D.C., where politics is the major employer and the *Washington Post* has built its reputation on providing comprehensive political coverage that includes a lot of the behind-the-scenes views of the business, the political reporters are realizing that they now have a broader audience that also needs to be served by their campaign coverage.

To the extent that it once was, this is no longer just a one-company town. . . . There are people who live in suburban areas who rarely come into the district and who are no more interested in the ins and outs of a lot of political stuff than the suburban reader in Philadelphia or Denver or Chicago or anybody else is. And I think we've all got to be conscious of trying to find ways to write politics that is accessible to readers like that, in addition to supplying the inside audience with the comings and goings of inside a campaign or inside the White House and that sort of thing.—Dan Balz, July 1999

The dramatic growth of the Internet and the ability to post stories, electoral maps and other information on the Web have made it easier for papers like the *Washington Post* to meet the needs of both political junkies and those less interested in every twist and turn of the campaigns, Balz said. Still, given that most people don't have as great an interest in elections and that the time they spend on news is shrinking, political journalists today face a tougher battle. They have to find ways to make the story interesting enough to draw the reader in, simple enough to make the point, and relevant to the criteria that they believe the reader will use when he or she evaluates the candidates. Reporters like the *Boston Globe*'s Ann Scales said readers won't stay with a story that is overly complex. Keeping the message simple, she said, is a better way to keep the reader interested. Charles Lewis, the Washington bureau chief for Hearst Newspapers, said that often means providing more explanation about the news of the day. That role sets up the journalist as the expert—a primary filter for the news—and reinforces his or her role as gatekeeper:

We need to make extra efforts to put on our educator's hat, which is to explain what a candidate stands for, explain what he or she represents, explain the culture or context of the candidate, and, yes, look at character. I'm unapologetic about looking at character. There's a line between the appropriate areas of examination and the inappropriate areas of examination, and I think I know where that line is.—Charles Lewis, July 1999

Certainly I am here to report on what they do . . . but if you are smart, you're not just regurgitating what they say. Your job is to take in what they say, analyze it, then apply common sense principles to their message. But it's never as clear-cut as that. When you're traveling, you have to think about where you're going with the campaign and why you're going there and what it means.—Wire service reporter, October 2000

A handful of reporters, however, argued that even though the journalists on the campaign trail should filter out the "noise" to provide readers with what's most important, that role shouldn't preclude covering what the candidates say. Benedetto said he has seen the amount of space given to what the candidate says grow ever smaller. In 1968, a candidate's quote on television averaged 42.3 seconds, and by 1988 it was down to 9.8 seconds (Wayne, 2000). During the 2000 and 2004 elections, the average candidate sound bite on television was down to 7.8 seconds, and compared to the candidates, journalists covering the campaigns had six times as much air time to talk about the election (Farnsworth & Lichter, 2007; Lichter & Lichter, 2000). Benedetto said that a similar shift away from the words of the candidates has occurred in the print media as well, which isn't serving the readers well. While the stories that provide the context and analysis of what's occurring are important, Benedetto and others said that the traditional role of journalist as scribe—as the one who brings the campaign to the voters—is one that should not be ignored in election coverage. Too often, he said, the traditional disseminator role is sacrificed for interpretive news coverage that puts the emphasis on the reporter and not the candidates.

What you have to remember is you are out there with the candidate and you're a surrogate for the people who aren't there. So therefore the more you can tell people who weren't there what went on, the better your reporting will be. And that's your job. You're a surrogate for the people. You don't have to handicap the race every day. It's far more necessary to report day-to-day what's going on out on the campaign trail, and I think that's become secondary today in reporting. . . . Sometimes what the candidate is saying today is important, even if he's said it before. He may say it 10 times a day, but the fact is the average citizen hasn't heard it once.—Richard Benedetto, June 2001

The decline of the disseminator role is apparent in most newspaper reporting (Hart, 2000). The shift to an interpretive role results partly from the fact that television, and now the Internet, are able to get the jump on breaking news, so newspapers need to provide greater context and analysis in their coverage in order to differentiate themselves from other forms of media. Also, readers increasingly want to know more than what happened; "they want to know *what it means* that something happened" (Hart, 2000, p. 97). Print journalists work to put the election and the candidates in a broader context than simply the backdrop of the campaign on any given day in an attempt to show readers the relevance of the campaign for their lives. This is particularly important, since one of the major reasons people don't vote is that they don't think the political system is relevant for their day-to-day lives (Doppelt & Shearer, 1999). Reporters who support an interpretive function for the media say that their stories can remedy that problem.

> I was taught in journalism school and by working journalists who were mentors to me to always consider the reader first—to, before you write a word, ask yourself, "So what? What does it mean? Why do I need to read this?" That has been the guiding principle for me as a political reporter. So what? Why should I care? How does this affect me? If you approach political reporting from that standpoint, the horse race becomes less interesting.—Ann Scales, July 1999

Viewing the issue from a slightly more cynical standpoint, Bill Lambrecht said that most voters are wary of the candidates for the White House and are driven by "a basic desire to know two things—who is this candidate and what's he or she going to do to me?" His job as a reporter is to couch the election in just those terms, whether through issue stories that compare the candidates to each other and that examine their records, or through profiles and character stories that give voters a chance to take the measure of the man or woman who might be sitting in the Oval Office. Dan Balz of the *Washington Post* said that with a readership that is becoming increasingly suburban, his newspaper has been gradually expanding its definition of what constitutes political coverage. The political junkies in Washington and the reporters on the campaign trail might delight in the behind-the-scenes stories from the campaign trail or "the latest sort of minicontroversy, which may be wonderfully delicious, but over time isn't going to have a great significance on peoples' lives," he said, but the outside-the-Beltway readers of the *Post* want something different.

> And so we have tried to broaden coverage and give different audiences different things. I mean, there are certain kinds of stories you write in a much more general way, and there are certain stories you write in a kind of inside way, and you have a political notes column or a politics column that kind of can do short bites to keep the political community happy, and you bring in particularly good writers to try to take a subject that's topical in a campaign and write it in a way that an outside audience can find interesting.—Dan Balz, July 1999

CHARACTER COUNTS

In covering the candidates for the White House, the one aspect of coverage that journalists universally agreed was important—both to making the story appealing to readers and to giving them important information for their electoral decisions—was coverage of the candidate's character. The interpretive journalist plays an important role in revealing to the reader something that goes beyond the facade of the candidate to better reflect the real person, flaws and all, who is running for office. A content analysis of candidate character coverage by the Project for Excellence in Journalism conducted in the summer of 2004 found that assertions about character traits—that George W. Bush was stubborn and arrogant or that John Kerry was very liberal—often were made without any evidence to support them, and were nearly as likely to come from journalists attempting to provide context as they were to come from the campaigns (2004a). The study also found that the media were shaping public perceptions about Bush and Kerry, noting that "the more people pay attention to press coverage, the more likely they are to match the character traits with the candidates the same way the press has" (Project for Excellence in Journalism, 2004a, p. 1). Campaign reporters say that the character traits—intelligence, temperament, honesty, consistency—are the criteria that voters use most to make decisions, so providing character coverage is even more important than providing coverage of the issues. Balz said the *Post* works hard to make sure that issues get coverage, but that stories about the horse race or about the campaign strategies "tend to drown it out." Still, the cry for more issue-oriented coverage may be a smoke screen, he said:

> What we have found is that there is, at least in the abstract, a desire both within news organizations and certainly with the public, for issue coverage. But we also find that those are the stories that we suspect are to most readers the least accessible, the first ignored, and in many ways the least satisfactory. In part, that's because I don't think we're very good at figuring out how you make certain kinds of issues stories interesting.—Dan Balz, July 1999

In part, however, the lack of interest in issue-oriented stories may simply be a reflection of what voters really want versus what they say they want. Just as the need for social approval will cause people to overreport their intent to vote in an election survey, the same need will drive them to overreport their interest in issue coverage when asked about the kinds of stories they want in election coverage, according to the reporters who cover campaigns. Instead, it's their gut reactions to the demeanor and personality of the candidates that often play a major role in voters' evaluations of those running for office. That was the case in the 2000 election, when public perception of the candidates' honesty was the issue that dominated voters' choices on Election Day (Frankovic & McDermott, 2001). And character became a key issue in the 2004 election cycle when Republican campaign strategists—knowing that John Kerry needed to concentrate on raising funds in the spring of 2004—focused on creating an image problem for Kerry by saying he flip-flopped on issues like the war in Iraq. Matthew Dowd, a chief strategist for the Bush-Cheney campaign, said the goal was to get voters to question Kerry's character.

> We understood the financial situation they were in. That's why we did what we did. … It was the beginning of a definitional period for John Kerry for the general election, and we wanted to impact his credibility to make an argument against us. That was the main point of what we were doing in the spring, so that his ability to affect our numbers would be reduced because, in my mind, for an incumbent president—especially this president—what our approval was and what our numbers were were more important than anything else. So if we can cause the voters to say, John Kerry is attacking the President on X—whatever it is, Iraq, the economy, health care, whatever—if they have a question in their mind that what they are hearing is true, it is a benefit to us. … That was the main reason we did it, and I think we were effective at it. (Institute of Politics, pp. 83–84)

The result is that candidates have to be concerned about the image they project in their own speeches and events, as well as through the lens of their opponents, because image and character often take center stage in the mass media.

In addition to putting candidates to the test by putting them under the glare of media scrutiny, Cragg Hines of the *Houston Chronicle* said that stories that delve into a candidate's character are a bigger part of election coverage because "people do, in large part, vote for someone because of gut instincts and gut feelings about someone—about their personality, about a candidate's ability to deliver. . . . I think that's an almost unspeakably important part of how a voter makes a decision." For Patty Reinert, who covered the Gore campaign for the *Houston Chronicle*, character coverage is important for undecided voters, as well as those who may have strong party affiliations or may have made a decision early in the campaign season.

> Say they've made up their mind in January and they're not voting until November—they still need to know that George Bush was arrested for DWI and hid it for all those years. They need to know if anything comes up on Gore's fundraising. It might change their mind, or it might just make them better informed as to what decision they're making.— Patty Reinert, June 2001

But most of the character-oriented stories are broader than simply a one-shot piece on an event in the candidate's past. At papers like the *Washington Post* and *New York Times*, multipart profiles of the major candidates began appearing more than a year before the 2000 and 2004 elections. The stories were attempts to reveal the interior characters of the candidates and the forces that shaped their personalities and their values. The *Post*'s Dan Balz said it's the kind of coverage that in 1992 brought David Maraniss a Pulitzer Prize for his coverage of Bill Clinton and Clinton's campaign.

> We understand that particularly in terms of presidential coverage, that people want to know as much as they can about who these people are who are running. Where did they come from? What have they done? What are their records? How do they portray themselves as opposed to what others say about them? That whole thing. So we've put a lot more into the kind of biographical work of campaign coverage than we used to. . . . I mean you've read it and seen it, too, this kind of personalization of the vote. And, as a result, people kind of take a measure of presidential candidates on a personal basis in a way they never do with a member of Congress, except someone like Newt Gingrich, who is prominent. So I think that that affects it. But there's no question that the coverage of Congress, coverage of the White House, coverage of politics have all become much more personality focused than it was 20 years ago.—Dan Balz, July 1999

The evolution from the coverage that emphasized the candidates' speeches and stump events, which predominated in the 1960s, to the contemporary model of coverage has been somewhat gradual. Most reporters agree that Theodore White's *The Making of the President* books on presidential campaigns started shifting the focus of coverage to closer inspections of the candidates and the campaigns, leading front-line reporters to look for stories that would be more revealing about the players and the campaign. And the candidates themselves drove some of the shift to coverage that makes character a key issue.

> I mean, go back to '84. In our coverage, we did the profile of Gary Hart that discovered that he had changed his name and changed his age. That was good investigative reporting that was revealing about a person that told us something we didn't know. But in '84, the coverage of the sexual life of a candidate was still an area that nobody really wanted to go to.—Dan Balz, July 1999

Four years later when Gary Hart was the front-runner, however, his sexual escapades with Donna Rice became front-page news after he repeatedly denied rumors about an extramarital affair and then essentially challenged the journalists covering him to prove otherwise. The *Miami Herald* did just that. And while most character coverage of the candidates does not focus on their sexual lives, it does "poke deeply into the lives and records of the candidates and present a coherent picture of who the candidates are," said Bill Lambrecht. He said that is a key role for the media, especially the print media, which have the space to devote to more lengthy probes into the candidates' personal and professional histories. In the *Dallas Morning News*, for example, stories in the summer of 1999 focused on George W. Bush and religion, looking at his beliefs, his own religious practices, and his view of religion and politics. The result, Carl Leubsdorf said, was a story that was "revealing" about Bush as a potential president. Cragg Hines said it's those profiles, which may get their genesis from a campaign issue, but then go much further, that are important in helping the readers better understand the candidates.

> As candidates come to discuss issues, it is incumbent on us to write about them. And then, as the campaign progresses, you write the comparative policy story. You write profiles, where you discuss the range of policies. And also, in addition to that, you discuss the motivation. What are the sort of bedrock tenets of the candidates that move them to the strange little business of seeking the presidency? After all, normal people don't run for president.—Cragg Hines, July 1999

Indeed, Walter Cronkite argued that since the political parties—which have been weakened by the party reform movements of the early 1970s and largely replaced by the primary election system—no longer vet the candidates for office, the media has an obligation to do so.

> The broadcast and print press today must be the monitors on the character of our candidates for public office. The days are gone when the political bosses, who knew the candidates well, screened them for drinking, gambling, womanizing, plagiarizing, or patronizing psychiatrists. With the candidates going directly to the public through the primaries, it's now up to the press to serve the public interest by doing the nasty but necessary job of screening through revelation. (Cronkite, 1998, p. 67)

But the profiles and candidate-focused coverage that campaign reporters specialize in today do more than examine a candidate's beliefs. They also examine a candidate's style—his comfort level on the campaign trail, his reception by the crowds, his energy for the job. Richard Benedetto of *USA Today* said that often the coverage of a candidate's speech talks more about the delivery of that speech than its content. And while that tendency is especially pronounced on television, Benedetto said that when a reporter is following a candidate, and hearing the same stump speech several times a day for weeks in a row, the speech itself is no longer news. Therefore, the candidate's delivery and the crowd response become the story.

> In 1988 I was traveling with [George H. W.] Bush in Columbus, Ohio. He goes to a steel plant and he's making a speech right in the steel plant. And I'm standing out in the crowd toward the back of the crowd and there are a bunch of guys who are wearing union T-shirts for Dukakis—hard-hat guys with their T-shirts on saying Mike Dukakis for president. And Bush is speaking and they're applauding. . . . So I went over to these guys and I said to them after the speech was over, "I notice that you're wearing Dukakis T-shirts and that you're applauding Bush." And they said, "Yeah, we have to wear these T-shirts. Our union's making us wear them." But they were for Bush because he was strong on defense. This was '88 when the Cold War was still on. So they were for Bush because he was strong on defense. So, see, there was a perfect example and I got a good angle out of that. And one of the things I concluded was, when I heard that, I said it's all over with. If Dukakis is not getting these guys, he's not going to be able to win.—Richard Benedetto, June 2001

Reporters look to the crowd for signals about how the candidate is doing among the rank-and-file voters. They look to the crowd for a new angle on what, by the third or fourth day of covering the same speech, is quickly becoming old news. And they look to the crowd because often there is little else that is different from one town to the next. While the speech or proposals may be new to the audience in Peoria, after the first day the candidate's words don't play well with the press.

> A lot of times they did say the same thing every day, and the only difference was who they were saying it to. So then I think it becomes more important to tell the reader what kind of a reception the candidate got. What was Gore's reception in West Virginia or Florida or whatever? How did the people react to him? Then the crowd becomes much more important than what the candidate actually said.—Patty Reinert, June 2001

While those in the audience may be the focus of some campaign stories, their role is simply to be a barometer. Journalists who canvass the crowd at a speech or rally are looking for ways to assess a candidate's style, as well as his or her chances of winning the election and the overall health of the candidate's campaign. These are stories that often involve a focus on the campaign strategies—called "inside baseball" stories among the journalists—and they are now common in election coverage. And while voters and media critics argue that there is too much emphasis on the behind-the-scenes, "inside baseball" story, the reporters who cover elections argue that the way a candidate runs his or her campaign can tell voters a lot about the kind of president he or she will be.

An example would be staff maneuvering with Al Gore, which began as minutia, but we're offering a story that tries to inform our readers about the turmoil that now surrounds his campaign staff and tries to put that in perspective. . . . [Gore] brought on a new pollster. He now has four pollsters, which is a bit. This speaks to a management style that may be somewhat unwieldy. It speaks to the potential confusion of message. It speaks to potential trying to be all things to all people.—Don Frederick, July 1999

Most often, these stories are triggered by ideas that the reporter has and things that he or she observes as the campaign progresses. One reporter for an East Coast daily said that the news features he did on Dick Cheney looked at how the candidate was preparing for his debate with Joe Lieberman, the Democratic vice presidential nominee, and examined Cheney's style, which most reporters described as uncomfortable. A story in the *Atlanta Journal and Constitution* in early October 2000 also made note of Cheney's awkward demeanor on the stump.

Cheney sometimes appears ill at ease in front of crowds and reporters, reluctant to make small talk and work a room full of supporters or undecided voters.

Even when he's on the attack, as he was last week when he questioned Vice President Al Gore's credibility, Cheney's criticisms often lack a pithy quote that helps distill an issue for his audiences. (Sherman, 2000)

The night she covered the presidential debates in the fall, Patty Reinert provided the same kind of description to give readers a sense of Bush and Gore under fire.

I tried to give a little color of the evening, like if someone would tell a joke or someone seemed very nervous or totally at ease or walked around the stage. You know, sort of factual things that would tell the reader what it was like to be there. But as far as analysis on who won or lost or whatever, we had someone else doing that who was sort of removed from the campaigns.—Patty Reinert, June 2001

Still, in the choices to cover style over speech and to characterize a candidate as comfortable or stiff, the journalists are shaping public perceptions of the candidates, as the research on second-level agenda setting shows (Lopez-Escobar et al., 1998). Readers pick up on the characterizations supplied by the press, even when the reporters aren't specifically saying that a candidate has lost ground or is uneasy in a crowd.

In addition to interpreting the actions of the candidates, reporters also said that they have an obligation to provide some perspective on the campaign itself, which often means interpreting the behaviors and the things that aren't being said, as well as the things that are said. Again, these are stories that spring from the observations of the journalist, sometimes to the chagrin of the campaign staff. One reporter, talking about his coverage of Cheney in the final days of the fall 2000 campaign, said he did a lengthy feature talking about how the Bush campaign would use Cheney in the last two weeks, including the campaign swing in Florida—obviously a close state—with retired U.S. Gen. Norman Schwarzkopf, a popular hero from the Persian Gulf War.

> You don't have to be captive to the daily news developments. My favorite stories are the ones that are forward-looking pieces or ones that go behind the scenes. . . . Half of reporting is to tell the readers why they're doing whatever it is they're doing. We're trying to go beyond what they're saying to talk about why they're saying it. That means you might call someone like Karl Rove to talk about the campaign strategy, or you might call on a political analyst.—East Coast daily reporter, October 2000

Stories about the campaign are designed to show voters how the candidates or the political parties may be trying to position themselves with the electorate, and they typically talk about the reasons behind the political maneuvering. In the case of the candidates, it's generally couched in discussions of electoral strategy. In the case of the political parties and the national nominating conventions, it's generally done to assess whether the political parties are in touch with the electorate and what the party leaders are trying to do to reflect an image that resonates with voters. Don Frederick of the *Los Angeles Times* said that his paper's coverage of the 1996 Republican Convention in San Diego focused more on the reporters' views of the image that the Republican Party intended to convey than it did on anything that was said from the podium.

> I think we try and use the convention to both elaborate on where the party is going, what the candidate is up to, and to read between the lines as to who is on the podium. In some cases it's more important, so that in '96 at the San Diego Republican Convention, the fact that they were really trying to put a more moderate face on the speakers that they paraded before the convention—more women, more minorities—showed they wanted a less combative face than the '92 convention in Houston. It was the key. . . . So what we tried to do in that coverage was not just report the speech, but try to give a more sophisticated look at why this person was picked and what it says about the party's message as a whole.—Don Frederick, July 1999

Journalists who advocate an interpretive role do see themselves as a filter to screen out the irrelevant noise of the campaign and even as a prism through which events are refracted and placed into a broader political context. But there are other reasons, perhaps more pragmatic ones, that print journalists cite when they talk about the shift to a more interpretive role. The first of these is competition. Revelations about the candidates—personal or professional—will be published by someone somewhere, so why not them?

> Today there's much more of an effort to reveal. And part of it is driven by competitiveness. If someone doesn't do it, someone else will do it. Some of it is because it will sell. Some of it is that the public has a right to know everything. Well, the public has a right to know most things if someone chooses to be president or run for president.—Carl Leubsdorf, July 1999

But more often, they say, it's the result of television, the Internet, and the 24-hour news cycle. In the 1960s and even into the 1970s, newspaper reporters tended to lead the pack when it came to campaign coverage. But gradually, as the campaign staffs began to realize the impact of television, events were scheduled with the six o'clock news in mind. In the late 1980s, however, with the growth of CNN and other all-news outlets, and in the 1990s with the 24-hour Internet, the role of the print reporter has shifted from one of being the eyes and ears on the campaign to one of being the analyst. Benedetto said that even in the 1980 campaign—his first national campaign—television and newspapers were keeping their coverage focused on events and speeches.

> The candidates would do their events, primarily hoping the evening news would broadcast something about them. And the networks basically sent their news crews on those trips for the purpose of something to put on the evening news that was a straight report on here was Ronald Reagan and here is what he had to say . . . period. Newspapers were doing the same thing. They were reporting back to their papers basically what the candidate was doing and what the candidate was saying. And at the end of the week they'd write a sum-up piece to say here is what we saw—more of an interpretive piece indicating what the candidate might have done over that particular period. Today it's very difficult for reporters who are on the road with the candidates to write a story that is straight because you have those 24-hour news channels where they're putting some of that on live. And therefore the newspapers and network TV news shows want something different. What they want is something more interpretive, something more analytical on a daily basis.—Richard Benedetto, July 1999

While newspapers may no longer be the medium to which people turn for breaking news, they do have the advantage of having longer deadlines, which means that newspapers can provide the perspective and analysis that television and the Internet don't have the time to do. Several reporters noted the increasing importance of this interpretive function for print journalism:

> People have no shortage of outlets for information. I think that the role of a print journalist is to help synthesize all of the information that's bombarding readers and voters and to help filter it for them. There's the Internet and the television and talk radio and the candidates' characters—one of the key roles print plays is to assimilate that and present a coherent picture of the candidate for office and how that person would impact the voters' lives.—Bill Lambrecht, July 1999

> You know, the cycles are 24 hours and everything is very quick. And you do have to spin every story forward. So the night that the Iowa caucuses take place, the story will be not only that Bush won, but how much he won by and who else is in the race in New Hampshire. You can't do the fallout the next day, you've got to do it that night. You've got to do all that that night because that's what you can have that the networks won't.—Carl Leubsdorf, July 1999

The shift in roles for print journalists from that of a news disseminator to an interpreter of campaign events has resulted in coverage that Cragg Hines of the *Houston Chronicle* argues is "much more savvy, much less 'he said, she said.'" But it comes at a cost. There is less room for the candidates in today's news, and there is more room for journalists to be wrong as they foreshadow a candidate's downfall—as they did with Bill Clinton after the Gennifer Flowers story broke in 1992—only to have events turn out differently. The journalistic "stargazing" is one thing that, according to Hanson (1996), is adding to the declining credibility ratings of the media. Perhaps more important is the fact that the shift to an interpretive role for print journalists has reporters sifting through each press conference and every event looking for signs of a candidate in trouble. Ed Chen of the *Los Angeles Times* said that print journalists, because they have more time to write and more space for a story, can report on the problems in a campaign "in infinite detail, which television doesn't have time for." The net effect is that the candidates and their staffs look at print journalists more warily, seeing them as more likely to cause trouble for the campaign. And as print journalists are pushed away and viewed skeptically, they become more skeptical about the confidence of the candidate. The catch-22 of it all begins to set up a relationship that can, at times, become almost antagonistic.

THE JOURNALIST AS ADVERSARY

With one week to go before the November 7, 2000, election, the Bush and Gore campaigns were traveling long hours and campaigning hard. For Dick Cheney, there had already been rallies and speeches in Minnesota, Iowa, Illinois, and Missouri before his stop in Hot Springs, Arkansas, on October 31. As he did at most stops, Cheney scheduled a short question-and-answer session for the local media in Arkansas just after his rally at the Hot Springs Convention Center. What was different at this stop, though, was that rather than being shuffled off to the makeshift filing center, members of the national press were invited to the interview session with the vice presidential nominee. The only condition, said Juleanna Glover Weiss, Cheney's press secretary, was that the members of the local media would get to ask questions first, and then she would open it up to the national press corps.

The reporters from the local media asked about the nation's military readiness and the relative experience of Al Gore and George Bush—topics Cheney had hit hard in his speech, including his often-repeated political mantra that Gore didn't have the right credentials to be president because he had never had to meet a payroll. After a few minutes, the national press started getting itchy. David Lawsky, a reporter for Reuters, was the first to jump in with a question about the campaign's final days, then Michael Cooper from the *New York Times* fired another question—this one about a Bush proposal to provide federal funds to faith-based organizations. Karen Gullo of the Associated Press followed up with another question on the topic, asking why the proposal to support the work of faith-based organizations was back on the campaign agenda. Martin Kasindorf of *USA Today* was next. Flipping to the back of his notepad, he pointed out to Cheney that former presidents Ronald Reagan, Franklin Delano Roosevelt, Teddy Roosevelt, and Abraham Lincoln also had never met a payroll prior to becoming president. So, he asked, is it really all that important as a qualification for the White House?

"That's it," Weiss announced, saying that Cheney had a radio interview to do. As the national press corps was being shuttled back to the press filing area, Lawsky exploded. After weeks of no access, he grumbled to Weiss, when the campaign finally did give some access to Cheney, why was it shut down before everyone traveling with the candidate had the opportunity to ask a question—let alone any follow-up questions? For the next hour or so, the filing room was unusually quiet as the journalists worked on their copy for the day. Several times through the afternoon and evening Weiss checked back with Lawsky and the rest of the press corps, trying to mend fences. "Are you okay? Do you need anything?" she'd ask. What they wanted, they said, was access to Cheney. But because candidates are wary of the national press, access is difficult to come by—even when the candidate is only a dozen rows away on the same plane.

Reporters, writes Rem Rieder of *American Journalism Review*, are a cynical lot. And while it would "do the electorate no favors to cover campaigns C-SPAN style, simply recording utterly disingenuous pronouncements with a straight face," it also doesn't serve the voters to let too much of that cynicism creep into news coverage (Rieder, 1996, p. 2). But journalistic cynicism does show up in what reporters have to say about the campaigns and even in what they write. Adam Clymer of the *New York Times* writes that there are three categories of candidate speech:

> The first category comprises candidates saying what they believe, as long as they think it will help them politically. . . . In a second category, candidates say what their handlers tell them to say—without believing or disbelieving it. . . . These two areas comprise almost all campaign speech. To be sure, there is a third category: when candidates simply lie about their beliefs because they think it will help them politically. (Clymer, 2001, p. 780).

What's notable here is that Clymer's typology doesn't have room for the possibility that a candidate might say something that he or she believes for principled reasons. Every word, in his view, is part of a larger political calculation. The cynical stance of some journalists translates into a more negative tone in news coverage, according to a July 2004 study on character coverage by the Project for Excellence in Journalism. The study identifies seven predominant themes, three about Bush and four about Kerry. For Bush, one theme—that he was strong and decisive—is a positive trait, but the remaining two—that he was arrogant and unwilling to admit mistakes, and that he lacked credibility—are clearly negative (Project for Excellence in Journalism, 2004a). For Kerry, the positive attribute was that he was tough and wouldn't back down from a fight, but three other themes were derogatory: that he was indecisive, that he was "very liberal," and that he was elitist (Project for Excellence in Journalism, 2004a). What's more significant is the proportion of these themes in news coverage. For Bush, 56 percent of the coverage was negative and 16 percent was positive; for Kerry, 23 percent was negative and 4 percent was positive (Project for Excellence in Journalism, 2004a). These themes become the "meta-narratives" of the campaign, write Bill Kovach and Tom Rosenstiel (2001b), and make it difficult for reporters who might want to write something contradictory to the conventional wisdom about the candidates.

Ed Chen of the *Los Angeles Times* said that the campaign views the members of the national press corps as being "out there to catch mistakes. We cover more ground and that often spells danger for the candidate. The national media feel like they have to play 'truth squad,' pointing out the errors or exaggerations in what the candidates are saying." That's the reason Kasindorf challenged Cheney on his assertion that good presidents are those who know what it means to meet a payroll. And it's the reason that many campaign journalists take a stance with the campaigns that is sometimes antagonistic and often adversarial.

> We don't take at face value anything that they say. Sometimes we make the news by challenging the candidate on his facts. . . . These guys talk about the accountability of the media, but reporters have a function to hold their feet to the fire to be accurate, just as they expect us to be accurate. Of course, this function may make no difference to the voters. For instance, we reported on Ronald Reagan when he said that trees cause pollution. But the people didn't care. They forgave him. So the journalists finally gave up. If the people don't want to hold them accountable for what they say, then we're shouting into the wind.—East Coast daily reporter, October 2000

Benedetto of *USA Today* said that there's a need for "truth reporting" in campaign coverage. Candidates may distort or exaggerate facts to their advantage, and in those cases simply reporting what they're saying is doing a disservice to readers. However, he also argued for some caution in the truth reporting, since it can cast a negative pall on the candidates and the political process. It also can underestimate the intelligence of voters, he said.

> For instance, I sort of have mixed feelings about ad watches. It's based on the assumption that the public is stupid. . . . To the degree that we try to interpret those ads or say, "Hey, wait a minute. This guy isn't being truthful," . . . I don't know. The public should be able to figure that out. And many times they do. I mean people aren't that gullible that they'll believe whatever comes across a TV ad. Now if a candidate is actually lying, maybe there's a purpose to them. But these are gradations, and the public isn't sucked in by most of that. They figure it out.—Richard Benedetto, June 2001

For the reporters, the rationale for ad watches and truth reporting springs from the idea that the candidates and their staffs will try to manipulate the voters and the press. The watershed for journalists came after Ronald Reagan's first term as president and his 1984 reelection campaign, which were high on image and, according to Dan Balz, "like a free advertisement as opposed to tough-minded coverage" of the campaign. Even in 1988, however, the coverage still followed the events and was less critical in its inspection of the candidates and what they were saying. The result, by 1992, was a pledge in most newsrooms that the press wasn't going to fall for any of those flag-factory photo-ops that made a mockery of campaign coverage in 1988. This year, the reporters vowed, candidates wouldn't be allowed to keep dodging the press, or their opponents, or tough questions on major issues. (Guttenplan, 1992a, p. 1).

Indeed, at the *Washington Post*, the lessons of 1980, 1984, and 1988 led to coverage that was less focused on the agenda of the candidate, with the *Post*'s editors and reporters fighting to control what they ended up writing. But that struggle has put the campaigns and reporters increasingly at odds in the battle for control over the message that reaches the voters on any given day.

I think '80 was a kind of the culmination of the Reagan talent of making the visual presentation of politics the message. And in '80 and '84, I think everybody marveled at it because it was newer to us, they were really good at it, and they were successful at it. But by '88 there was a feeling that the politicians and political operatives were more skillful at understanding how we did our jobs and how we would respond to certain stimuli than we were at kind of piercing through some of the phoniness of that. And by the end of the '88 campaign, I think people just kind of said the way we've covered campaigns these last few cycles, we've got to figure out a different way because, you know, they'd take us to a nice backdrop and have a nice message and we'd report it and show it, and it was like a free advertisement as opposed to tough-minded coverage about, you know, Bush or Dukakis and what they've done and what they've said.

And so, here at the *Post* we had long discussions after the campaign about what aspects of it were not satisfying in terms of our coverage, where did we think we kind of got off track, how could we do it better in '92. And I think that led to a little less attention on the daily stuff coming out of the candidates and more rigorous looks at the backgrounds of these candidates. I mean, just to make the coverage less dependent on where the candidate was on any given day and what that candidate chose to talk about. You cover major speeches—there's no question about that. But the little hit of the day, you say we don't need to do that every day. You know, they can buy their ads for that, but we don't have to pay all this money to travel with them to just write what they want us to write, just because they show up and say it.—Dan Balz, July 1999

On the Gore plane in 2000, the tensions were high at times, going "somewhat beyond adversarial and short of animosity" (Mnookin, 2000b, p. 33)—particularly between Gore staffers and three women journalists who came to be called the Spice Girls. The reporters—Ceci Connolly of the *Washington Post*, Katharine Seelye of the *New York Times*, and Sandra Sobieraj of the Associated Press—were criticized for being biased against Gore and writing stories with an especially negative undertone. Mnookin (2000b, p. 33), writing for *Brill's Content*, argues that "there's no 'there' there" in the criticism of the stories written by Connolly, Seelye, or Sobieraj.

> For instance, Connolly described how Gore slammed the pharmaceutical industry by writing that "Gore's rhetoric included such words as 'baloney,' 'collusion,' 'cahoots' and 'loopholes.'" . . . The *Times* reporter [Seelye] poked fun at Gore for occasionally calling his "progress and prosperity tour" a "prosperity and progress tour." But given the inanity of political slogans, that's the humorous point: Even the candidate sometimes can't keep it straight. (Mnookin, 2000b, p. 33)

While the coverage of Gore may not have been biased or negative, it was aimed at pointing out the candidate's weaknesses and the problems in the campaign process. And the Spice Girls weren't the only ones doing it. Don Frederick said the *Los Angeles Times* sent a reporter to New York in April 1999 to cover a speech by Bill Bradley on race relations, but that story and others on Bradley "also made the point that so far he is refusing to flesh out his position." Benedetto said that reporters come to the table with the idea that the candidates typically are hiding something. In the case of George W. Bush, for instance, it was the idea that he was hiding something from his past about his use of alcohol or drugs. And in fact, less than week before the election, a television station in Maine broke the news about Bush's 1976 arrest for driving under the influence over Labor Day weekend. It's that kind of news that feeds the media's cynicism and sends reporters off looking for more evidence of a candidate's shortcomings.

The effort to unmask the candidates crosses the line into a more active adversarial role when reporters choose to test candidates on what they know. Andrew Roth (2005, p. 29) writes about "campaign 'pop quizzes'— on topics ranging from the identification of international leaders to the price of groceries—as one specific form of hostile questioning that journalists selectively use in attempts to vet, and potentially discredit, candidates." Roth's review of pop quizzes turned up early instances in 1984 when *Nightline*'s Ted Koppel asked Geraldine Ferraro, the Democratic vice presidential nominee, to delineate the details of military strategy, and in 1991 when David Duke, who was running for governor in Louisiana, was quizzed on his knowledge of the state's economy. But in recent elections, quizzes have taken on a more combative tone, as evidenced by the interview Andy Hiller, a reporter with WHDH-TV in Boston, did with George W. Bush on November 3, 1999 (Neal, 1999):

Hiller: Can you name the president of Chechnya?

Bush: No, can you?

Hiller: Can you name the president of Taiwan?

Bush: Yeah, Lee.

Hiller: Can you name the general who is in charge of Pakistan?

Bush: Wait, wait, is this 50 questions?

Hiller: No, it's four questions of four leaders in four hot spots.

Bush: The new Pakistani general, he's just been elected—not elected, this guy took over office. It appears this guy is going to bring stability to the country and I think that's good news for the subcontinent.

Hiller: Can you name him?

Bush: General. I can't name the general. General.

Hiller: And the prime minister of India?

Bush: The new prime minister of India is [pause]. No. Can you name the foreign minister of Mexico?

Hiller: No sir, but I would say to that, I'm not running for president.

Bush: What I'm suggesting to you is, if you can't name the foreign minister of Mexico, therefore, you know, you're not capable about what you do. But the truth of the matter is you are, whether you can or not.

The exchange, which was reprinted in the *Washington Post* two days later, made headlines in papers in the United States and abroad, and was still a topic in the *Boston Herald* more than a week later when the paper speculated that, based on his performance on Hiller's quiz, Bush would likely fail the Massachusetts Comprehensive Assessment System test, a series of exams given to primary and secondary school students. Hiller's questions were less about Bush's actual knowledge, however, than they were about unmasking the candidate and showing that he may not be worthy of the Oval Office. For some reporters, as Hanson (1996) noted in his analysis of the campaign coverage in 1996, this unmasking is just part of the game:

> In this campaign season's early phase, the game was even more diverting than usual. We didn't just kill candidacies off. We resurrected them and killed them again, as in playground wars of old. Each week, at times every couple of days, our sand castle consensus was kicked down and eagerly rebuilt. But then, on or about March 12, far sooner than we had hoped, the dreaded specter was upon us: game over, drama dead. Bob Dole—bob dull, as *The Washington Post* called him in one headline—sews up the nomination. (Hanson, 1996, p. 1)

For others, it's part of the job:

> I want to know if, for example, a candidate is against gay rights but is a closeted gay. It is nonsense for us not to report that. . . . We have to point out the contradictions between what the candidate says and what he does.—Ann Scales, July 1999

> The media plays a huge role in emphasizing to the public to have a negative view towards their politicians. Some politicians have done it through their own actions because it's not like they're perfect either. But I think that we go in with a negative attitude and it's up to them to prove they're not crooks.—Richard Benedetto, July 1999

And for some, it may even be the path to professional glory:

> You know, it's too easy to fall into the idea that all of these politicians are corrupt or that they're lying most of the time or that they're purely manipulative. I mean, there is this notion that in order to sort of make our bones journalistically you've got to prove that these people are inadequate to the task of what society needs them to do. There's no question that we need to be rigorous in pointing out those flagrant examples of ones who aren't, and we're long past the point where the deification of politicians is the routine as it was in the '50s and '60s, when no matter what they did in private it didn't matter to anybody. In general, we had so much respect for the institution of the presidency that we kind of closed our eyes to things that Kennedy did, or just the notion that authority figures are authority figures and therefore we defer to them. We're never going back to that and we shouldn't. But I sometimes sense that we've almost gone too far in the other direction.—Dan Balz, July 1999

While the battle lines seem to be drawn largely over the concept of controlling the message that gets to voters—David Lightman, for instance, said that the candidate and his staff "can talk about what they want to talk about, but I'm going to write about what I want to write about. And that's not necessarily their agenda"—there also seem to be broader influences at work in the creation of an adversarial relationship between journalists and the campaigns in election coverage. Dan Balz said the adversarial attitude is stronger among younger journalists "probably because of what they've grown up with." Richard Benedetto said that journalists coming to the profession today typically bring an activist orientation, "therefore they see government as an enemy." And the editors who are mentoring them "are the products of Watergate. They're people who came into this business thinking that Watergate was the epitome of good journalism."

They're a lot more cynical about politics and politicians. You can't always say that the government is lying to you or the government is doing something wrong without it having an impact. We shouldn't leave the voters or the citizenry with the view that all politicians are bad. A politician shouldn't have to die to have a good story written about him. But you can turn in a profile of someone and have an editor say it's not negative enough.—Richard Benedetto, July 2006

The end result, according to both Benedetto and Balz, is a view of the candidates and campaigns that is often cynical. And it's a view that is too often reflected in the coverage, which only feeds the adversarial role conceptions of reporters and campaign officials. Balz is optimistic, though, believing that if they pay attention, journalists can limit the cynicism while maintaining a healthy skepticism:

This is probably sort of a self-correcting process, and maybe the pendulum swings back a little bit. . . . But one of the things we have to think about in journalism is the degree to which we allow the cynicism . . . that clearly is there among people in the media, to infect the coverage that we provide. I mean, you can't ignore the fact that there is public cynicism toward politics, and to some extent you have to factor that in to how you assess campaigns and politicians. On the other hand, I think it's sometimes kind of easy to feed that back to people. And that is something that I think we—as institutions and as individuals—need to work hard at avoiding.—Dan Balz, July 1999

Kovach and Rosenstiel (2001b) argue that in recent elections, journalism has focused more on campaign reporting than political reporting. The distinction matters because the former focuses on the minutiae of the electoral process, while the latter puts its emphasis on what the election and the campaign mean for the country. In the turn to campaign reporting, issues become political maneuvering and voters become abstractions measured by percentage points in public opinion polls. And that perspective fuels a cynical view of politics. But strategy and poll numbers are safer than assessing policy differences, and, according to Benedetto, that kind of reporting "is easier than the real legwork of covering the campaign, but we should know about strategy so we can improve our own coverage, not so we can show how much we know about strategy." In today's campaign environment, voters would not be well served by a return to a "just the facts" kind of news reporting. Campaign strategy is sophisticated, and the public is less attentive to politics, so journalists need to provide the context. But in doing so, they need to stop short of casting the electoral process in a light that discourages citizens from taking part in it.

4

The Goals of the
Campaign Managers

It was the second day of a three-day campaign swing for Vice President Al Gore. The message for this late-September trip during the 2000 election was Medicare, and except for a brief stop at the University of Michigan in Ann Arbor to tape an MTV *Choose or Lose* special, Gore would stay meticulously on message. At a series of events in Florida, Michigan, and Iowa, he outlined—mostly for elderly voters—his plans to revamp Medicare and provide them with a prescription drug plan. For the nearly 70 journalists traveling with Gore, including James Gerstenzang of the *Los Angeles Times*, finding a story on the first day wasn't a problem.

"There were elements in the speech that he hadn't raised before. Some of it was new, so it was actually quite possible to write a story with some news in it that will help the reader," Gerstenzang said at the end of the second day of the trip.

> Today there's nothing very interesting. I ended up with a short bit that was "Al Gore said today. . . ." There were some questions from the audience that were different, but most were the same. Tomorrow might be very different. If they're [the campaign staff] doing their job, they'll find some new nugget. If not, would I write something? Yeah, I would. Early in the primary season I wouldn't have had to write about those speeches that weren't news. But at this stage we feel compelled to tell the reader what Gore's been doing every day . . . but it might be as part of a roundup rather than a story.—James Gerstenzang, 2000

Gerstenzang's take on his coverage of the campaign reveals two important truths about how reporters think about the news. The first is that the news is, almost by definition, the element or nugget that is new to the journalists covering the candidates. The same speech that was news in Florida on the first day of the campaign swing was not news on the second day in Michigan. The second truth is that even when there is no news coming out of a campaign, there is pressure to find some story to file. The fact that Gore was a major party nominee for the White House drove the decision by the *Los Angeles Times* to have at least one reporter traveling with the candidate full-time and drove that reporter's decision to have at least one story—even if it was short—every day. And what Gerstenzang would write, whether it was the speech, audience reaction to it, or Gore's strategy in Florida, would become the reality of the Gore campaign for the readers of the *Los Angeles Times*.

MEETING THE NEEDS OF THE JOURNALIST

Campaign managers understand this, and their goal is to make sure—as much as is possible—that the reality that is presented to readers and viewers is one that benefits their candidate and sways voters their way.

> Candidates and their campaign strategists have little incentive to help voters choose well. After all, candidates are in the business of winning votes, not satisfying some ideal of democratic life. In formal terms, this means that they will set agendas and frame issues in ways that promote their candidacy. . . . Candidates will, for instance, parse the truth to exploit facts convenient to their cause and obscure others. They will highlight an issue that seems to help their cause even when it is only tangentially connected to the responsibilities of the office. And they will ignore issues of paramount importance if they seem [to] negatively affect their campaigns. (Ryfe, 2005)

The political strategist, the campaign communications consultant, the senior adviser—whatever the title, contemporary presidential campaigns feature at least one person and typically several people whose primary job is to manage the candidate's media image. Campaigns have always had to consider the media since most people get their political information from media, rather than from any direct contact with the campaign. But the introduction of television to electoral politics in the 1960s, and the quick ascendancy of television as a key source of information for voters, led to the need for political consultants to manage the chaos of the campaign trail and insulate the candidate from any misstep. Joe Klein, in an excerpt in *Time* of his book *Politics Lost*, describes consultants as funny, creative, and smart.

> But their impact on politics has been perverse. Rather than make the game more interesting, they have drained a good deal of life from our democracy.

They have become specialists in caution, literal reactionaries—they react to the results of their polling and focus groups; they fear anything they haven't tested. (Klein, 2006, p. 66)

They also fear the things they can't easily control, including the reporters from the national press who travel with the campaigns, who provide day-to-day coverage of the candidates, and who often set the agenda for voters in the election. And the interpretive journalism that predominates in today's campaign coverage puts the emphasis on "dissection, rather than repetition, of the candidates' messages" (Iyengar, 2005, p. 3), which means that the media serve as a critical filter for the campaign. Iyengar writes that campaigns try to frame their messages around issues that seem central to voters, but "that much of what the public encounters during the campaign is journalistic commentary inspired not by the guiding metaphors of political elites but by the agendas of their own profession" (2005, p. 5).

While campaign managers and consultants can't control what journalists ultimately write, they can control the flow of information to the media. Sometimes that means getting out in front of an issue before it breaks against them. Sometimes it means holding press "gaggles" to give the media a fresh quote or story angle. Often it means avoiding the press, either by ignoring their questions or by shutting down access altogether. On the long and sometimes bumpy road to the White House, the goal is simply to win, and the media are simply a tool for reaching potential voters with whatever message will help them reach that goal. Paul Burka, the executive editor of *Texas Monthly* who covered George W. Bush when he was governor of Texas, told a group of journalism educators at a conference in August 2005 that the members of the Bush administration "treat the media as a special interest, just like any other special interest. They use the media when they can, and ignore them otherwise." Reporters covering the White House and Bush on the campaign trail in 2000 and 2004 had similar complaints about the administration's view of the media and the message discipline of the Bush staff. Julie Mason, a *Houston Chronicle* White House correspondent who covered John Kerry in 2004, told the same group of journalism educators that "it's like throwing questions at a wall. They're impenetrable. We already know going in what they're going to say every time. There's no getting through no matter how aggressive you are."

While the Bush campaign and Bush administration may have perfected the notion of message discipline, they certainly didn't create it and they're not the only ones to use it. Often referred to as the "issue of the day" or "message of the day" strategy, the idea of shaping a candidate's image through control of the flow of information got its foothold in the

Reagan years. The strategy "reduces the frequency and increases the formality of candidate contacts with the media while emphasizing a single issue over an extended period of time. It encourages the media to portray the candidate in terms preferred by the candidate" (Covington et al., 1993, p. 783). In the early stages of Reagan's 1980 campaign, the candidate held press conferences and could be found talking informally with members of the press. When the news coverage during that time didn't follow the script that the campaign hoped for, and in fact was critical, the campaign responded by limiting access to Reagan and making the access that did exist more formal (Covington et al., 1993). In their study of the effect of Reagan's press strategy on his news coverage, Covington, Kroeger, Richardson, and Woodard found that it worked—at least partially. The message control plan was successful in keeping reporters talking about the issues that the campaign wanted to stay focused on, especially for television reporters, and it also "was overwhelmingly successful in preventing Reagan from shooting himself in the foot with off-the-cuff remarks, by eliminating the opportunity for such unplanned statements to be made" (Covington et al., 1993, p. 796). But the strategy didn't result in a more favorable tone in the news coverage of Reagan (Covington et al., 1993).

The Reagan campaigns taught a lot to campaign strategists. They learned that they could manage the news—both what gets said and what visual images are projected—by controlling the flow of information to the media. They learned that the forum for meeting with the press matters— that more formal settings with more ground rules can contain the media better. So reporters are allowed to ask a question, but not a follow-up; or they're buried in paper on a tight deadline; or the candidate will take two or three quick questions, but go to the writers for the wire services who more often will ask about the issue of the day. As William Rhatican, an associate communications director for former President Gerald Ford, said, "It is not a conscious evil decision to evade the press, but more a desire to answer those questions that you want to answer in a way that you want to answer them" (Grossman & Kumar, 1979, p. 45).

But the journalists learned, too. Martin Kasindorf of *USA Today* covered presidential campaigns in the 1960s and 1970s, then took a few election cycles off before coming back to the campaign trail in 1992, when George H. W. Bush ran for reelection against Bill Clinton. In the earlier elections, he said, print ruled the press plane. But the steady influx of television and its predominance in the American home meant that by 1992, all that concerned the campaigns was getting a good picture on television. "That's a Republican thing. Roger Ailes [a Republican strategist] said that it really doesn't matter what the reporter is saying, it's the picture that resonates with voters," Kasindorf said. So the press would be taken to a rally with flags waving or some other backdrop that would serve the campaign, and the camera crews would film it, the photographers would shoot it, and the reporters would write it up. But journalists were skeptical about the value of that kind of campaign reporting.

Tom Rosenstiel, director of the Project for Excellence in Journalism and a former journalist who covered the media and politics for the *Los Angeles Times* and *Newsweek,* in his study of television coverage of the 1992 presidential campaign, writes that journalists covering Ronald Reagan in 1984 "had allowed themselves to be used" by the campaign, which relied on "empty photo opportunities" (1994, p. 29).

> Ronald Reagan had mastered nearly all the techniques, from Nixon's staging of events to Carter's spinning the press. Reagan's team also perfected how to inject their candidate into nonpolitical events, like stock car races and rodeos. Even as it decried his campaign as phony, the press used the pictures, and the idea became popular that the words spoken on TV didn't matter. The average length of a sound bite dipped to below ten seconds.
>
> By 1988, candidates had adapted to the point that even the issues were picked to fit the abbreviated grammar of television. George Bush ran in favor of the Pledge of Allegiance and against prison furloughs. (Rosenstiel, 1994, p. 32–33)

Dan Balz of the *Washington Post* said that kind of candidate-driven coverage amounts to little more than unpaid advertising for the campaign. While reporters have a responsibility to cover the major campaign speeches and events, they also have duty to be more "tough-minded" on the campaign trail.

In an effort to accommodate the media's need for new information each day, while still keeping the candidate at a safe distance from the press, campaigns turn to the use of surrogates to speak on behalf of the candidate. In each of the 2004 presidential debates, the surrogates lined up in "spin alley" even before the debates themselves ended. The surrogates included the campaign spokespeople—Karl Rove and Karen Hughes speaking for the Bush campaign, and Mary Beth Cahill, Mike McCurry, and Joe Lockhart speaking on Kerry's behalf—and they included other political figures, like former New York Mayor Rudy Giuliani, who appeared for Bush, or Arizona Gov. Janet Napolitano, who appeared for Kerry. And they also included celebrities—actor Ron Silver worked as a Bush surrogate; actor Michael J. Fox was a Kerry surrogate. The surrogates, of course, are carefully chosen, and they're given the campaign's script for the message of the day. And even in less high-stakes settings than the debates or the fall campaign, those who might interact with the media are told to be careful. At a breakfast meeting of the Colorado delegation during the 2004 Democratic National Convention, delegates were told where to pick up their credentials, what activities were planned for the day, and when they had to be at the Fleet-Center for the evening speeches. They were told to dress brightly and to wear hats or other attention getters so that the Colorado delegation could get some television time, but they also were cautioned by Julia Hicks, the first vice chair for the state Democrats, "to be careful about what you say to the media" (J. Hicks, personal communication, July 27, 2004).

Reporters, of course, will push for an interview or press availability with the candidates themselves, but they say that a fresh quote from a surrogate can at least give them enough for the next day's story. And in the closed-off world of the members of the traveling press corps, the availability of spokespeople helps, said Martin Kasindorf, who covered the Kerry campaign in 2004.

> Even if the candidate doesn't talk to you, you can talk to the strategists. The rules are changing these days, and they're less and less willing to have people talk on background. But to the extent that you can, you try to get one of the strategists on the plane or on the phone or in a corner somewhere. They give you the background about what's going on, why the candidate is saying something, and what personnel changes might be coming. They would talk policy, too. Of course, when you talk to [Joe] Lockhart or [Mike] McCurry or someone like that, you do get a certain amount of spin. But sometimes it's useful just to get your questions answered, just to get something new for your story.—Martin Kasindorf, July 2006

Unlike the candidates, campaign strategists and press secretaries try to accommodate the media—as long as doing so won't put the candidate at risk. Charged with the care and feeding of the Gore traveling press corps in 2000, Chris Lehane, Gore's press secretary, made it a point to step off of Air Force II on occasion to spend some of his travel time on the press plane. Typically he'd grab a seat next to one of the reporters from a major media outlet, but he'd also take a few questions from smaller organizations or the small cadre of Internet journalists.

> Chris was pretty available. He would ride the buses with us. I found myself sitting next to him on occasion and everything was fair game. You could sit and talk to him about the weather, or you could grill him with questions the whole ride. And he would talk. So I didn't have too much trouble. And usually some staff people would be wandering around the press area as you were working, and you could corner them and say, "What about this, this, and that," and there would be sort of an impromptu little gaggle or press conference there.—Patty Reinert, June 2001

And in the closing weeks of the fall 2004 campaign, Mike McCurry, a senior adviser to John Kerry, often talked to the members of the traveling press corps, sometimes in the filing center and often on the Kerry plane, which meant, of course, that the reporters on the press charter for that leg of the trip would be left out. But briefings on the plane were covered by the pool reports, which would get shipped out to the Kerry press at the next stop. The gaggles, as the reporters call them, typically were a mix of policy and strategy. On an October 15, 2004, flight from Des Moines, Iowa, to Milwaukee, Wisconsin, for instance, McCurry talked to the media about some endorsements that were coming out for Kerry that weekend, about Kerry's speeches in the coming week that would focus on the economy and the federal deficit and other "closing arguments" to reach the voters, and about "the extensive and unprecedented effort" the campaign had in place to get voters to turn out on Election Day. When the reporters got to ask some questions during the 19-minute briefing, they asked about allegations of voter suppression and other irregularities in voter registration; about a memo that Matt Drudge had; whether Kerry got a flu shot; if the cancellation of a campaign stop in West Virginia meant Kerry was giving up on the state; and for a press availability with Kerry himself, to which McCurry said only, "That's worth thinking about." Other press gaggles with McCurry focused on other issues, but the range of questions typically covered recent claims and counterclaims by the campaign as well as some strategy for the final weeks of the election season. But the danger of relying on surrogates and spokespeople, and especially the campaign strategists, as regular sources is that their focus often is on the tactics that will lead to a win in November. Journalists who turn to strategists for fresh material run the very real risk that "their perspectives come to reflect those of the consultants and managers who necessarily see voters as an abstract mass that can be manipulated and moved with just the right mixture of fear and promise" (Kovach & Rosenstiel, 2001b, p. 3).

Some of the reluctance on the part of political campaigns to make candidates more available to the media comes from the fear that the candidate will misspeak or commit some other kind of gaffe that will dominate the news cycle. Unscripted interaction with the press can lead to moments like the one President Gerald Ford had during the second debate in October 1976. Asked by a *New York Times* reporter about Soviet influence in Eastern Europe, Ford responded, "There is no Soviet domination of Eastern Europe, and there never will be under a Ford administration" (Commission on Presidential Debates, 1976). The comment was covered as a major error, given the political context in Eastern Europe at the time, and it was a turning point in the campaign, which Jimmy Carter narrowly won. And although Ford's gaffe occurred in a more formal setting—an official presidential debate—the debate itself was set up more like a press conference, with a panel of reporters asking questions of the two candidates. But the coverage that focuses on the misstatement, or on Bob Dole's fall leaving a podium in 1996, or on John Kerry's windsurfing is a distraction for the candidates and the campaign, so they try to limit the potential for that kind of coverage by insulating the candidates and, in the eyes of many reporters, trying to manipulate the media.

> I think that the campaigns and the consultants have figured out what plays in the media and what doesn't, and I don't see a lot of effort on the part of anyone trying to depart from that and trying to improve the communication. People might think about it, and a political consultant, when he's between jobs, might talk about making a candidate accessible and staying on the high road. But once the campaign starts, it's like combat. I haven't seen a lot coming out of the campaigns about how to improve it.—Richard Benedetto, July 2006

The result is a sometimes strained relationship between the campaign consultants or the media spokespeople and the members of the press corps. And while the campaign staffs and the reporters on the campaign trail understand each other's needs, the wariness on the part of the campaigns and the skepticism on the part of the press can make those relationships difficult to navigate. Former White House press secretary Scott McClellan told Howard Kurtz that part of his job was "to mix it up a bit" with the reporters in the White House press corps (Kurtz, 2005, p. A6). McClellan summed up his view of the press corps saying, "The media's trying to get under our skin and get us off-message. My job is to help the president advance his agenda" (Kurtz, 2005, p. A6). Reporters respond by getting increasingly irritated and may start to be more pointed in their questions. Or they can get testy, as David Lawskey of Reuters did when a press availability with Dick Cheney in October 2000 was suddenly shut down after another reporter asked a tough question. Back in the press filing center, Lawskey confronted Cheney's press secretary, Juleanna Glover Weiss, telling her that the vice presidential candidate should have been able to handle the question and that shielding him from the press wasn't going to help the campaign. Reporters covering John Kerry also got irritated by what they saw as attempts to manipulate the press. During a trip to Cincinnati in mid-September, Kerry's aides told reporters that the candidate would be speaking to the media, "raising hopes for some unscripted give-and-take. But as reporters scrambled into position, Kerry came to the microphones, read a brief statement about the 'tragic milestone' of the 1,000th U.S. war death in Iraq and walked off, ignoring shouted questions" (Farhi, 2004, p. A9). But the antagonism that the two camps may feel in those moments doesn't go too far because "both sides have such fundamental needs for each other that strong elements of cooperation remain at all times" (Grossman & Kumar, 1979, p. 49).

When the antagonism does escalate, however, there are other tactics at a campaign's disposal. A reporter who consistently asks questions that a candidate or campaign doesn't like can be left out of press pools or ignored in the few press availabilities that are held. One journalist said that his experience with the Cheney campaign was that if the press staff "doesn't like what you're writing, they'll ice you out." That sense was shared by other reporters, who believed that the campaign's dislike for news coverage by the *New York Times* was behind the decision to cut the *Times* reporter from the press plane. Rick Lyman wrote about his experiences chasing after the Cheney campaign using commercial flights.

> I am told not to take this personally. Nor, I am told, is this intended as a slight against the paper, which normally maintains a seat (paid for handsomely) on all campaign planes, presidential and vice-presidential.
>
> Frankly, there are some colleagues who suspect that antipathy toward the newspaper may be behind it. Anne Womack, the vice president's chief spokeswoman, says such suspicions are baseless. There simply are not enough seats for all of the press, and other publications got their names on the list before us. If someone drops out, they'll let me know.
>
> So I stalk: Flying commercial, I hopscotch around the country, booking my own flights, trying to keep one step ahead of Mr. Cheney. (Lyman, 2004, p. 1)

From the perspective of the campaign consultant, the media are a necessary part of the election process, but the media's agenda doesn't always serve the campaign or the voters. One campaign spokesperson said that the focus that the national press corps puts on the process story—campaign strategy and tactics—is a real source of frustration. "A good amount of attention is given to the political context. That's what's going to be covered," the spokesperson said. And Mike McCurry, a Kerry senior adviser in 2004, said that the problem stems from the fact that the story, for political journalists, "is the game and its insides, not the larger issues and forces that shape the environment for the campaign. Good campaign coverage has to attack politics from all fronts," including issues and policies put forth by the candidates. He said some of the problems in campaign politics are due to media coverage. "People are anxious about the fact that they're not hearing the arguments that allow them to make real choices," McCurry said.

Because the journalists on the campaign trail do view it as their job to fully reveal who the candidates are, they say they need to cover not only what the candidates are saying, but also what it means—the bigger picture—so that readers have the context for the story. Fiedler (1992) says journalists also should test the candidates' grace under pressure to see whether they can hold up under the rigors of the presidency. And they operate under the belief that the candidates' issues may not be the concerns that are most relevant for voters. Often, therefore, the members of the national press corps are asking questions that pull the candidate "off message"—that put his or her focus on something other than the idea that the campaign staff has decided should be the story of the day. For members of the campaign staffs, controlling the message means limiting the access that the national press will have to a candidate while, at the same time, making the candidate more available to local news reporters who tend to ask "grateful" questions.

MAKING POLITICAL NEWS LOCAL

After the final presidential debate and a postdebate rally in Tempe, Arizona, on Wednesday, October 13, 2004, John Kerry headed to Las Vegas, Nevada, where he was scheduled to talk to the national conference of the American Association of Retired People the following day. The speech wound up at about 12:30, and the national press had about 45 minutes to file a story or check in with editors, while Kerry took time to talk to reporters from five local television stations—four based in Las Vegas and one from just outside Las Vegas in Henderson. The ground rules gave each reporter three questions, and each one asked about allegations of voter fraud in Nevada. But with only three questions, there wasn't room for a follow-up, and the reporters from the local stations weren't used to covering national politics. And while the pool report that went out to the reporters in Kerry's traveling press corps summed up the local media interviews by saying there was no news coming out of them, the questions asked by the local television reporters were just the kind of questions that the campaign wanted. The KTNV reporter asked about Kerry's plan for Iraq, the KVBC reporter asked about Kerry's views on stem cell research and energy independence, the KLAS reporter wanted to know about Kerry's take on the minimum wage and Social Security, and the WB reporter asked about Kerry's support for veterans and his Vietnam experience. In fact, the only local reporter to pose a question related to campaign strategy was the reporter from KVVU, who wanted to know what Kerry thought it would take to win Nevada.

Kerry spent much of the fall campaign season doing interviews with regional media in battleground states and taking advantage of the stops along the campaign trail to do interviews with local reporters. And Kerry wasn't the only candidate turning to the local media to get the message out. The Bush campaign in 2000 and in 2004 made interviews with the local and regional press a key part of their campaign communications strategy, said Republican National Committee press secretary Tracey Schmitt, who served as the Western states spokesperson for the Bush campaign in 2004. In fact, during one four-day period on his last campaign swing in 2000, Dick Cheney did interviews with local media in 10 different cities—starting in Rochester, Minnesota, on October 30, going through several stops in the Midwest and in Florida on October 31 and November 1, and including a November 2 local availability in Gallatin, Tennessee. In that same four days, however, the national press corps was invited to only one of those local availabilities, and the press briefing was cut short once the questions were opened up to the traveling press, which is when the questions got tougher. And in that same four days, despite repeated requests from the national press to interview Cheney, the candidate came back to the press section only once, and that was for an off-the-record chat.

For the reporters who travel with the presidential and vice presidential candidates, the increasing number of local press availabilities—especially when they're being shut off from access—is troublesome. But Schmitt and others defend the practice, arguing that the local media provide a better way to reach voters.

> Here in Washington, we tend to get wrapped up in the Beltway news cycle, but the reality is that candidates don't win or lose elections as a result of coverage in the *New York Times* or *Washington Post*. In the 24-hour news cycle, the national newspapers are, of course, critical, and ultimately responsible for shaping daily cable news coverage, which is important. But the bottom line is that the five major newspapers in the United States make up only 12 percent of newspapers circulated nationwide. The other 88 percent are local and daily papers. Not only do voters get more of their information from local sources than national outlets, but regional media are usually more likely to cover issues with a real impact on the local level.—Tracey Schmitt, September 2006

In 2004, she said, the Bush campaign put a communications director on the ground in every "target state" nearly a year before the election to work exclusively with the local and regional media. And the campaign made sure that Bush and Cheney, when possible, and other people prominent in the campaign—Laura Bush, Lynne Cheney, cabinet members, and others—spoke to the local press. "There was a constant drumbeat to book local and state officials who were identified with the campaign on radio, TV, and in print interviews," she said.

Campaigns are turning to the local media for several reasons. Schmitt said that while the national news organizations can set the agenda for news coverage for regional and local media, there also is a "trickle up" effect from local news organizations to national ones. "Regional media opportunities serve as springboards for campaigns to raise the profile nationally of a state issue that might otherwise be overlooked," she said. For example, she said, elements of a press conference with local media in Nevada denouncing a Kerry proposal for national parks—which the Bush campaign claimed would cost thousands of jobs in Nevada—were covered in the local media and eventually made their way into the national press.

Dan Pfeiffer, the Northeast communications director for the Gore campaign, said in an interview in September 2000 that the local media are more consistent about picking up on the candidate's message. When Al Gore was spending time in local schools, which he did on seven days during the campaign, the national press was not particularly interested. Members of the local media in those communities, however, covered the story in great detail. "We dominated media coverage in Maine for four days because of the time Al Gore spent there," Pfeiffer said. He also said that while the national press corps can shape opinion, the journalists for those organizations are much more critical of the candidates than the reporters working for regional and local newspapers. They also ask questions that members of the national press corps call "softball questions."

Asking a candidate to state his policy on Iraq or on minimum wage or on Social Security—as Kerry was asked to do by the local reporters in Las Vegas—lets the candidate rely on his "playbook" and doesn't push him or her in the same ways that a national reporter would. In a *Los Angeles Times* story on the reporters from the *Concord Monitor* in New Hampshire, who have unprecedented access to national candidates during the primary season, John M. Glionna noted the difference that a few more years of political reporting experience can make.

> One cub reporter asked bachelor Dennis J. Kucinich out on a date because she thought he was cute. Another boarded a plush campaign bus to interview Rep. Dick Gephardt and suddenly gushed: "Hey, sweet ride, Congressman!" Then they talked about pies. (Glionna, 2004)

Alec MacGillis, a reporter who worked for the *Concord Monitor* in 2000, but was working for the *Baltimore Sun* in 2004, lamented that he had more access to Gore in 2000 as a reporter from a small paper than he did in 2004 to any of the major candidates. In 2000, he said, one of Gore's staff "would motion toward a back door and I'd ride with [Gore] to his next stop while the national media was left behind screaming at him" (Glionna, 2004). His step up the professional ladder to a larger newspaper meant that by 2004, MacGillis was "just part of the pack" (Glionna, 2004).

Toby Eckert of Copley News Service said he's seen the differences in how presidents and presidential candidates—Democratic and Republican—deal with the national and local press. The fact is, he said, that candidates think that the national press puts a negative spin on the news.

They consider the national media a filter, and they believe they can get their message out more clearly and more positively by going to the local media. The reporters at that level are more likely to be a little starstruck by Dick Cheney or Condoleezza Rice coming to their town. And they're not as up on national issues as someone who's covering politics for a national news organization full-time or even part-time. So they're not as likely to challenge the candidates or point out contradictions. And that's not to denigrate local media, but it's just not their primary focus. And I think that's why the candidates turn to them as much as they do.—Toby Eckert, July 2006

Eckert said that reporters with the national press corps are going to work more to hold the candidates accountable for what they're saying, and they're going to add some of the political context to the story and bring in viewpoints from the opposing campaign. The campaign managers, he said, "see going to the local media as a way to blunt some of that impact and as a way to reach local voters."

TURNING TO NEW AND NONTRADITIONAL VENUES

With the audiences for mainstream news shrinking, campaigns also are looking for other venues to reach out to potential voters. Bill Clinton, for instance, played "Heartbreak Hotel" on the saxophone on *The Arsenio Hall Show* during his first presidential campaign in June 1992, and, in his first term in office, appeared on MTV, where he faced the question, "boxers or briefs." But Clinton's courting of voters—especially younger voters—through such nontraditional media outlets has caught hold, especially among Democrats. Al Gore, in the 2000 election, appeared on an MTV *Choose or Lose* program where he was asked about his grocery bag preference—paper or plastic. And in the 2004 campaign, candidates hit the late night talk shows, and John Kerry showed up on Comedy Central's *The Daily Show* in August while the Swift Boat Veterans for Truth controversy was still swirling.

While it was the first time a presidential nominee had appeared on *The Daily Show*, hosted by Jon Stewart and known for putting a slightly sardonic spin on the nightly news, it wasn't the first time the program had featured a heavy political hitter. Joe Lieberman appeared on the program in 2000 when he was the vice presidential nominee, and in 2004, John Edwards announced that he was going to run for the presidency on Stewart's show. Still, the interview with Kerry was a first. And it was an important venue since increasing numbers of people are turning to Jon Stewart, Jay Leno, and David Letterman for information about presidential campaigns because they see it as entertaining and, oftentimes, because they think it is just as reliable and accurate as traditional media (Sella, 2000), despite the fact that Stewart refers to himself a "good fake journalist."

While *The Daily Show* made a big splash, especially in the 2004 campaign season, the expanding reach of the Internet provided candidates and campaigns with direct access to voters and contributors that didn't rely on the filter of mainstream media. The Internet was a factor in the 1996 presidential campaign, but mainly as a mechanism to provide fast communication, said Mike McCurry, a senior adviser to the Kerry campaign. It became a political tool in 2000, when John McCain beat Republican front-runner George W. Bush in the New Hampshire primary and the McCain campaign brought in more than $2 million in four days—raising almost $21,000 an hour—from its website (Cornfeld & Seiger, 2004). In the wake of the New Hampshire win, the McCain campaign also saw its e-mail list jump from 60,000 subscribers to 142,000 subscribers, making it easier for the campaign to let more people know about McCain's appearances in the hopes of drawing bigger crowds at his rallies and speeches (Cornfeld & Seiger, 2004).

But perhaps the biggest impact of the Internet in 2004 was to take the fledgling candidacy of former Vermont Governor Howard Dean and turn him into a media darling and a front-runner for the Democratic nomination through the spring and fall of 2003. Dean started that year with $157,000, seven staff members, and a network of 432 identified supporters nationwide (Cornfeld, 2006). Within a year, Dean's Internet campaigning, and the media coverage that followed it, had helped the candidate raise $40 million, and his network of "Deaniacs" had grown to 552,930 supporters (Cornfeld, 2006). Dean started by setting up his own blog and soliciting campaign contributions via the Internet. He even held a fundraising dinner online, spoofing a $2,000-a-plate Republican luncheon, by eating a turkey sandwich while chatting, via the Internet, with his supporters about the issues of the day. The "fundraising gimmick netted the Dean campaign $500,000 from 9700 people, and great publicity about its grassroots enthusiasm and prowess" (Cornfeld, 2006, p. 213).

Patrick Ruffini, the eCampaign director for the Republican National Committee, said that the Internet is bringing dramatic changes to political communication. With more people going online for news, he said, the campaigns are working with audiences that not only want to read what's going on, they want to "interact with the news 24 hours a day."

The mainstream media are no longer the sole gatekeepers for political information. Increasingly, they're joined by bloggers and other online influentials who are increasingly setting the agenda for what news gets reported. The blogosphere acts as a free market for news, and the best stories—even those with humble origins on the Web—eventually make their way into mainstream media.—Patrick Ruffini, September 2006

He also said that campaign websites are seeing traffic double every election cycle, "and the rise of social media like MySpace or YouTube . . . dramatically broaden our horizons in reaching people beyond our website."

Mike McCurry said he sees greater possibilities for the Internet in 2008, with campaigns having to look for ways to reach voters through the Web, through their iPods, and through whatever else comes along.

> The Internet has changed political fundraising forever, and that is the most significant change. Real grassroots action is possible, and real grassroots candidates can emerge and challenge established incumbents. Next, all technologies—the Web, satellite, cable, iPods—are eroding the hold of the 30-second spot on political communication. The marginal cost of sending an effective persuasion message to a potential voter is declining and will go lower. That means the cost of campaigns will go down and the need for massive budgets will diminish. That is a hopeful and positive change, but one that has not been fully realized. . . . In short, campaigns will cling to "traditional," that is, "old media," techniques and blend them with Internet-based communications for a while. But over time, the Internet modes will proliferate and new campaign communications innovations will occur in that space.—Mike McCurry, August 2006

McCurry did say that in the short term, bloggers will add zest to the political debate, but their electoral impact will be limited until they can reach an audience that approaches the size of the audience for traditional media outlets.

5

Life "In the Bubble" of the Campaign

With less than a month to go before Election Day and less than a week to go before his third and final debate with George W. Bush, John Kerry was trying to fit in several campaign stops before heading to Santa Fe, New Mexico, for a day of debate prep before heading to Arizona. For the 75 people in the press corps traveling with Kerry, that meant getting up on Saturday, October 9, in time to make a 6 a.m. baggage call so that their luggage could be swept by the Secret Service, and a 7:10 a.m. press call time in the lobby to catch the buses to the St. Louis airport. From there, the campaign would make several stops throughout the day, with the press corps hopscotching across the Midwest and East, sometimes trailing and sometimes slightly ahead of Kerry, until they would RON—rest overnight—in Florida:

7:15 a.m. CDT	Traveling press depart Radisson Hotel en route Lambert-St. Louis Int'l Airport
7:45 a.m. CDT	Traveling press arrive Lambert-St. Louis Int'l Airport
8:15 a.m. CDT	John Kerry departs Westin en route Lambert-St. Louis Int'l Airport
8:40 a.m. CDT	John Kerry arrives Lambert-St. Louis Int'l Airport
8:45 a.m. CDT	Press plane departs Lambert-St. Louis Int'l Airport en route Cleveland-Hopkins Int'l Airport
9:00 a.m. CDT	[Kerry] Wheels up Lambert-St. Louis Int'l Airport en route Cleveland-Hopkins Int'l Airport *Open press departure*

11:05 a.m. EDT	Press plane arrives Cleveland-Hopkins Int'l Airport
11:20 a.m. EDT	John Kerry arrives Cleveland-Hopkins Int'l Airport *Open press arrival*
11:30 a.m. EDT	John Kerry departs Cleveland-Hopkins Int'l Airport en route rally *Traveling press accompany in motorcade*
12:00 p.m. EDT	John Kerry arrives rally *Traveling press proceed to riser/file*
12:15 p.m.– 1:30 p.m. EDT	Rally for a Stronger America Lorain County Community College Elyria, OH *Open press*
1:30 p.m.– 3:00 p.m. EDT	Press file Gymnasium adjacent to Ewing Center *File: Workspace, power, audio, and Internet. Lunch will be served.*
3:00 p.m. EDT	John Kerry departs rally en route Cleveland-Hopkins Int'l Airport *Traveling press accompany in motorcade*
3:30 p.m. EDT	John Kerry arrives Cleveland-Hopkins Int'l Airport
3:35 p.m. EDT	Press plane departs Cleveland-Hopkins Int'l Airport en route Ft. Lauderdale-Hollywood Int'l Airport
3:45 p.m. EDT	Wheels up Cleveland-Hopkins Int'l Airport en route Ft. Lauderdale-Hollywood Int'l Airport *Open press departure*
6:40 p.m. EDT	Press plane arrives Ft. Lauderdale-Hollywood Int'l Airport
6:50 p.m. EDT	John Kerry arrives Ft. Lauderdale-Hollywood Int'l Airport *Open press arrival*
7:15 p.m. EDT	John Kerry departs Ft. Lauderdale-Hollywood Int'l Airport en route Broward Community College *Traveling press accompany in motorcade*
7:30 p.m. EDT	John Kerry arrives Broward Community College *Traveling press proceed to riser/file*
7:30 p.m.– 9:00 p.m. EDT	Town Hall Meeting Broward Community College Central Campus Davie, FL *Open press*

9:00 p.m.–	Press file
9:45 p.m. EDT	2nd Floor of Gym
	File: Workspace, power, audio, and Internet.
	Dinner will be served.
9:15 p.m.–	Regional press time
9:35 p.m. EDT	
9:50 p.m. EDT	John Kerry departs Broward Community College en route
	Miami, Florida
	Traveling press accompany in motorcade
10:20 p.m. EDT	John Kerry arrives Sheraton Bal Harbour
JK/Press RON	Sheraton Bal Harbour
	Bal Harbour, FL

The next morning started early for those in the small press pool, who went with Kerry to a service at St. James Catholic Church in Miami. A slightly larger pool headed to Liberty City, where Kerry showed up at 10:50 a.m. for a second service—this one at Friendship Missionary Baptist Church that also featured Rev. Jesse Jackson and Rev. Al Sharpton, who ran against Kerry for the Democratic nomination. Later in the day, the campaign headed to New Mexico for a quick rally at the Albuquerque airport before the motorcade headed north to Santa Fe. The two days of campaigning, though, barely broke into the nation's newspapers—six of the country's top papers carried stories about Kerry's speech at the Baptist church, and most of those stories spent more time on Revs. Jackson and Sharpton than they did on John Kerry. And the rally in Elyria, Ohio, showed up in a photo and caption in the *Houston Chronicle*, as part of a short story in the *New York Times*, and as a stand-alone news story in the Cleveland *Plain Dealer*.

THE REPORTERS "IN THE BUBBLE"

The print journalists who are assigned to cover presidential campaigns are typically at the top of their profession. They are working for a handful of the nation's leading newspapers, and within their own organizations, they have risen to the upper echelons of the professional ladder, where they are "rewarded with greater freedom" in terms of deciding what to cover and how to cover it (Soloski, 1989, p. 145). Despite this status and freedom, there is a striking similarity in the campaign coverage of the reporters who travel with the candidates. And there are a number of reasons for that similarity. Breed (1955) discussed the socialization of journalists that occurs as they work in the newsroom among other reporters and editors. By reading the stories that other reporters at the newspaper are writing and by observing what doesn't get into print, new reporters are "taught" what is newsworthy. Learning the rules and conforming to the newspaper's norms are the keys to succeeding. As Breed (1955) notes,

> The newsman's source of rewards is located not among the readers, who are manifestly his clients, but among his colleagues and superiors. Instead of adhering to societal and professional ideals, he redefines his values to the more pragmatic level of the newsroom group. (p. 120)

For reporters who travel with the candidates for long stretches of time, their newsroom becomes the press plane and their newsroom group becomes the journalists from competing organizations who travel with them. Reporters manage the dissonance of working so closely with journalists from other news organizations by adopting norms that allow for controlled competition (Bantz, 1997). Because they work for long months in a confined environment, journalists develop standards among themselves that

> may permit reporters to provide competitors [with] factual information (something publicly available and the withholding of which would be seen as petty) or even to delegate one member the task of gathering all the information for sharing. . . . At the same time, the reporters may subtly compete for additional details that will differentiate their story from their colleagues. (Bantz, 1997, p. 132)

Therefore, as they think about what's newsworthy on any given day, they take their cues from each other, and sometimes even discuss both facts—such as what the candidate said or how large the crowd was—and story ideas with each other, despite the "greater freedom" they receive from their home organizations. On the campaign trail, reporters freely share tapes of speeches and talk about their impressions of the candidates—Kerry's "more presidential" demeanor through the debates in 2004 or Bush's verbal misstep in the second debate in St. Louis when he talked about rumors on the "Internets."

Still, the freedom that Soloski (1989) refers to is constrained by other factors for those who cover candidates. Editors at home are expecting their reporters to have a story that's similar to what other news organizations are reporting, and reporting something that is dramatically different means having to jump through more than a few hoops to get the story in print. Of course, finding something different is difficult. The members of the traveling press corps are herded from one place to another on chartered buses and chartered planes, and even at campaign events, those in the traveling press typically are escorted into either a filing center with the sound piped in or a cordoned-off area reserved for them. And while they can venture outside of these areas, doing so at the beginning means they have to find people who would rather talk to them than listen to the candidate. Venturing out into the audience toward the end of the speech or rally means taking the risk that they'll miss the chartered bus back to the airport. So while reporters do talk to people in the audience, it's not something they do at every stop, or even at most stops. Instead, the members of the traveling press corps spend most of their time with each other and with the few campaign staff members assigned to the care and feeding of the press. And it is these people who become their primary reference group.

The ability of media outlets to influence the coverage of other news organizations extends beyond the plane, however. Most mornings the members of the traveling press corps can open up their hotel room doors to find a copy of *USA Today* waiting for them. And often they can find copies of the *New York Times* and several other major newspapers, depending on the city, on hand in the press baggage area or in a room set up with coffee and breakfast. Each of these newspapers is scanned first to make sure that it doesn't have something new or different—that it doesn't have a major scoop that needs to be followed that day. While the journalists do travel together and share information, reporters are always on the lookout for a scoop, said Patty Reinert of the *Houston Chronicle*, so checking out the competition is an important part of a campaign journalist's daily routine. The newspapers also are scanned to find out what's going on with the other candidates' campaigns. Throughout the day at the various press filing centers, journalists also log in to their own web pages and their competition's websites to check on the news. And if they don't have the time to do it, their editors at home are checking for them and relaying the "news" to the campaign reporters by e-mail and cell phone.

Evidence of the intermedia agenda setting in a presidential election was found by Just, Crigler, Alger, Cook, Kern, and West (1996) in their study of the 1992 campaign. The authors determined that news coverage of the campaign becomes more homogenous over the course of the election, and concluded that "many of these similarities in coverage presumably arise from standard routines, shared journalistic norms, and similar definitions of news and how it should be covered" (Just et al., 1996, p. 118).

Gans (1979) wrote that this kind of intermedia agenda setting also occurs because a story appearing in one newspaper or on its website—particularly a major newspaper like the *New York Times* or the *Washington Post*—will have already been vetted by respected journalists and have been deemed newsworthy. And by checking the competition, journalists can assure themselves that they haven't missed anything that is important (Reese & Danielian, 1991). Additionally, there is a kind of informal intermedia agenda setting that occurs as reporters on the campaign trail collaborate, checking with each other for crowd estimates, important quotes, and sometimes even to see if their assessment of what was new in a candidate's speech is the same as that of their colleagues in the traveling press corps. As a result, the influence of the media on themselves is quite strong.

BEING PART OF "THE PACK"

More than 15,000 press credentials were handed out for both the Republican and Democratic national conventions in the 2000 and 2004 election seasons. Taking into account the fact that many of those credentials were issued to technicians and support staff for the news organizations present or to people who were not working for daily news organizations, there still were more than 5,000 "working journalists" on hand at the conventions trying to find news. In some cases, they manufactured it. During the 2000 conventions, for example, *USA Today* held twice-daily roundtable discussions with political leaders and party officials in their makeshift newsroom at the conventions. The roundtables were broadcast to Gannett television stations and covered by *USA Today* political reporters.

Others at the conventions simply followed the people who seemed to make news, including actress Angie Harmon and her husband, former New York Giants player Jason Sehorn; model Christie Brinkley; actor William Baldwin; and former pro-wrestler-turned-actor "The Rock." And some simply followed the crowd. So, when the camera lights went on for a live webcast interview with Doug Bailey, the Freedom Channel's founder and president and the founder of Youth-e-Vote.net, being held in "Internet Alley" at the 2000 Republican Convention, a small group gathered. Within minutes, nearly a dozen reporters were huddled around the small set taking notes and keeping their tape recorders pointed at Bailey and the moderator. Toward the back of the huddle, a journalist who was furiously taking notes leaned over to the reporter next to him. "Who is this?" he asked. "I don't know. I just saw a lot of people standing here and figured I'd better get some of this down," came the reply.

Traveling with the press in 1992, Ken Auletta saw the same phenomenon, and wrote that it was driven by

> the same mindless conformity one witnesses every time a Clinton or Bush handler stops to chat with a couple of reporters and within seconds a hive surrounds them, panicked that they are missing some vital spin from the candidate. Once after a Clinton-Brown debate in New York, Dan Balz of the *Washington Post* played for a colleague in the NBC lobby a tape of what Clinton had said to reporters that morning about how he had avoided the mili-

tary draft. Although they had no idea what Balz was playing and could barely hear it, a hive soon formed and aimed their tape recorders at Balz without knowing what it was they were recording. (Auletta, 1993, p. 79)

Sometimes referred to as "pack journalism," the tendency of many reporters to literally follow each other during the campaign—to seek out the same sources on the road and to keep an eye on who other people are talking to—is an element of intermedia agenda setting. And perhaps even more than the kind that scholars traditionally think about, which involves the practice of monitoring each other's coverage, this kind of intermedia agenda setting preempts other stories or other people from ever making it into the news. Tim Crouse, who traveled with the George McGovern campaign in 1972 for *Rolling Stone*, said that as a result of being confined to the press buses and planes, reporters "began to believe the same rumors, subscribe to the same theories, and write the same stories" (1973, p. 8).

For reporters at the top of the pecking order on the campaign press plane—those from the major daily newspapers or the networks—the pack mentality comes into play as they talk to each other between events. "The *New York Times* and the *Washington Post* are always talking to each other mainly because neither wants to be too far off from the other guys because they know they're being watched pretty closely by their editors" and by the rest of the press pack, said Richard Benedetto of *USA Today*. He said journalists also tend to seek each other out socially, and increasingly Washington journalists have married other Washington journalists, "so that you have two reporters living in the same household, maybe working for different organizations. They hang around together, they socialize with each other. So as a result you have this kind of inbreeding of ideas." The problem with the socialization among reporters is that they then start to write for each other, rather than the reader. And given the close confines of a campaign press plane, the tendency to write for other journalists only increases.

They don't think in terms of what the public wants to know, how can I help them know. They think of it in terms of . . . what does my colleague want to know? What can I show my colleagues that I know that they don't know? That's what's going on. I think that journalists today in Washington basically write to each other—or report to each other—to show each other up, to be a member of the club. There is this kind of close-knit clubby kind of group of people and everybody—they all hang out together and they talk together, think alike. They all want to scoop each other by finding out a piece of information that the other one doesn't know. But they won't really get far off the reservation from what everybody else is reporting. A lot of that stuff, the public is not interested in. So therefore, they don't read it or pay much attention to it.—Richard Benedetto, July 1999

Thus, what is newsworthy typically is determined by a relatively small group of leading national reporters who often are writing with more of an eye toward what other reporters will find interesting rather than what a more general audience needs to know about the campaign. And once the leading newspapers and networks determine what the story is, "it becomes difficult for any . . . correspondents to deviate from it without being second-guessed by colleagues or editors" (Rosenstiel, 1994, p. 61). The thinking of those at the leading news organizations becomes the conventional wisdom, and doing something different, even for a veteran reporter, isn't easy. Guttenplan (1992b), in his review of campaign coverage in 1992, said the pack mentality results in a "crushing consensus about what is, and is not, subject to political debate" (pp. 2–3). Cragg Hines of the *Houston Chronicle* said that newspapers often assign someone on their political team to monitor other media outlets—particularly television.

> Everybody kind of thinks the same and it draws a conclusion and therefore it becomes what they call the conventional wisdom. . . . It's tough to march to your own drummer. You know, you have to have something that's really going to convince them [the editors] that you're right. It's not that it's going to fall on deaf ears, but it's a much harder sell if you've got a story that's flying against the grain of what everybody else is reporting. . . . And in a lot of ways that's kind of too bad because part of what we should be doing is to write with a lot of different views, not just with the same one everyplace you go.—Richard Benedetto, June 2001

But in the 2000 and 2004 elections, as in previous campaigns, the view that readers got from the campaign trail was largely homogenous—no matter which newspaper they read or television station they watched. When Toby Eckert, a reporter for Copley News Service papers who was covering the Gore campaign, stepped off of the press plane in Clearwater, Florida, on September 25, 2000, he pulled out his cell phone and called his home office. He pitched several ideas to his editor, who relegated one to a short piece and settled on yet another story about money.

"Yeah, we just landed in the 90-degree weather here. I guess we're in St. Petersburg," Eckert said into the phone, then paused. "He's on Medicare again. He's put out this booklet on it. It's basically a rehash, but there are one or two things in it that are new, unless you want me to do that finance thing we were talking about." Another pause. "Yeah, I do too, because I don't see much new in here. I wanted to do the Florida story this week—the battleground angle, especially since Jeb [George W. Bush's brother] is the governor here—but Finlay was on the Bush trip last week and he did that."

A few minutes later, Eckert was sitting on the press bus with 16 or so other reporters. He pulled out his phone again and started making calls to officials with both the Republican and Democratic parties to begin collecting information for a weekend story on campaign financing. He would end up filing a Medicare story that day, as well.

Talking to another reporter after he got off his cell phone, Eckert resigned himself to being part the pack. His editors, he said, "are more interested in the resource gap between Bush and Gore. You know, you can't do anything original here."

At the national political conventions, the coverage was focused on the evening speeches—or at least snippets of them—and the protests outside of the convention halls. And because most reporters at the conventions called them merely coronations—the nominees and their running mates had already been chosen—very few reporters actually spent time in the convention halls during the morning, when the day's speakers and entertainment would rehearse for the sessions later in the day or B-list speakers would try to rally electoral subsets—especially younger delegates and voters.

On the campaign trail, the reporters sought out the same sources, even at events like Al Gore's Medicare speech in Clearwater. With four hours of filing time after the event, the reporters had the luxury of being able to move through the crowd after the event to get audience reaction to the candidate's speech. But many of the reporters in the press corps followed the camera lights, interviewing the same random citizens that everyone else was talking to. The pack also set the news agenda for the second day of Gore's campaign trip, when the MTV *Choose or Lose* event was the lead story of the day and the candidate's rapport with the young audience at the University of Michigan was the angle that most newspapers took on it. And invariably the reporters covering the event looked for the 2000 equivalent of the "boxers or briefs" question that former President Bill Clinton got from a similar audience when he campaigned in 1996. The closest they got was about grocery store bags—"paper or plastic?" Gore's response: "I've never figured that one out. Just lump it up in your arms and take it all like that. I usually get paper."

On the third day of Gore's late-September campaign swing the story was Winifred Skinner. Skinner was one of the senior citizens in the audience at a speech in Altoona, Iowa, where Gore made his first stop of the day to talk once again about Medicare. The journalists, who had heard Gore's speech several times over the previous two days, were underwhelmed. When they arrived at Altoona, the reporters made a beeline for the press center, which was set up in the community room, rather than going to the gymnasium, where Gore was going to speak. In the gymnasium, the local media were setting up on the press stands, and photographers from wire services were getting their equipment ready so they could transmit a few pictures from the event. But the members of the traveling press corps were largely absent. Even when Gore took the stage at 10 a.m., most of the national press reporters stayed in the filing center, where they could check e-mail, call up the Internet, have a late breakfast or early lunch, and monitor Gore's speech through the audio feed that was being piped in from the gymnasium a few hundred feet away. Because the speech itself was old news, no one needed to see it or the audience reaction to it.

When Gore's speech ended and he opened the floor for a question-and-answer session with the audience, some of the traveling press corps wandered in. They opened their notebooks but wrote down very little—until 79-year-old Winifred Skinner made news. Gore had called on an elderly man, but when he stood up he pointed to Skinner, who was seated on the other side of the gymnasium, and said that she had something to say that Gore should hear. Skinner stood up and told the vice president that she was retired and trying to make it on a monthly Social Security check of $782 and a pension benefit of $130 a month. From that, she had to first pay out $111 for heath insurance and $250 for prescription medicines. The balance wasn't enough to cover her living costs, so every day Skinner spent several hours scouring the streets for tin cans and using the money she got from those to buy food. As she spoke, Gore did the math in his head. Then he asked her, "About how much do you make from the cans?" Skinner hesitated. "You aren't going to tell the government, are you?" she replied. Gore nearly doubled over laughing and the national press poured in from the filing center to get the story. Within a few minutes Nathan Naylor, a Gore press aide, was coming around with a sheet of information on Skinner, including the spelling of her name and the fact that she was a retired quality control inspector for AAMCO auto parts. He didn't have her age—he said he didn't want to ask her that—so Andrew Kane, a *Washington Times* reporter, snaked his way through the crowd to ask her how old she was. When he came back, that information was passed through the press corps as well. Gore, meanwhile, had moved on. And while the members of the national press were checking with each other to make sure they had Skinner's quotes and figures down, another senior citizen stood up and told his story. He and his wife, who had suffered a stroke, were living on even less than Skinner because their combined monthly prescription bills chewed up most of his retirement income. But the national press corps had the story for the day—the same story everyone who was there would have—so no one paid attention to the gentleman who spoke after Winifred Skinner. The journalists on the campaign trail knew that their editors would be tracking what the competition was writing. And anyone who didn't have Winifred Skinner on that Wednesday would have faced some tough questions from the desk at home.

Typically reporters on the campaign trail take their lead from the reporters for the major national newspapers, like the *New York Times* or the *Washington Post*, or from the wire service reporters. However, in recent years journalists also have had to follow nontraditional media and even the tabloids. Auletta (1993) reported that in the 1992 campaign, writers for the nontraditional media, including the *Star* and *Hard Copy*, "established the peer pressure. They set the pace. And they did it by relying more on rumor than reported fact" (p. 67). The *Star*, for instance, broke the story about Bill Clinton's affair with Gennifer Flowers. And while members of the traditional press held off on the story for a few days, the pressure to cover the Flowers allegations as news built quickly, and as soon as Bill and Hillary Clinton appeared on *60 Minutes* to talk about the story, it became legitimate news. "Reporters insisted that once the story was out and the president of the United States was asked about it publicly, they couldn't ignore the story" (Auletta, 1993, p. 85).

The "pack" also emerges because the journalists who cover campaigns have limited access to anything original. As Crouse (1973) noted when he wrote about reporters covering the 1972 campaign, journalists covering the presidential candidates get their information from the same events, the same press releases, the same speeches, and the same (albeit infrequent) opportunities to question the candidates. "To follow a candidate you must join a pack of other reporters; even the most independent journalist cannot completely escape the pressures of the pack" (Crouse, 1973, p. 15). Auletta (1993) and Lewis (1997) drew similar conclusions as they wrote about the presidential campaigns. The result of traveling with a candidate, Auletta (1993) wrote, is a kind of inbreeding among the press corps:

> From early morning to late night, they were sequestered as if in a witness protection program, moving from hotel to chartered bus or plane to rally to bus to plane to rally. They had little time to talk to voters, or shop in a supermarket, or watch television. Their transit and food and lodging were arranged, their sources were nearby, deadlines always loomed, and days and speeches blurred. (p. 71)

It was no different in 2004, when days often started with a stop at the baggage room before sunrise and then a cup of coffee while waiting for the press bus, and ended with a late check-in at a hotel in a new city. And in the days just before the election, the pace can be grueling. On the first day of Dick Cheney's final campaign trip in 2000, which began on Monday, October 30, and ran through Election Day, reporters met up with the campaign plane at 6:45 a.m. at Dulles International Airport in Virginia. Five cities and 16 hours later reporters were finally able to settle into a hotel room in Kansas City, Missouri, for the night. The day had taken them to a speech at Lourdes High School in Rochester, Minnesota, and rallies at Loras College in Dubuque, Iowa, and at an outdoor park in Peoria, Illinois. Cheney's speeches that day—and for the next few days—were strikingly similar. And at each speech and rally, the national reporters traveling with Cheney were escorted into and out of the event by someone from Cheney's press staff. The tight travel schedule made it nearly impossible to work the crowd after the events, and so reporters stayed "in the bubble," getting little or no exposure to the world outside the campaign.

The emergence of the Internet has only increased the pack mentality, reporters said, and has increased the speed with which the pack mentality can dominate more rational thinking about a story. Dan Balz of the *Washington Post* said that the Internet means that the view of the mainstream media as the primary gatekeeper is less applicable.

Balz and Carl Leubsdorf of the *Dallas Morning News* both said that Internet publications, such as the *Drudge Report*, have created even more sources of rumors that the traditional media have to track. Even if a story can't be verified, the pressure of the pack means that campaign reporters spend some of their time getting ready with the information in case it breaks somewhere else. The competition between news organizations, Leubsdorf said, means that newspapers have less control over determining whether to print a story.

> In the old days a newspaper such as ours certainly was determining what the readers of Dallas learned about some subject. But our control over that is far less than it once was. If something's all over television all day, . . . we clearly don't have the freedom to handle it that we once did. . . . The first day of the Gennifer Flowers–Clinton story, the *New York Times* didn't run it, or they ran a little brief, like three-paragraph story inside. But most papers won't do that. Most will run it because it's out there.—Carl Leubsdorf, July 1999

In addition to the pressure from the pack, Balz said there is a pressure to publish that comes from within the news organization that is influenced by the pack. Tracking down rumors and getting ready for a story, like the story that ran in the *Wall Street Journal* in 1999 about the rumors that George W. Bush had used cocaine, means investing a lot of a reporter's time in researching the piece. In the case of the *Wall Street Journal* story, no one that the reporter talked to confirmed that Bush had used cocaine or any other illegal drug. But the story ran. "It was sort of like an anatomy of a rumor proving conclusively that the rumor was untrue," said Carl Leubsdorf. "Well, you can't prove a negative, and the story didn't really prove anything. Mainly it got the story all over page one." While the *Dallas Morning News* didn't pick up on the *Wall Street Journal* story, the *Morning News* editors soon found out the story was going to run in the *Los Angeles Times*. The newspaper then quickly went to print with another story that its reporters had already been working on about Bush and his service in the National Guard. The pressure from the pack, therefore, creates an additional pressure to publish, said Dan Balz.

> Every organization now spends more time running down rumors, trying to figure out whether things are true or not, or partly true or not partly true, even before you then decide do you put it in the paper. And that takes a lot of resources. And once you go down that road to do that, we're in the business of publishing. We're not in the business of not publishing. And so there's a pressure that builds up. Well, if we know all this we ought to be able to figure out a way to get it in the paper. And, you know, there are systems in place, and checks and balances, and discussions and editors ask tough questions. But in general, my sense now is that if there's bad information about one candidate or another from his or her past, in the heat of a campaign it's going to become public.—Dan Balz, July 1999

Pack journalism is a reality of campaign reporting. Once the campaign moves past the New Hampshire primary, journalists covering presidential elections have to become part of a "tarmac campaign," Balz said. Journalists covering the candidates can no longer travel independently because the logistics of the travel schedule make it virtually impossible for reporters to stay with a candidate unless they sign on with the press plane. So the journalists covering the candidates become captive to the arrangements that are made by the campaign staffs, and they travel, often for months on end, with a band of other reporters. Through the socialization of the press plane, the conversations they have with each other, and the observations they make about what the other news organizations are doing, the pack becomes an important factor influencing news coverage of the presidential campaigns.

THE PRESS POOL

The 15 members of the Kerry press pool on October 13, 2004, the day of the final debate at Arizona State University, included three wire reporters, one newspaper reporter, one radio reporter, one magazine reporter, six still photographers, one television producer, and a two-member camera crew. These journalists trailed Kerry throughout the day, chronicling his debate walk-through in the morning, some crowd interactions, and the scene inside Gammage Auditorium, the site of the debate, which was closed off to the rest of the press corps who came to Tempe for the event. The early pool reports started at 9:08 a.m. when Kerry left the hotel, and included some quotes from Mike McCurry, a senior adviser traveling with the campaign who held a press gaggle while holding the debate walk-through. McCurry told reporters that the debate would focus on jobs, the economy, and health care and that the comments from then-treasury secretary John Snow that job losses under George W. Bush were a "myth." After a little talk about the Red Sox–Yankees playoffs, the questions turned to Kerry's wardrobe—he'd be wearing a "powerful red" tie, according to the pool report. There was some optimism in an earlier pool report that Kerry might talk to the pool, but at 12:46 p.m., David Jackson of the *Dallas Morning News* wrote that "not only did Kerry not speak, poolers had to run to avoid being left behind. Walk-through appeared to last about 20 minutes."

That evening, while most of the Kerry traveling press were watching the debate on the televisions in the filing center—along with roughly 500 other journalists—the pool reported on the event from the top balcony of Gammage Auditorium. From that vantage point, the pool reports described the empty seats in the auditorium, which could hold 3,000 people but was restricted to 350 for the debate, as well as the crowd reaction to the occasional jokes from Bush and Kerry. "The mood seemed to tense up as the candidates attacked each other over Iraq and the war on terror. The only other sounds were occasional coughing and the constant clicking and shuttering of news cameras," Jackson wrote in an 8:19 p.m. pool report.

For the members of the traveling press who weren't part of the pool, the reports from that day weren't critical. They had enough from their view in the press filing center and at the rally after the debate to craft a story for the next day. But that's not always the case. In fact, often the pool reporters are the only access to information about the candidate or campaign. In late January 2000, for instance, Arizona senator and Republican presidential candidate John McCain was campaigning hard in New Hampshire for a win in that crucial first primary. A win could give him the momentum he'd need to pose a serious threat to George W. Bush. McCain, who had picked up a second busload of journalists along with his status as the candidate most likely to challenge Bush, had just arrived in Windham, New Hampshire, for his second town hall meeting of the day. As McCain stepped off his campaign bus, the "Straight Talk Express," Elaine Povich, a reporter for New York's *Newsday* who had been a pool reporter on the first of the two buses with McCain, stepped onto the "Straight Talk Express II"—the overflow bus for the rest of the reporters traveling with the candidate.

Povich perched herself on the edge of a table in the back of the overflow bus. Flipping through the pages of her four-by-eight-inch reporter's notebook, Povich said, "Well, he talked a little about his tax plan and about his stand on abortion. He also went into his bit about paying down the debt, but that's not news." None of the nearly dozen reporters from other news organizations who had gathered around her raised an eyebrow at Povich's declaration. They were ready and willing to accept her definition of "news" from the Exeter-to-Windham leg of the trip.

The press pool is generally a handful of journalists—a mix of print and broadcast reporters and photographers—who travel with the candidate or go into an event where space is tight. Their job is to take notes and to report back to the rest of the press corps about what happened. The *Washington Post's* Dan Balz said that pools, while considered a necessary evil among reporters, are a fact of life on the campaign trail and in many other situations where the entire press corps simply can't be accommodated. At the White House, it's "standard operating procedure," he said. And for the journalists traveling with the major presidential candidates, press pools are common.

For example, on the Monday before the February 1 New Hampshire primary, Al Gore toured several diners and small restaurants, stopping to chat with the patrons. In Tilton, New Hampshire, he stopped at a small place called the Tilt'n Diner. The restaurant was small, and Nathan Naylor, Gore's press assistant, announced that a "tight pool"—a smaller-than-normal press pool—would go in. The pool for that stop included a reporter from the *New York Times*, a video crew, and a still photographer. The fact that the *Times* reporter was in the pool caused some grousing among the other reporters who were left standing out in the parking lot, cordoned off behind a plastic yellow rope, on a brisk winter day—"the *Times* always gets in," one reporter complained. Pool reporters are rotated, but campaign staff members know that the Associated Press and the *New York Times* are heavy hitters. Typically someone from those organizations makes it in the pool. Afterward Gore left the diner, and the pool report was brief. Gore shook a few hands, poured a couple of cups of coffee, and asked the people in the Tilt'n Diner to vote for him. The pool, said Patty Reinert of the *Houston Chronicle*, is the "eyes and ears" of the press corps whenever the full press corps isn't allowed in.

Any reporter would rather be there than to rely on another reporter's pool report. But all of the people in the pool are professional journalists. They know what to look for. They know what to ask if they get a chance. For the most part, they'll give you a totally unvarnished view of what happened there. They'll report everything. They're not allowed to hold back anything for themselves. In other words, if you forget to put something in a pool report and then later you want to use it in your

own story, forget it. You've got to share that with everybody.—Patty
Reinert, June 2001

Violating the rules of the pool means losing your right to be a pool reporter. Reinert said that occasionally someone does hold something back
in a pool report, but if the rest of the press corps finds out, then the of-
fending reporter gets pulled from the pool rotation, which means less access to the candidate. "So that's a pretty good incentive to share everything. If you want any access, you've got to share," Reinert said. Still, the
pool works as a disincentive to come up with anything new or different,
since the requirement to share all of your notes means that the pool reporters won't have anything extra for their own stories (Lewis, 1997). As a
result, pool reports are typically very factual or, alternatively, rich in details
that no one would actually use in a story. On the final night of the American League playoffs, Charlie Hurt of the *Washington Times* was one of the
pool reporters watching Kerry watch the Red Sox take on the Yankees. His
7:47 p.m. pool report on October 20, 2004, had those rich details that would
never see the light of print:

> About 17 of us, with a smattering of agents and staffers, choked into fifth
> floor hallway at 9:30 to pay Kerry a visit. Doors lining the hallway had little
> staffer name signs with graphics of Canada geese on them as if they were
> children's rooms.
>
> Entered low-ceilinged room with another ten or so staffers jammed into a
> long L-shaped couch watching the game. Kerry was in the corner, with Setti,
> Wade, Cutter, Shrum, Sasso, Dobson and others.
>
> They were all drinking the King of Beers with a few more sitting in a pa-
> per ice bucket. On the kitchenette was a paper bucket of Sam Adams on ice.

In 2004, the prevalence of BlackBerry handhelds meant most pool reports came through e-mail. But some, like the pool report that Povich provided from the McCain bus, were verbal updates given on the press bus
or plane or in a press filing center—generally a quick rundown of what
the candidate said or did, with the pool reporter slowing down to read
verbatim quotes. And often, whether electronic or verbal, the pool reporter would sum up the report by deciding, as Povich did, what was
news. The pool report from Al Gore's MTV appearance in 2000 made sure
to note that no news occurred.

> The VP showed up in khakis and a sage green shirt, and worked the crowd of
> 150 a bit before the cameras went on. . . . A few things you might not have
> caught from what they showed in the filing center: During the video they
> showed of Gore's early life, he laughed when The Kiss was described as a
> PDA, and commented "That's not me" at the footage of what appeared to be
> Woodstock. However, when the narrator made reference to the fact that Gore

once smoked "the herb," Gore was silent. At the reference to his having picked "a simpatico running mate," Gore punched the air triumphantly, as he did when the video made reference to polls that showed him ahead of Bush, and the comparison between his proposal for education spending and Bush's.

During breaks in taping, he answered a wide variety of questions—many of them quite sophisticated—from audience members he selected at random.

None of the answers made major news.

What was most interesting was that no one from the press corps seemed bothered by the pool reporters' decisions about what was newsworthy, and none of them pressed for more details on the statements deemed "not news" by the pool reporters. Patty Reinert of the *Houston Chronicle* said that the people traveling with the candidates often appreciate the fact that the pool reporter is signaling what is newsworthy, particularly reporters who may be new to the campaign trail or to that particular candidate.

You may have people who have been on the Gore campaign for a month and a half—and you've seen how isolating that can be—and then they switch over with McCain or Bush. And they don't keep track of every word that candidate has said. So a lot of times, even though you feel like you're very well informed and you're totally immersed in all the coverage and you're reading the papers every day and you're catching the TV reports when you can, sometimes you do find yourself going, "Well, is this new? Is this a new part of his economic plan? Or did he announce this last summer?" And a lot of times the campaign can make it look new, when actually there's nothing new about it. They're just trying to get a daily headline out of it. And someone who's been on the campaign for a while can help with that. For the benefit of the people who might have just come on board, a pool reporter might say, "Well there was no news, but this is what happened," so that people know right away that nothing earthshaking happened.—Patty Reinert, June 2001

The tendency to accept a pool reporter's version of what is new and, therefore, newsworthy is one of the practices that is common on the campaign trail. Rosenstiel (1994) calls it part of the "more subtle side of pack journalism" (p. 61), where consensus among the press corps determines what readers and viewers ultimately learn about the candidates and the campaigns.

COLLABORATION AND COMPETITION

Martin Kasindorf, a *USA Today* reporter, stepped onto the third press bus after John Kerry's postdebate rally in Tempe, Arizona, and pulled out his BlackBerry. The final debate between Kerry and Bush had ended maybe 30 minutes earlier, and Kasindorf already had the early Gallup Poll numbers—52 percent thought Kerry had won; 39 percent gave the debate to Bush. Kasindorf shouted out the numbers to the other reporters on the bus—partly because it was fresh information, partly because he knew they'd have e-mails themselves soon enough, and partly because there is a camaraderie that develops among the traveling press corps. Today's campaign press plane isn't the one that Tim Crouse wrote about, which featured card games and drunken revelry between campaign stops (1973). The presence of more women and the ability to work on laptops and cell phones between stops has changed the tenor of the press bus. But there is collegiality that develops, which leads to lots of information sharing—especially if it's fact based—and lots of talking about what the polls mean or what candidate bus is better or the image-building attempts behind Kerry's barn jacket or Bush's flight jacket.

That collegiality shows up in the news in typically small and subtle ways. During the 2000 campaign, the reporters traveling with Dick Cheney formed a solid bond. First, there were only a dozen or so, compared to the 70 or more that travel with the presidential candidates, so it was easier to get to know the rest of the pack. Second, since the vice presidential campaigns don't typically generate as much news, there was less of a need to be competitive, even from the first day of Cheney's final campaign swing in the last week before the election. Third, according to Richard Benedetto of *USA Today*, the journalists assigned to the vice presidential candidates typically don't have as much experience as those assigned to the presidential candidates—the "primaries" as they're sometimes called. While more senior reporters might travel with a vice presidential candidate for a few days to get information for a larger story package, the journalists who regularly cover the vice presidential candidates are in a lower stakes venue that makes collaboration the norm.

USA Today's Martin Kasindorf, who had joined the Cheney campaign that morning at the airport at Dulles, Virginia, was taking down a few quotes from Cheney's speech at a rally at Loras College in Dubuque, Iowa. And, from his perch on the press stand, he was sizing up the crowd. As soon as Cheney finished speaking, Kasindorf and several other reporters in the traveling press corps huddled to negotiate a crowd estimate. Kasindorf put the crowd at 400, someone else said it looked like 600, and the press corps split the difference between the two and settled on 500. Then they talked about the crowd reaction. One reporter asked, "How many would you say were clapping?" "Maybe half," another said. Since Dubuque was considered a Democratic town, the press corps figured Cheney got a good response.

Of course, collaborating on crowd estimates and even a sense of the crowd reaction isn't unusual. Journalists reporting on events such as speeches, rallies, and other events that often draw large audiences typically report on the crowd size, and they typically check with each other or with other officials, such as the police, to arrive at a consensus on the crowd size. Michael Lewis, a writer for *The New Republic*, noted the same thing in his travels with the candidates for president in 1996.

> The reporters from AP and Reuters do what they always do in these difficult situations when a candidate draws serious crowds. Each makes a rough guess of the number of people in the room. They then average these together to create a fact for posterity. (Lewis, 1997, p. 40)

But the collaboration among campaign reporters in 2000 didn't end with crowd estimates. The Cheney press corps, for example, huddled again on the evening of October 30 after an outdoor rally in Peoria, Illinois, to compare quotes. Three days later in Gallatin, Tennessee, the reporters gathered around Associated Press reporter Karen Gullo after Cheney's speech at the Gallatin Civic Center. Gullo had been traveling with Cheney since the Republican Convention in August 2000, so when Cheney—who had been focusing on the nation's military preparedness in his speeches—mentioned later in his Gallatin speech that public schools were in disarray, Gullo noticed the addition. In the huddle after the rally, Gullo mentioned that Cheney hadn't talked about education in more than a month, and later the press corps asked Cheney's press secretary, Juleanna Glover Weiss, whether the campaign was shifting gears in the final week to return to the "compassionate conservative" message that Bush had been pitching since he entered the race.

Reporters on the campaign trail do compete with each other, but since the "bubble" that they travel in—going from hotel to press bus to speech, then back to the bus and on to the press plane and the next city and next event—means long hours together, they compete in an environment that has its own social norms. And unlike the norms for reporters based in the home office, who collaborate with each other but rarely do so with reporters from competing organizations, journalists on the campaign trail come to view their colleagues on the plane in much the same way as they would their colleagues at their own organizations. The result is a greater degree of collaboration among campaign reporters, especially since they typically all have access to the same information (Bantz, 1997). It's not unusual to find reporters on the press planes or in the filing centers sharing a tape or calling out the latest poll numbers to each other, as Kasindorf did on the Kerry bus in 2004 or as David Lawsky of Reuters did on the Cheney press bus each evening. Patty Reinert of the *Houston Chronicle* said that while the reporters on the press plane are looking for a "scoop," the tenor among the campaign press corps is largely one of cooperation.

Especially on the campaign trail, the reporters work much more cooperatively than you might imagine them working elsewhere, because they're all going to get the basic information. . . . There's kind of a sense that you're all in this together, in a way. And everyone's exhausted and everyone's working under deadline. In some cases you've spent months with the people, so you get to know them, and you sort of begin to treat them like someone from your own paper—not that you share your story. You know, if you get a hot tip on something, obviously you're not going to share it with your competitor. But just basic day-to-day stuff—you know, factual questions or, "I don't understand what he said about this or that," or "My tape is garbled, could I borrow your tape," or "Did you catch that quote," or "I don't understand where he's getting the figures or the budget plan." You might go to someone like Reuters, who deals with financial news all the time, and those guys know what they're doing, and they can help you with the math.—Patty Reinert, June 2001

Reporters who cover presidential campaigns, as well as those who cover presidents, also recognize that they're up against some pretty powerful forces when it comes to shaping the message for the day. So they collaborate not just on the information that comes in the form of quotes or crowd sizes, but sometimes on how to approach an opportunity to ask questions. Candidates don't often hold press conferences or even press availabilities. So on the campaign trail, reporters—especially those who have covered the White House and have a better sense about how to manage those rare opportunities—sometimes work together to develop a line of questioning, according to Bill Douglas, a Knight-Ridder reporter. Douglas, who spoke at a panel on political reporting in Austin, Texas, in August 2005, said that reporters will collaborate on "a line of attack, even in a two-question press conference. If you can get your ducks in a row, [the campaign] can't change the subject," he said. Campaigns, of course, battle back by going to reporters they know and trust as much as they can for questions or by going to someone who might have a different story agenda than the rest of the pack. "For example, if there is some hot scandal going, and a candidate has a news cycle to show that the candidate is unaffected by said scandal, a reporter with a different interest—say, gasoline prices or interest rates—might get the first question. That's the campaign or a candidate's way of trying to control the questioning," Douglas said.

A LONG AND WINDING ROAD

While press pools, pack journalism, and the norms of traveling press corps are important factors that shape the content of campaign news coverage, the fact is that the culture of the press plane and grueling travel schedule also exert powerful influences on the reporters and, consequently, on what they write. On Al Gore's press plane, a chartered Pan Am 727, the seats were assigned by organization. On most seats the assignment was announced by a blue card labeled "White House Two," which was attached to the headrest with black electrician's tape. Print was toward the front—labeled NYT, LA Times, WP, Wash Times, Newsday. Broadcast reporters and then camera crews were toward the back of the plane, mostly for logistical reasons since the camera crews leave by the back of the plane because they have so much equipment to carry.

John Kerry's plane didn't have seat signs, but being on Kerry's press plane in 2004 was, in itself, a kind of statement. About half of the traveling press could fit on the campaign plane, with a small section of business class seating for the broadcast networks and the reporters from the elite newspapers and the rest of the journalists behind them in a section that ran six seats across. And the other half of the press flew on the press charter— a comfortable plane with lots of leg room (it sometimes was used for basketball teams)—but absolutely no access to the candidate or, often, to his key advisers.

Richard Benedetto of *USA Today* said the demarcation isn't simply one of logistics.

> There's a certain invisible barrier that exists, say, between the print reporters and the camera crews. There's not often a lot of fraternization. They don't socialize together. It's just a sense that many of the camera crews don't necessarily have a lot of interest in the news story itself. You know, they've just got to get the pictures. So they're not necessarily worried too much about the news story itself. And so they don't tend to want to talk too much about it, whereas the print reporters are all interested in the story itself and they flock together.—Richard Benedetto, June 2001

On the Gore press plane, the line of demarcation became fully evident after the Clearwater event, when the press corps headed north to Ypsilanti, Michigan, so they could be at the MTV *Choose or Lose* event on Tuesday. A few minutes into the flight, the camera crew members who were sitting in the back of the plane began rustling around. They taped miniature Christmas lights along the overhead bins in the back half of the plane and tossed around a beach ball. They played music on a boom box and sang along to Eric Clapton's "I Shot the Sheriff." They put on yellow plastic hard hats about 15 minutes before the plane landed in Michigan as a way of joking about the hard landings that the plane had been making. In the front of the plane, the reporters either worked on weekend news features or swapped war stories from earlier in the campaign or from previous election seasons. Some war stories weren't even their own. A *Washington Times* reporter who brought along a paperback copy of Timothy Crouse's *The Boys on the Bus* handed the book to the *Los Angeles Times* reporter sitting across the aisle. "Have you read it yet?" he asked. "It really resonates. Except for some of the technology, it's really pretty much the same." Someone else remembered the opening of the book when Crouse writes about a 6:45 a.m. wake-up call:

> The media heavies were rolling over, stumbling to the bathroom, and tripping over the handouts. Stooping to pick up the schedule, they read: "8:00 – 8:15, Arrive Roger Young Center, Breakfast with Ministers." Suddenly, desperately, they thought: "Maybe I can pick McGovern up in Burbank at 9:55 and sleep for another hour." Then, probably at almost the same instant, several score minds flashed the same guilty thought: "But maybe he will get shot at the ministers' breakfast," and then each mind branched off into its own private nightmare recollections of the correspondent who was taking a piss at Laurel when they shot Wallace, of the ABC cameraman who couldn't get his Bolex to start as Bremer emptied his revolver. A hundred hands groped for the toothbrush. (Crouse, 1973, p. 4)

"Poor slob," the *Washington Times* reporter said. The thought of missing the big story, like the attempted assassination of George Wallace in 1972, is every reporter's worst nightmare. It's why Toby Eckert of Copley News Service said that despite the long stretches of waiting and early morning baggage calls so that his luggage could be swept by Secret Service agents and sniffed by trained dogs, he'd rather travel with the candidate's motorcade than catch up with the campaign at a later event. And it's why the reporters traveling with Gore the day before the November 7 election were still trailing at 3 a.m. on that Tuesday when he stopped at a hospital in Florida to talk to the workers on the night shift, even though they knew the stop would never make it into the next day's news cycle.

> For the last days before the election, Gore did a 36-hour run with no sleep in the end. . . . By that point, you've filed your story and you know the next day is Election Day, so very little of this is going to make it into your next day story. So when we arrived at the hospital, I mean people literally just laid down on the floor right in the place where he was sitting in a circle talking to these people. Reporters were just crashed out everywhere because it was the only option. And a lot of people went back to the plane and slept on the plane while he was doing this overnight stuff because they knew by the next day your story is going to be about who won the election and what Gore did the day of the election. You don't really care what he said in the middle of the night. You

only care that he made four stops on the way there and didn't sleep. On the other hand if he trips on the way onto the airplane and gets a black eye, you kind of want to be there. Or if he gets in a car accident in the motorcade, you want to be there. You're kind of the body watch at that point. If someone tries to assassinate him, you want to be there.—Patty Reinert, June 2001

However, as Dan Balz pointed out, once assigned to a campaign, reporters are not content to simply be the "body watch" for the duration of the election season. Newspapers are in the business of publishing stories, and reporters, who get some of their professional satisfaction from seeing their stories in print, are in the business of writing them. The reporters on the campaign trail typically are hungry for a nugget of new information—something that will make the long days and weeks or months away from home worthwhile. Geoff Boucher, the *Los Angeles Times* reporter who was traveling with the Cheney campaign in late October, was frustrated by the lack of news coming from the vice presidential candidate. "It's five days before the election and he's got nothing new to say," Boucher complained one afternoon. "I just want something to write." On the morning of October 31, 2000, when Michael Cooper of the *New York Times* had a 14-inch story "downpage"—played lower on the page—in the *Times*, the rest of the Cheney press corps wistfully congratulated him, wishing aloud that they could get that kind of space in their own publications.

And while the campaign staff, if they're doing their jobs, will try to give the media something new to write about each day, often the agenda of the media is different, so the "new" news is deemed not newsworthy. And sometimes, dulled by the rigors and the sameness of the campaign trail, numbness sets in.

Reporters are only human, and when you've been on the campaign trail for six months and you are going sometimes literally 18 or 20 hours a day, you're exhausted. I mean you are physically and mentally spent when you're doing that. And still you've got to do your job every day. So that does figure into the product that you're producing. You're not only totally isolated in the bubble of the campaign, being fed what the campaign is feeding you, but they are controlling your every movement, your diet, your sleep, everything. So it can be very grueling, and I would not be honest if I didn't say that that affects your coverage.

Question: In what way?

I think sometimes you might miss something or you might skim over something that if you had another day to explore you'd write a better story on it—a more in-depth story. But the next day you're onto something else and you don't have time. I found it frustrating because sometimes you would see a good story, but you have no time to write it. You know, you say, "Oh, if I could just go back to my office right now and spend three days on the phones and talking to people I could write this great weekend story that would be more meaningful than the day-to-day coverage that I'm doing." But you just don't have that option in the throes of the campaign.—Patty Reinert, June 2001

In time, Ken Auletta (1993) wrote, the frustration of being with a candidate for long stretches of time can feed the cynicism among some members of the press corps. The result is tougher questions for the candidate and the members of his or her staff. In Campaign 2000, a trio of women reporters who were known among the press and the press staffs as the "Spice Girls"—Katharine Seelye of the *New York Times*, Ceci Connolly of the *Washington Post*, and Sandra Sobieraj of the Associated Press—became a story in themselves for the kinds of questions they asked Al Gore and his press secretary, Chris Lehane.

> Speaking of Connolly, Seelye, and Sobieraj's relationship with Gore, Cox Newspapers reporter Scott Shepard says, "It seems to go somewhat beyond adversarial and short of animosity. It's certainly different from anything I've seen on other campaigns." (Mnookin, 2000b, p. 33)

Benedetto said the questions that Seelye, Connolly, and Sobieraj asked went beyond the journalistic role of being skeptical of the candidates. Instead, he said, their questions were largely "a product of that total cynicism. Nothing met with their approval—the way the candidates were conducting themselves or what they even had to say or how they were saying it. They were grousing about everything." Benedetto said that the cynical attitude of the three women showed up in their coverage of Gore. However, because reporters on the press planes are isolated from the "real world" and because these were reporters from agenda-setting news organizations, their cynicism affected the rest of the press corps as well.

> Well I think there's a tendency to somewhat follow the tone. Though I don't think that some went to the degree that some others did. But I think there was varying degrees of it. Sure.—Richard Benedetto, June 2001

KEEPING THE VOTER IN MIND

But even if a reporter remains immune to the cynicism that can crop up on the campaign trail, the travel schedule and isolation can lead to a loss of perspective about what matters to the average voter. Some papers combat this by assigning two or three reporters to a candidate and having them trade shifts on the press plane. Ann Scales of the *Boston Globe* said her paper had two reporters covering Al Gore. So when Scales returned to Washington, D.C., after the New Hampshire primary, she had a couple of weeks off the plane while her counterpart took to the air. Other reporters rely on their editors at the news desk or on phone calls home to get an outside view of the campaigns. Toby Eckert said he checks in with his family when he's on the road to see what they're paying attention to from the campaigns.

> Your job is to take in what the candidates say, analyze it, then apply commonsense principles to their message. But it's never as clear-cut as that because you're inside the bubble and you have to think outside the bubble. A lot of reporters I know will call up their friends and relatives from the road just to get some perspective on a story.—Wire service reporter, October 2000

Benedetto works the crowd, as do other reporters. Mike Allen, who covered the Kerry campaign for the *Washington Post* in 2004, typically was one of the first to leave the press filing area and talk to voters at Kerry stops. The quotes from voters rarely made it into the stories that Allen wrote, but the sense that he could get of the audience is something that most reporters say is helpful, even if the interaction is brief. And reporters who aren't chained to one candidate, like David Lightman of the *Hartford Courant*, try to battle both the fatigue of campaign travel and the loss of perspective by getting off the campaign trail as often as they can—even if it's only for a day or two. Lightman said he always makes sure he gets home for part of the weekend. "You've got to remember that there are people out there who don't care about this," Lightman said in October 2000, when he was traveling with the Cheney campaign. Patty Reinert said that reporters do a better job of keeping their readers in mind if they do get a chance to step out of the bubble for a day or two, but often—especially after Labor Day—that doesn't happen. Then, she said, a reporter has to rely on the people back at home on the editorial desk to help him or her realize what "the story of the day" really is. Still, that relationship is not without its frustrations for a campaign reporter.

> You have to realize that they're on the outside of the bubble and they can see things a little clearer than you can. So there's a trust issue there, I guess. But on the other hand, sometimes you're screaming at them, "No, I'm right here and I can see what's going on."—Patty Reinert, June 2001

Even just a few days on a campaign plane can become disorienting. Reporters have to check their press schedules to know what city they are in, and it is a rare luxury to end up at a hotel long enough to be able to get any laundry done. In the final days of the 2000 campaign, Gore was "following the sun," Reinert said. In order to get in as many stops with as many voters as he could, Gore would start in the East and travel across the country each day, making campaign stops on the way. At the end of a long day, he and the press corps traveling with him would fly overnight back to the East Coast and start the cycle again. By the end of October, the journalists on the campaign trail were looking forward to Election Day—mostly because they thought it would bring an end to election coverage and the chance to return to their normal lives and routines.

6

A Battle for Access

At a rally in Elyria, Ohio, on October 9, 2004, Democratic presidential candidate John Kerry made a rare appearance in the press filing center. Dressed in khakis and a mustard-brown barn jacket, the candidate wasn't there to talk to the national media about health care or jobs. He simply was using the filing center as the easiest path to get to the stage, where he gave a speech on those issues. To the 80 or so reporters traveling with him to cover the campaign, Kerry gave only a quick wave as he passed through the room, flanked by his aides and Secret Service agents.

It wasn't much better a few days later when the campaign made a stop in Santa Fe, New Mexico, for a rally and then a day of debate prep before heading to Tempe, Arizona, on October 13 for the last of three debates with incumbent President George W. Bush. After deciding to stay in Santa Fe for an extra day so that he could catch the first game of the American League Championship on the night of October 12, Kerry spent much of the day in debate prep sessions. His only interaction with the 15 members of the press pool that Tuesday came at 3:50 in the afternoon when he went out for a bike ride. For a few brief seconds, while Kerry slowly pedaled out of sight, the pool reporters got in a few quick questions and got back a few noncommittal responses. According to a pool report filed by Scott Shepard of Cox Newspapers, Kerry said that he wasn't ready for the Wednesday debate, but he was taking a break from the prep sessions. Shepard's pool report then notes, "As he rode away, the pool asked whether he was ready for the Red Sox–Yankees game tonight. He turned his head back toward us and said, 'That I'm ready for.' The senator was not wearing his helmet, but was seen putting it on a block away from the pool." The 30-second exchange was the only interaction between the candidate and the members of the traveling press corps that day.

But the Kerry reporters weren't the only ones being shut out by the campaigns. Reporters covering Bush's campaign also went for long stretches without any direct contact with Bush. In an article in the *Los Angeles Times* on October 15, 2004, staff writers Maura Reynolds and Edwin Chen noted that when Bush came back to the press section of Air Force One on the morning of October 14 for a five-minute chat about the debates, it was the first time the president had set foot in that part of the plane in more than three years (Reynolds & Chen, 2004).

For the campaigns, it's just part of the strategy. In order to develop and manage the image of a candidate, strategists need to control the flow of information to the media. They accomplish this by controlling access—and generally by limiting it—and by setting the ground rules for the rare occasions when they do allow media access to the candidate (Covington et al., 1993). The great fear is that giving the members of the press corps the opportunity to ask the candidate any questions will, at best, risk pulling the candidate off of the message for that day. At worst, the candidate could commit some major gaffe that will make headlines in all the wrong ways. But the battle for access on the campaign trail, which is a prominent feature of contemporary political campaigns, may well be one factor contributing to the increasingly negative tone of news coverage of presidential campaigns and to the focus, especially late in the campaign, on stories about strategy and electoral polls.

WHY ACCESS MATTERS

Journalists traveling with the candidates do so partly in order to get closer to them and to see them in moments that are less orchestrated than the speeches and rallies. And they know that their news organizations are paying a fair amount of money—at least $1,000 a day and sometimes more—to get the stories that reveal something about the candidate and his or her suitability for the office. So the fact that those in the traveling press corps spend most of their time in press filing centers or corralled behind a security line watching the candidate is a source of frustration for reporters, said Patty Reinert, a *Houston Chronicle* reporter. Journalists begin to view the candidates suspiciously, seeing the lack of access as an attempt by the candidates to avoid questions they don't want to answer (Mnookin, 2000a). On the other hand, candidates who are readily available to the media—especially those who are considered to be serious contenders—can benefit. Access to the candidates is rare once the Republicans and Democrats have settled on a nominee, but during the early caucuses and primaries, some candidates try to court the media by being available. That's one reason that journalists love to cover the New Hampshire primary. The state is small, which means reporters don't have to rely on the campaign to organize their transportation and housing. With a rental car and a map, they can get anywhere they need to go. Also the New Hampshire primary is dotted with more candidates—many of whom want the national press exposure to help fuel support and create momentum. The result is that most candidates, except for the heavy favorites, freely invite the press corps onto their buses. Lesser known candidates like Gary Bauer and Al Sharpton would offer to take journalists out with them for a day or more in hopes of generating some coverage for their campaigns and the issues that mattered to them, a practice that was much common before political strategists and polls came to dominate the campaign environment.

> Years ago, you could go off and spend a day with a candidate. Going out with a candidate for a day and riding in the same car with him or her, rather than on a press bus, is really helpful, but you rarely get to do that anymore. The best chance to get to the candidate is during the primaries, the New Hampshire primary especially. That's when they go into people's homes and the venues are small. Then that's it. You're into campaign mode. So the time to start to get close to the candidates for 2008 is now, as they're starting to make their early forays into important states. But newspapers don't want to spend the resources to have someone in the field with John Edwards in Iowa right now.—Richard Benedetto, July 2006

> In the primaries, the candidates talk to the press a lot more because they need the press to get their name known. As the campaign moves on, their advisers tell them not to talk to the press because they don't want to make a mistake. Certainly with the press, the advisers, the consultants, say just hunker down and stay on message and don't risk straying from your message and certainly don't make any mistakes.—Martin Kasindorf, July 2006

John McCain, the Arizona senator who posed the most serious threat to George W. Bush in 2000, clearly benefited from his accessibility early in the campaign season—during late 1999 and early 2000. Reporters were enamored with him because he was a "quote machine" (Wolper & Mitchell, 2000) who would talk to them whenever they called. On his campaign bus, McCain would take any and all questions from the pool reporters who traveled with him.

> He just wears the press out. There's a point at which he could say anything and it would just go into the void. We're suckers for anyone who

will talk to us. . . . And so, because of his accessibility, he probably has gotten better press coverage.—Dan Balz, journalists' roundtable, February 2000

Ed Chen of the *Los Angeles Times* said that for journalists, the accessibility issue is tied to the candidate's willingness to be open and truthful with the media. So McCain wooed the press not simply by being available, but also by his apparent candor. The media are less likely to latch onto an issue if the candidate is forthcoming about it, which is one reason Chen was surprised by the November 2000 story about George W. Bush's DUI arrest. Chen was traveling with the Bush campaign the night the story broke and said that as word of the report started making its way through the press corps, members of the Bush staff finally came by and said that Bush would meet with the press. "So they decided to defuse it right away," Chen said. "But what baffled me is why they didn't get all this out at the beginning of the campaign. They should have put it in Bush's book and gotten it all out there. That's what John McCain did."

Gore also sought press coverage to defuse an issue in 2000—in his case it was a concern about fundraising. But in that case, Gore talked to the press late in the day so that reporters would have enough time to get his version in print, but not enough time to make a lot of follow-up phone calls. The strategy, said the *Houston Chronicle*'s Patty Reinert, was to let Gore's message sit for a full day before there could be any response from the Bush campaign or anyone else.

That day, Gore, who hadn't had a press conference in three weeks or so, came back on the plane and said the truth is my friend in this and did an on-camera briefing. And he just bombarded everyone with his financial statement—you know, his transcript of his testimony at the deposition. And so they [the campaign] just papered you to death with 40 or so pages—it was a thick stack of papers—so you could spend all day reading those papers. It's definitely a campaign tactic to appear as if he's totally giving you everything and you can sort through it on your own. But what it did was it sort of delay the full story for a day while people tried to sort it all out. And he got on camera saying, "I have nothing to hide. The truth is my friend. I'm giving it all to you."—Patty Reinert, June 2001

Occasionally the candidates will meet with the press, either in a briefing for the press corps or in short one-on-one sessions, but even in those instances, there's little new information. A reporter traveling with Gore in 2000 talked about a five-minute interview he had with Gore. He had several questions for the candidate, ranging from prescription drugs, which was Gore's message of the day, to education to answering criticisms that he sometimes exaggerated his record. No matter what he asked Gore, the candidate quickly circled back to the message of the day. In 2004, the experience was no different. One journalist who had been on the campaign trail in 2004 with Howard Dean, John Kerry, and George W. Bush said that Bush held more press availabilities with the media than Kerry did just to get in the news cycle, but that the availabilities were essentially useless. "You could ask him anything, even about the weather, and he'd say, 'Well, John Kerry has flip-flopped on the weather,'" the reporter said.

Typically, however, the front-runners simply wall themselves off from the press (Mnookin, 2000a) since they see no real advantage to talking to the national press corps. The conventional wisdom is that the national press will not cover the issues that the candidate thinks are important, and the overall tone of national press coverage has a greater chance to damage a candidate than it does to help him or her. Bill Clinton, once he became the front-runner in 1992, began to limit his meetings with the national press, and in 1996, as the incumbent, he ran a "Rose Garden" campaign—sticking close to the White House and using the trappings of his office to keep the media at arm's length. Mike McCurry, a senior adviser to the Kerry campaign in 2004 and Bill Clinton's press secretary from 1995 to 1998, said in a July 2006 interview that he and the rest of Clinton's staff "basically kept Bill Clinton away from the press corps for six whole months because the conversation they're trying to have with the candidate is not the conversation we want to have with the voters, and the voters matter more than the press."

Stuart Rothenberg (2000) wrote that when news coverage of a candidate pulls him or her off message it's generally pulling the discussion from issues on which the candidate has an advantage to areas where he or she will lose ground to an opponent. That was the case with Al Gore early in the summer of 2000, when the media were talking about the security problems at Los Alamos. The only way for Gore to prevail in the press, Rothenberg wrote, was to fall out of the media spotlight.

> The coverage [of Gore] has been bad because it has taken the vice president far off message, away from issues such as gun control, a patient's bill of rights and the cost of pharmaceuticals, where Gore has an advantage. . . . The only way for the vice president to make up ground against Bush is for the electorate to focus on the potential problems and weaknesses of the governor. This could happen at the GOP's Philadelphia convention, during one of the debates, or even now, but only if Bush becomes the subject of media scrutiny. If the media's focus remains on Gore, the vice president is likely to be stuck in his rut, trailing Bush by a half dozen points or so. (Rothenberg, 2000, pp. 1–2)

Gore successfully walled himself off from the press in 2000, as did George W. Bush later in the 2000 campaign. But access to the candidates has been a growing problem for several election cycles. Reporters covering the 1988 campaign said George H. W. Bush also favored the "Rose Garden" strategy, using his position as vice president to fend off significant contact with the national press.

I remember in 1988 George Bush was campaigning for president in the fall, and he had gone quite a few days without any press availability, and it got to be a news story. Reporters were counting down—"on day 10" and "on day 13"—until finally they smoked him out by saying it's been so many days since he's answered any press questions. And so finally they smoked him out into holding a press conference. That didn't happen this time around. I didn't see anybody in a concerted way raise the issue. Everybody seemed to be concerned about that particular point—that [George W.] Bush was hiding. But now reporters seem to accept it—that the candidate, that it's not in his interest to get involved in a give-and-take on a day-to-day basis because the message gets stepped on.—Richard Benedetto, June 2001

As the presumptive Republican nominee in late spring 2000, George W. Bush started making more trips to the press section of the campaign plane, but he kept everything that occurred in those impromptu sessions off the record, McCurry said. Still, little that occurred on the plane would have been really newsworthy. Bush schmoozed the press by circulating through the press section with a tray of sodas, by handing out nicknames to most of the regulars on his plane, and by chatting about baseball or other non-campaign matters with the press. On one flight, Bush—surrounded by the press corps—spent the time before takeoff talking to the media about his family pets (Mnookin, 2000a). Even though none of that was on the record or even substantive, the contact with the candidate did leave journalists with the impression that Bush was a nicer guy.

As a correspondent for Copley News Service, Toby Eckert spent a large part of the 2000 election season traveling with Al Gore's campaign. He knew going in that it would be difficult to get to the candidates, so he wasn't surprised that there was little access to Gore—even when, just after the Democratic convention, Gore boarded a riverboat for a 400-mile campaign trip down the Mississippi River. Despite the close quarters, the candidate was kept at a safe distance from the national press. That message was driven home for Eckert when he went looking for Chris Lehane, Gore's press secretary, and "kind of wandered into a section of the boat where I guess I wasn't supposed to be and Gore was there." Eckert tried asking a couple of questions, but Gore, who also seemed surprised by the unscripted interaction with a reporter, wasn't talking, and Eckert was quickly shuttled out. "I was just struck by how controlled the candidates are. They're just very hard to get to. They're isolated from the media for the most part during the campaign, and they're just giving the same speech over and over," Eckert said during a July 2006 interview. Gore suffered particularly in comparison to Bush, who made himself more available once John McCain beat him in the New Hampshire primary and before McCain withdrew from the race on March 9, 2000, making Bush the de facto nominee of the Republican Party.

> It created the image that Gore was out of touch or that he was afraid to talk to the media. I don't think that the media were more anti-Gore, but I think that the media traveling with Bush were schmoozed by Bush, and in some ways were starstruck in that they were sort of charmed by Bush, and that affected their coverage, as much as Gore's reticence and distance may have affected coverage of him.—Toby Eckert, July 2006

The lack of access to the candidates sometimes becomes a story in itself. Once the fall campaign season started gearing up in 2004, both the *New York Times* and the *Washington Post* featured articles on the distance that the candidates were keeping from the traveling press corps. In the September 16 edition of the *Washington Post*, Paul Farhi (2004) noted that the reporters covering Kerry were keeping track:

> In the section of John F. Kerry's campaign plane reserved for members of the news media, calendar pages marking the days until the Nov. 2 election hang from a prominent spot on a bulkhead wall. A date on one of the pages, Aug. 9, is circled several times in dark ink. Above it, someone has written the words "Last Press Avail!!!" It is a pointed, if silent, comment from the media pack that follows Kerry on the campaign trail. (p. A9)

Farhi wrote that Kerry, like Bush, also had cut back on the number of informal conversations he had with the press members on his plane—partly because the campaign risks losing control of the message of the day, and partly because of the risk that comes from a misstep when a candidate answers a question. Bush, for instance, made headlines during an August 30, 2004, interview with Matt Lauer of *Today* when he said he didn't think the war on terror could be won. In that moment, the Bush campaign lost control of the news for several days as the media focused on the Lauer interview. Access on the Cheney plane became an issue when Rick Lyman of the *New York Times* was denied a seat in the press section and wrote about the experience in a column that ran on September 19, 2004:

> The vice president travels on Air Force Two, a tech-packed, wide-body with private areas in the front, a Secret Service buffer in the middle and a media cabin in the back. A crew of about 10 reporters flies with him, representing all the networks, the wire services and two or three newspapers. There are snacks, cable television and camaraderie.

But there is not a seat for me.

Nor has there been a seat for the previous two *New York Times* reporters sent to cover the vice president. (p. 1)

And Reynolds and Chen (2004) wrote about candidate access for the *Los Angeles Times*, noting that when Bush did step into the press section of Air Force One for a few minutes on October 14, 2004, the day after his final debate with Kerry, it was the first time he had done so during the campaign, and it was a maneuver aimed at courting the press in the final weeks of a tight race. But stories about the access issue are rare since, unlike other "inside baseball" stories about strategy, the question of candidate access is one that puts the journalists in the limelight.

McCurry, who said he's "a strong believer in doing more availabilities and having more interviews," said one problem with creating more access for the media is that journalists typically not only want to talk to the candidates, they want to keep the conversations on the record. In 2004, McCurry said he tried to negotiate with the press for a series of off-the-record sessions, but the Associated Press wouldn't go for it.

> The decision by the AP not to participate in any backgrounding or off-the-record sessions made it impossible to create the discussions that I think are helpful, or would seem to me to be useful for the media. I wanted to create some sessions where Kerry would talk to the press about how he thought the campaign was going—deep background sessions with no direct quoting. But the AP takes a strict, purist view of these things. And if the AP takes that view, then there is no such thing as background. I had a long roundabout with the AP on this, but for them it was just the principle, and I understood it because they get jerked around so much.—Mike McCurry, July 2006

McCurry said a key advantage to the campaign of interactions with the press is that it prepares the candidate for tough questions. Without that, he said, it's easier for someone to get "unhinged" when he or she does have to face the press. And while reporters certainly prefer on-the-record sessions, most would take an off-the-record session rather than the lack of access they typically face on the campaign trail. David Lightman of the *Hartford Courant* said that even a short, off-the-record session lets him get a sense of the candidate as a person, which is helpful as he writes his stories. Candidates sometimes realize this. Bush, in the spring of 2000, said as much in his interview with Seth Mnookin:

> "I think probably the best thing I've done is interface with the press," he says. "They get to see the human, that I'm a human person, that I've got feelings, I care, I've got priorities. It gives them a better sense of who I am as a person." (Mnookin, 2000a, p. 77)

Martin Kasindorf of *USA Today* said the off-the-record interactions he had with Al Gore in 2000 gave him a very different impression of the vice president than he otherwise would have had. During the steamboat ride down the Mississippi, Gore hosted a rock party and included the press corps. The event was simply a chance to kick back, but Kasindorf said it also helped him realize that Gore wasn't stiff, which was the conventional wisdom about his style. After the party, Kasindorf said, "Privately I discounted other people's reporting that he was a wooden, stiff person, and I did not repeat that characterization in my stories."

WHAT HAPPENS WHEN ACCESS IS DENIED

Richard Benedetto of *USA Today* said the lack of access to the candidates results from the conflicting goals of the media and the campaign. The goal of the campaign is to reach the voters with the issues that favor their candidate, and "our goal is to get them on something," Benedetto said. For the front-runners, talking to the national press is considered a losing game, and the closer it gets to Election Day, the less accessible they become since there is even less time "for digging oneself out of a hole" that a major story might create, said Ed Chen of the *Los Angeles Times*. In fact, Chen and other journalists on the campaign trail said that especially late in the campaign, reporters can count on *not* getting to talk to the candidate very often.

> Many times what we're going to do when the candidate stands in front of us is we're going to say, "Why are they criticizing you for being tight with the oil companies?" or "Why are they criticizing you for not being relaxed enough on the campaign stump?" You're not going to ask them, "Where do you stand on this?" Most of the questions that the national press are going to ask are going to be questions that deal with some kind of a political controversy that many times are conjured up by the press. So there's very little percentage for the candidate to get involved in that unless he's getting bombed on something and he has to get his own voice in there just to defend himself.—Richard Benedetto, June 2001

> They certainly don't make themselves available if everything's going well for them. They also don't make themselves available if something has just broken that's harmful to them, unless they want to get their word in and try to defuse it.—Patty Reinert, June 2001

Left with little or no access to the candidates, the journalists on the campaign trail have to find something else to cover. The campaigns hope that they'll focus on what the candidate is saying on the stump—the message of the day. And to some degree, it's a successful strategy. In their examination of news coverage of Ronald Reagan's 1980 campaign, Covington, Kroeger, Richardson, and Woodard found that the message of the day strategy "was increasingly effective with print journalists, and always effective with television journalists at setting the news media's substantive agenda during the campaign" (1993, p. 792). While the strategy has been less effective since the Reagan years, as reporters have gotten wiser to the tactic, it still influences news coverage of the campaign—but perhaps not in the same ways. Even in the 1980 campaign, the message of the day tactic didn't result in more positive news coverage for Reagan (Covington et al., 1993), and more recently, the strategy has led some reporters to set the agenda themselves—sometimes through the kind of candidate "quizzes" that caught George W. Bush off guard when he was asked, by a Boston reporter, to name the leaders in several world "hot spots," and sometimes by leading a journalist to look for the gaffe or misstep.

Bush accommodated the media in its quest for a political gaffe 2004 by saying, in a *Today* interview, that he didn't think the war on terror could be won. And he did it again when he said he hedged, during the second presidential debate, on identifying three mistakes he had made during his first term. Kerry also struggled with verbal missteps on topics ranging from the Iraq War to football. After Kerry mistakenly referred to Lambeau Field, home of the Green Bay Packers, as "Lambert Field" during an August campaign event, the slipup was carried in newspapers and on television news and was posted on ESPN's website. A month later, the blunder resurfaced as news when two lawyers who were supporting George W. Bush's reelection started their own 527 group, Football Fans for Truth, to "get out the political humor about John Kerry's unsuitability to be sportsman-in-chief," Jeff Larroca, one of the attorneys, said in a news interview (Tumulty, 2004).

Auletta (1993) said that the focus on the gaffe results from the fact that it isn't scripted. The mistakes, he argues, provide the moments that journalists believe strip away the protective veneer of the campaign and show the candidates for who they are. While the mistakes may reveal the candidates as human, the focus on them portrays the candidates as bumbling and takes the attention away from the real issues of the day.

Those lessons lead political strategists to advise against much direct interaction with the media. "Everybody's afraid of making a gaffe, and I think that's what drives it," said Mike McCurry, a senior adviser to the Kerry campaign. "They're afraid of getting off message. It's not a very honest way to deal with the voters, but they feel that if they don't, it's just going to be a 'gotcha-fest.' And there's too much journalism today that runs in the direction of 'gotcha.'"

From a journalist's perspective, the reluctance to talk to the press is a sign of weakness, a signal that the candidate may not be worthy of the White House.

> In a perfect world, a man or woman who is going to run for president of the United States should be ready to face the media. But the point is message control. We're the closest thing to them that they can't control, so it's pretty scary for them. They're scared to death that someone's going to make fun of the candidate and that it will be remembered.—David Lightman, October 2000

One reporter for an East Coast news organization who also was assigned to the Gore campaign said the lack of access creates tension between the campaign staff and the members of the media.

> They dollop him [Gore] out to us when they need something, but that engenders this attitude that we are not going to let them use us. That sets up a struggle between us and the campaign, which can get in the way of what we should be doing for the voters. Earlier we had been pushing for access, but he wouldn't do a press conference for two months. . . . They [the campaign staff] said we asked stupid questions about fundraising and the use of White House e-mail. But he should be more available, and probably we should ask better questions.—East Coast daily reporter, October 2000

The frustration that journalists feel—especially those covering the campaign from the confines of the press plane—is partly because the lack of access to the candidate means there is less news to write about, which leaves them no option but to cover polls and strategy stories, since the campaign managers are much more available. "We're substantially controlled by one man's agenda, and because of the constant travel, we don't have the latitude to go poking around, to do real reporting," said one journalist in 2004. But reporters also are frustrated because they spend long months away from their homes and families to travel with the candidates—sometimes for very little return on the investment. One reporter on the Cheney plane in 2000 said she was hoping Bush would lose the election because it would mean she'd get home sooner. A Bush victory would mean she'd have to spend an extra week in Austin, Texas, she said. Of course, the unprecedented result in 2000—with an election that went undecided until mid-December—had her on the road for much longer.

The resentment that can build among the national press corps is only made worse by the candidates' apparent willingness to talk to local reporters for "happy little interviews," as Patty Reinert of the *Houston Chronicle* described them. And the tension that develops from the candidates' inaccessibility increases the journalists' sense that they're being manipulated and that the campaign is hiding something. Trained to ferret those things out, the campaign reporters do start to ask tougher questions and take on a more adversarial view of the candidates and the campaign staffs.

AN UNEASY SYMBIOSIS

For days the members of the traveling press corps had been sitting in the back section of Dick Cheney's plane waiting for the chance to talk to the Republican vice presidential candidate. Separated by 15 rows and a contingent of campaign staffers and Secret Service agents, the reporters covering Cheney were edgy. Cheney had been meeting with members of the local press at nearly every campaign stop, and, with the exception of one opportunity to join in on that press availability in Hot Springs, Arkansas, on the second day of the campaign swing, the members of the national press corps had not been able to talk to the candidate. And the Hot Springs press availability was shut down as soon as the national press began asking tough questions, which had only added to the tensions between the campaign and the journalists. So it was a little surprising when Juleanna Glover Weiss, Cheney's press secretary, walked to the back of the plane during an early evening flight from Chicago to State College, Pennsylvania, on Thursday, November 2, 2000, to say that Cheney was coming back for an off-the-record chat with the press. David Lightman, a reporter for the *Hartford Courant*, was anxious for the chance to size up the candidate, and while he would have preferred an on-the-record talk, he said he could still get a measure of the man from the informal session. A few minutes later, Cheney walked down the aisle of the plane and stopped at the front of the press section. The reporters gathered around him as well as they could, crowding into the aisle and spilling over into nearby seats. They asked about the strategy for the final days of the campaign and about the poll standings that showed Al Gore might pull off an Electoral College victory. Cheney was relaxed and confident, saying that he and George W. Bush would work hard over the next several days to reach as many voters as they could and to convince them that they had a better plan for the nation's future. Fifteen minutes later, Cheney went back to his section in the front of the plane to finish getting ready for a rally at Penn State University in State College. And the reporters were satisfied—at least until they could call their home offices on the ground in State College.

While Cheney was courting the media at 30,000 feet, a television station in New England was breaking the news that George W. Bush had been arrested for driving under the influence on September 4, 1976. Given the allegations earlier in the campaign season about Bush's alcohol use and rumors about cocaine use, the DUI arrest was a potential bombshell coming this close to Election Day. So after the Penn State rally on the flight from State College to Harrisburg, Pennsylvania, where the campaign would stop for the night, the reporters flagged down Weiss once more. They needed a few minutes with Cheney to ask him about the DUI arrest. Not possible, Weiss responded, "after all, he was just back here talking to you all. He can't keep coming back every time you have a question for him." And so the day ended much as it had begun—with the journalists in the traveling press corps being frustrated by the 15 rows and lack of access that kept them from getting the quote they needed for the next day's paper.

Lightman, who had joined up with Cheney's campaign in New Orleans, Louisiana, on the second day of Cheney's final campaign swing, was already feeling a little put out—even before Weiss rejected the journalists' request for a chance to question Cheney about the DUI story. Lightman had been scheduled to travel with George W. Bush, the primary candidate, but got bumped from the Bush plane at the last minute to make room for journalists from news organizations in Florida and Pennsylvania. It was a new experience for Lightman, but not entirely unexpected since Al Gore's running mate, Joe Lieberman, was a U.S. senator from Connecticut.

> I've been doing this since 1980 and I've never been bumped before. But Connecticut is gone—it's Gore's state. They only wanted people on Bush's plane who served his needs.—David Lightman, October 2000

While Lightman knew he didn't fit in that camp, he found himself struggling for an angle on the campaign from the Cheney plane that would be right for his paper. Fortunately the next day had both Cheney and Lieberman campaigning in Florida, so armed with his cell phone, Lightman made a few calls and wrote a piece about the two vice presidential candidates campaigning in Florida in a frenzied attempt to take the state. The story wasn't what the Cheney group most wanted—they would have preferred a piece that focused on Cheney's speech about U.S. military forces, especially since they added retired U.S. Gen. Norman Schwarzkopf to the campaign lineup for the day—but Lightman had his own agenda.

Still, reporters who cover the presidential and vice presidential candidates say they have to be somewhat careful about how far they go— especially if they are doing something different than the rest of the members of the press corps. Breaking a news story, especially one that puts a candidate in an unfavorable light, may please the editors back home, but it can make life pretty lonely on the press plane. Reporters say that if the candidates like what they're writing, they're more likely to get a scoop on a story or to be included in the press pool (Crossen, 2004). And a writer who breaks away from the pack and writes something critical about the campaign or the candidate can find himself or herself left out of press pools and cut off from even the limited access that traveling journalists are given to the candidates. It's a way of "punishing" the reporters that the campaign staff members think are uncooperative or unfair. Some journalists suspect that the Bush administration's view that the *New York Times* gave it unfavorable coverage is the reason that Cheney had no room for a *Times* reporter on his plane in 2004.

> A lot of that goes on on the presidential planes, I'm sure. Let's go back to the "major league asshole" remark that Bush made about Adam Clymer [of the *New York Times*, on September 4, 2000]. That was a reaction to a piece Clymer wrote about how poor medical standards and insurance coverage are in Texas. It was not what the Bush campaign wanted the influential *New York Times* to say to the opinion makers and the television stations who follow what the *New York Times* does. . . . Sometimes they do leak stories to favored reporters.—East Coast daily reporter, October 2000

Another reporter put it more bluntly: "If you screw your sources, they'll screw you back. They'll shut off access," she said in an October 2000 interview.

It's something that journalists—especially those who travel on the press planes and have to work for months or years with the people on the campaign staff—keep in mind as they weigh the value of running with a story or holding it back. For example, after George W. Bush selected Dick Cheney as his running mate in late July 2000, the political pundits watching the race were writing that Cheney was a drag on the ticket. Rumors started to fly that Bush was thinking about replacing Cheney with Colin Powell.

> In fact, it turns out the rumors were being fanned by the Gore camp. Cheney was asked about it kind of off the record. We [his newspaper] said we wouldn't be the first to run the rumor. Then one of the Gore staffers called a reporter on the Cheney plane to ask what was new with the rumor. At that point, we had to consider whether we would run with the rumor about Powell. My editor pushed me to put it in the lead, so initially we did go with that. Then Juleanna [Cheney's press secretary] said she would have a real problem with any reporter who would print the rumor because there were no Republican sources for it. At that point I called my editor and said we would have bad problems, serious problems, if we didn't change the lead. We pulled it and ran with something else.—East Coast daily reporter, October 2000

Bantz (1997) described these kinds of decisions as a "calculus that includes . . . balancing their relationship with sources and the demands for work" (p. 128). The tendency to tip the scales in favor of the sources is greater when the sources and reporters have long-standing or intense working relationships, as they do in a national political campaign, or when the sources have a lot of power over the reporters, as is the case once the two major party nominees have been determined—something that now typically occurs in March once the Super Tuesday primaries have passed. Generally at that point, even though there may still be some primary contests to be held, one candidate in each party has enough delegates to secure the party nomination, or has such a lead in the delegate count that the challengers simply can't catch up. At that point, the candidate's campaign picks up more funding, more staff, and more security, and the national press corps gets relegated to the back of the bus. However, there are limits to what Bantz (1997) calls a "nonconflict" mode of interaction between journalists and their sources. In the event of a major breaking story or a tight deadline, journalists will become more confrontational, particularly if they believe that the candidate or the campaign staff members are shading the truth or avoiding them.

And despite the fact that the candidates can shut out certain reporters or news organizations, Cragg Hines, a political columnist for the *Houston Chronicle*, said he'd never hold back on a story for fear it would "queer a deal" with one of the candidates. But Hines said that he sees evidence of it in other publications. Pressure from the campaign staff, he said, can result in an unfavorable story being held or a favorable one making it into print. Carl Leubsdorf of the *Dallas Morning News* said that sometimes campaigns or politicians can get a favorable story in as part of the newspaper's strategy to build good relationships with sources, but only if the story itself isn't especially important. It's how relationships are built, he said, particularly inside the Washington, D.C., Beltway. And it's especially important for papers like the *Dallas Morning News*, which have bureau offices in Washington but aren't based there.

> You sometimes write stories for the sources, but not on page one. You sometimes cover something in Washington because of the source that's involved with it. Like a confirmation hearing, it won't be much of a story, but we'll do something with it because it's someone we want to cultivate and you'll do it to show interest. Sources like reporters who show interest in what they're doing. . . . We need to do enough so that when you call the White House person who is handling [a story], they'll know you and they'll call you back.—Carl Leubsdorf, July 1999

And while journalists will do what they can to build good working relationships with the members of the campaign press staffs, the staffers also try to cultivate cordial relationships with the journalists on the press plane. They do this by scheduling events around the needs of the media— especially the network television stations—and by trying to make life on the campaign trail a little more pleasant. John Kerry's campaign provided wireless Internet access to the traveling press and tried to schedule filing times to serve the deadline needs of television and daily print reporters. And on the first day of Al Gore's late-September 2000 campaign trip, the press staff scheduled four hours of filing time in St. Petersburg after Gore's speech on Medicare at the Coliseum, meaning that the press buses wouldn't leave for the airport until 6:15 p.m. They did this to accommodate the television reporters who wanted to do live shots from the site. But Nathan Naylor, who coordinated the press travel for the Gore campaign, knew that the print reporters—most of whom had filed for the day by 4 p.m.—might resent having to wait around for the television crews, so he commandeered one of the three press buses for a few hours and took a small group of journalists to a nearby bar. Later on the plane, Naylor and Chris Lehane, Gore's press secretary, chatted with some of the reporters, particularly those for the major news organizations. In the final weeks of the 2004 campaign, Bush campaign strategist Karl Rove and senior adviser Karen Hughes also made frequent visits to the press filing centers to comment on the race and to court the press (Reynolds & Chen, 2004). But riding the press buses and planes or hanging out in the press filing area serves another purpose, according to Ed Chen of the *Los Angeles Times*. Campaign staff members would "take the temperature" of the press, he said, and sometimes change the candidate's speech as a result. Wayne (2000) said that the effect of the media on the campaign can be quite substantive. If an issue is emphasized in the press, the candidates will sometimes alter their agendas to address that issue in their campaign speeches. "In this way the news media affect the conduct of the campaign, which in turn influences the decisions of the electorate" (Wayne, 2000, p. 231).

Sometimes the media's influence is subtler. On one trip through Iowa that Chen was on in 2000, Gore talked about a patient's bill of rights and told the audience that his was the biggest and most ambitious plan in 35 years. Back in the press filing area the reporters on the campaign trail started comparing it to the proposal floated by the Clinton administration shortly after Bill Clinton became president, and Chen asked about it. "It wasn't a big deal, but it was catching him in something that was not accurate," Chen said in a June 2001 interview. Gore's next speech simply said that the plan was ambitious—the reference to the past 35 years had been dropped. Lehane didn't want Gore's exaggeration to be the story and he knew if that's what the press was talking about, then it might be. While the reporters noticed the change in the rhetoric, they were more forgiving since it was corrected by the next stop, Chen said.

Still, with that forgiveness comes some degree of skepticism. Journalists in the traveling press corps are aware that the campaign staff members are advocates for their candidate and that they are well schooled in how the media work. Events are tailored for the media, especially television, with backdrops that provide good visuals and scheduling that accommodates press deadlines. But journalists are wary of being used by the campaign staff, particularly since they still feel the bruises of the 1980s, when campaign managers seemed to understand the job of the media better than the reporters themselves. The master of that, said the *Washington Post*'s Dan Balz, was Ronald Reagan. But even in 1988, the Reagan style of campaigning, with its emphasis on photo opportunities, was prevalent.

> Eighty-eight was a kind of the culmination of the Reagan talent of making the visual presentation of politics the message. During the Reagan presidency and in '84, I think everybody marveled at it because it was newer to us, they were really good at it, and they were successful at it. But by '88 there was a feeling that the politicians and political operatives were more skillful at understanding how we did our jobs and how we would respond to certain stimuli than we were at kind of piercing through some of the phoniness of that.—Dan Balz, July 1999

One reporter for an East Coast daily news organization who traveled with the Gore campaign in 2000 said that because of the lack of access and the staged events, Gore essentially viewed the press as "just a microphone," which the reporter resented. And while those in the traveling press corps realize that the campaign staff members are hired guns who are supposed to make the candidate look good, they get tired of the volume of press releases and the constant attempts to spin a story or offer it up to a favored writer. The *Los Angeles Times*'s Ed Chen said that on several occasions Gore's campaign staff went to extreme lengths to manipulate the media. Early in the fall of 2000 at a campaign stop in Cleveland, Ohio, Gore was scheduled to give a major policy address outlining his top 10 economic goals. When the press corps arrived in Cleveland late in the afternoon on the day before the speech, Chen said, everyone was trying to get an advance copy of a paperback book that outlined the goals. The campaign leaked copies of the policy book to the major media outlets—the *New York Times* reporter got a hand-delivered copy of the book. Reporters for the *Washington Post* and the *Los Angeles Times*, including Chen, were sent copies by e-mail. The rest of the reporters in the traveling press corps, who were from smaller news organizations, were selectively sent e-mails that had only a partial list of the 10 goals, although each of those e-mails had a slightly different list. "Those reporters hung out in the lobby of the hotel and began comparing goals so they could come up with 10. It really set a tone with the press corps, and it ticked off just about everybody that they would try to manipulate us that way," Chen said.

Another East Coast daily newspaper reporter said that although the people who worked for the campaigns understood the needs of the press, the candidates and campaign officials view the media's role differently than the members of the press corps do. "They kind of resent us ever being a prism of interpretation" for the day's events, he said. Thus, the typical relationship between press liaisons on the campaign staff and the journalists they work with is laced with some antagonism. In a column in the *Los Angeles Times*, for instance, David Shaw wrote that the Bush administration's view of journalists was dismissive.

> Bushites don't see journalists as representatives of or surrogates for the public. They don't even see them as conduits. They see them as, in effect, lobbyists, pleaders—bleaters—for special interests: their own. *Their* access. *Their* scoops. *Their* headlines. *Their* careers. *Their* egos. And that means the policymakers in the Bush administration have no obligation to talk to them. (D. Shaw, 2004a, p. 2)

Ken Auletta, in a 2004 story on the Bush administration and the media for the *New Yorker*, says that Bush and his staff have been especially adept at keeping control of the news agenda while, at the same time, keeping the press at bay—oftentimes opting not even to return phone calls from reporters. Elisabeth Bumiller, a *New York Times* reporter who covers national politics, told Auletta that the members of Bush administration "treat us with contempt. . . . This crowd has a wall up. They never get off their talking points" (Auletta, 2004, p. 55). The press, Auletta writes, sees "the White House as a fortress," and "Bush sees the press as 'elitist' and thinks that the social and economic backgrounds of most reporters have nothing in common with those of most Americans" (2004, p. 53). The tension that exists within the White House between the press and the administration is mirrored on the campaign trail, although it's somewhat softened by necessity. Candidates can't entirely bypass the national press corps—news organizations provide candidates with "free media" that lets them get their message to potential voters, even if that message is refracted a bit through the journalist's sense of what's newsworthy. And news organizations benefit from cultivating good relationships with sources so that they can have better stories. That means that any antagonism is softened by both a mutual need and a degree of respect for each other—at least in most cases. Toby Eckert of Copley News Service described the relationship between the campaign and the media as "ambivalent."

> They realize that they need the national media to get their message out to the broadest audience. But it's an adversarial relationship because the reporters are trying to get at the truth and hold them accountable. It does keep the candidate from just getting their kind of "press release"

message out. Any reporter is going to try to balance the story by including the opposing candidate's viewpoint and is going to put some context to the story. So I think there's just a natural tension there.—Toby Eckert, July 2006

Tracey Schmitt, the Western states spokesperson for the Bush campaign in 2004 and now the press secretary for the Republican National Committee, said the problem is an intractable one, given that journalists and campaign communicators have different jobs but work in close proximity to each other in the final months and weeks of a campaign. Still, she said, "there are usually strong professional, if not positive personal relationships. A good working relationship between a campaign and a news organization is mutually beneficial, and any smart campaign recognizes this." Mike McCurry, a senior adviser to John Kerry, said the tension is inherent since the goals of the campaign are different from the goals of the journalist.

Journalists tell you "news" and having done that, move on to the next subject. Political communicators know that persuasion takes repetition and multiple deliveries of messages that have impact. Those are almost 180-degree opposite goals, which creates some of the tension between campaigns and the journalists who cover them. The answer is for campaigns to be much better in making important messages "newsworthy" and for journalists to realize that their assignment is unfulfilled until they can make the news vivid enough to have real impact.—Mike McCurry, August 2006

Still, one reporter who had been on the campaign trail in 2000 for close to a year characterized the relationship with the press staff more harshly. In a September 2000 interview, he said that after a story that was critical of Al Gore ran on the network news one night, he talked to Chris Lehane about the story. Lehane, he said, didn't mind the negative tone of the piece because "Lehane said the pictures look good and the pictures are 70 percent of TV coverage." The journalist said Lehane's attitude—one that reflects a kind of disdain for the press—is more common than it should be.

Both sides have almost contempt for each other. It's kind of a Machiavellian struggle. And the game that's played between the campaign and the media gets in the way of the real reason for the campaign, which is to give voters information.—East Coast daily reporter, September 2000

Much of this, as Eckert, Schmitt, and McCurry noted, is driven by the conflicting goals of the reporters on the campaign trail and the candidates they cover. Journalists need new stories every day, and candidates work to stay on message. Reporters in the traveling press corps believe they should have greater access to the candidates, when the reality is that they have very little access. And the power imbalance between the press secretaries who work for the candidates and the members of the traveling press, who do have to rely on the campaigns for their logistics and for the opportunities to talk to the candidate, fuels a journalistic instinct to be aggressive in order to avoid appearing too cozy with the candidate or his or her staff. For news coverage, that means more stories about strategies as the journalists try to reveal the character of the candidate and the timbre of the people who are his or her closest advisers.

In 1972, when Timothy Crouse traveled with the presidential campaigns for *Rolling Stone*, journalists in the national press corps had regular access to the candidates and often talked to them informally on the flights between one rally and another (Crouse, 1973). However as campaign reporting has changed—focusing more attention on the candidate's private life and on the political strategies and gaffes that reveal the candidate as merely human—candidates and campaign managers have become more wary of the national press corps because of their belief that the journalists in the traveling press corps will take advantage of any opportunity to focus on the candidate's foibles. While there is some truth to that, since many journalists believe they need to give voters information that lets them assess the candidate's mettle, the lack of access leaves reporters for the nation's top newspapers with little else to write about other than polls and the "inside baseball" stories that talk about campaign strategy.

Moreover, the lack of access to the candidates, which campaign staffs use to try to control the message getting out to the voters, only adds to the level of frustration among the press corps and the increasingly adversarial attitude among journalists traveling with the candidate. The tension is heightened when local news stations are given opportunities for interviews at nearly every stop on the campaign trail, while the national press corps is herded off either to a press filing center or back onto the bus.

Reporters in the traveling press corps are at the mercy of the candidate's campaign staff for their food and lodging, for their phone and Internet connections at filing centers, and for information that they can put in tomorrow's edition. They know—or at least believe—that if the press secretary gets angry about a story they've written, it can mean being left out of a press pool or accommodations in a "spill-over" hotel rather than the same hotel as the candidate. And just as candidates and campaign managers are wary of the national press, those in the traveling press corps resent the campaign tactics that result in the media becoming "just a microphone" for the candidate.

The struggle to shape the news agenda leaves its scars. Journalists, wary of being used by the candidates and their campaign staffs, look at every press release, every event, and every leak for the political motivations behind it. Even the policy proposals of the candidates are viewed under that microscope. One reporter for an East Coast daily said that after Al Gore announced a proposal to use the Federal Trade Commission as a venue for addressing violence in the media, his first question to Chris Lehane, Gore's press secretary, was whether the announcement was motivated by Gore's need to distance himself from Hollywood. Lehane, in a September 2000 interview, said questions like that miss the point and don't help voters understand the differences between the candidates. The disconnect between campaign staff members and journalists sets up what Patty Reinert of the *Houston Chronicle* calls a "love-hate" relationship between the press corps and the candidates and their staff.

> They need the press to get their word to the American people, but they also want to manipulate the press to make sure that the word that gets out is their campaign message. So it's kind of a big game of them trying to get the word out in the way that they want it reported, and it's up to reporters to sift through that, balance it from the other side, do some investigating, and see if what they're saying is what they're doing. But definitely the campaign is not there to have a balanced story every day. They're there to get their message out. And they will use the reporter to do that. And it's up to the reporter to decide when they're being used and when they're being helped.—Patty Reinert, June 2001

The reality of campaign travel, then, is an odd battle over message control between the candidates and their staffs and the reporters who are on the press planes. It's a friendly battle—press secretaries and campaign managers joke with the reporters and often sit in the press section of the plane—but it's still a battle for control of the news.

7

Deciding What's Newsworthy

The 2004 presidential election was nearly three weeks away, and George W. Bush was scheduled to square off against his Democratic challenger, John Kerry, in their final debate in just a few hours. But before the debate got started, representatives from the Kerry campaign held a press conference to highlight two issues—the first was a letter sent by Democratic National Committee Chairman Terry McAuliffe to his Republican National Committee counterpart, Ed Gillespie, accusing Republican groups of various attempts at voter disenfranchisement and voter fraud; the second was to fill reporters in on the Kerry campaign's strategy to take the Southwest and mobilize the Latino vote. On hand at the press conference, in addition to the roughly two dozen reporters who attended, were McAuliffe, Kerry senior adviser Joe Lockhart, and Henry Cisneros, a cochair of the Kerry campaign and former secretary of Housing and Urban Development.

The press conference started off with McAuliffe reading excerpts from his letter to Gillespie but quickly turned to the latest polls from the Southwest states showing Kerry ahead in Nevada and New Mexico, even with Bush in Colorado, and closing in to within five percentage points in Arizona. Cisneros said that Kerry's support from the Latino community would exceed 70 percent—more than Gore got in 2000—and that the growing Latino population in Ohio could swing that very close state to Kerry (it was close, but the state ultimately went to Bush). They then talked about the "ground war" that would bring out Democratic voters to the polls and that would be critical for Kerry to win on Tuesday, November 2. And although the candidates would meet in their final debate of policy issues that evening, for a good chunk of the day, the focus of the campaign and the media was, once again, squarely on matters of strategy and the daily hit of poll numbers.

The final debate, of course, dominated the next day's headlines. But even the debate stories showed "the tendency of the press to ignore the policy aspects of the debates and highlight instead the tactics, particularly to see the debates and performances (43%), and as a reflection of campaign strategy (10%)" (Project for Excellence in Journalism, 2004b, p. 3). The Project for Excellence in Journalism study also showed that candidates' statements on policies were covered in only 13 percent of the stories reported in the media in the final stretch of the campaign.

Journalists who cover presidential campaigns say they do cover the issues, but that a candidate's issue position won't be news for more than a day, so the focus on strategy stories and poll numbers comes, at least in part, from the fact that there's little access to anything else on the campaign trail. Each day the campaigns would have a message they were trying to get out to the electorate, which sometimes was considered newsworthy, but "the rest of the day was stump speeches, and we didn't write about those," said Martin Kasindorf of *USA Today*. "We'd heard it a thousand times already. But the stump speech evolved over time, so then you'd frantically make some calls to get perspective on that."

The perspective, according to Adam Clymer of the *New York Times*, was typically a view through the lens of campaign strategy. Campaign journalists, according to Clymer, often assume that the candidates' speeches and statements are a matter of political expedience—that candidates will say what will help them win votes rather than what they really believe. That assumption results in news stories "that put motive and tactics up front, beginning with phrases like 'Seeking to burnish his conservative credentials,' or 'In another bid for the crucial soccer mom vote'" (Clymer, 2001, p. 780).

Editors and reporters also are skeptical about the public appetite for in-depth issue coverage. Early in the campaign season—often in the year before the political primaries get started—news organizations, and especially newspapers, will run long stories on potential candidates. While these stories focus on the likely candidates who are ahead in polls or who are raising a lot of money to support a campaign, they are stories that provide readers with insight into who the candidate really is and how he or she has been shaped by history and life. And the stories get little response.

It's kind of a quandary that political journalists have been dealing with for some time—the horse race versus substantive issues coverage. We keep hearing that readers want to read about the issues, but you wonder whether people really read these serious issue pieces. People say they don't have much time or patience for the longer stories that explore issues.—Toby Eckert, July 2006

And reporters like Clymer and *USA Today*'s Richard Benedetto say that despite all of the hand-wringing about political coverage, the polls are news. Voters, they say, want to know who's ahead and by how much.

TRACKING THE CANDIDATES

With six days to go before the 2000 election, Republican vice presidential nominee Dick Cheney had spent a full day campaigning in Florida—first at the South Ocean Grill, a diner in West Palm Beach, then at a private home, and finally at rallies in Port St. Lucie, Punta Gorda, and Weeki Wachee Springs near Brooksville. The day brought some new faces for the journalists covering Cheney on the campaign trail. Sure, Senator Alan Simpson was still around from early in the week and was still telling the same jokes to the crowd. But retired Gen. Norman Schwarzkopf joined the campaign at the Port St. Lucie rally and stayed for the rest of the day, and Florida's Governor Jeb Bush spoke to the Weeki Wachee audience. And there were miniconcerts along the way. Lee Greenwood warmed up the crowd at Port St. Lucie, while the Bellamy Brothers did a few numbers for the people who had come to the evening rally in Weeki Wachee Springs, a Florida tourist attraction best known for its mermaids. Still Cheney's speech throughout the day was essentially the same speech he had been giving for the past several days, so it was with slightly dulled senses that the journalists covering Cheney got back on the press bus to head to Hernando County Airport for a two-hour flight to Nashville.

Once on the press bus, most of the roughly dozen reporters in the Cheney press corps pulled out their cell phones for a final check with their editors. David Lawsky, a reporter for Reuters, scribbled furiously on his notepad as he talked to the people at the home office. When he hung up, he had new numbers: George W. Bush was up by about three points. More importantly, Lawsky had state-by-state poll numbers showing Al Gore was ahead in some key states that could give him the Electoral College, even if he didn't take the popular vote. But Gore was running well behind Bush in Tennessee, where the Cheney campaign would be tomorrow. The rest of the press corps listened and took notes as Lawsky went through the numbers from the latest Reuters poll. Several reporters made quick calls back to their editors to make sure that their news organizations got the new poll results, and the buzz on the bus turned to what the numbers meant for the campaigns. Questions and opinions flew freely. Gore couldn't win Tennessee, but could he afford to admit that without sacrificing votes in key states like Pennsylvania, Florida, and Ohio? Should Gore try to campaign in Tennessee just for appearances? Should he send his running mate, Joe Lieberman? Could Bush and Cheney capitalize on the fact that Gore was losing in his home state? And with a three-point difference between Bush and Gore, could Gore make up the lost ground? Did he even need to if he was ahead in the states with the most electoral votes? Out of a full slate of events, with four stops in four different Florida cities and the addition of both Schwarzkopf and Jeb Bush to the campaign lineup that day, the reporters on the Cheney bus still looked to the poll numbers to tell them the story.

The media clearly have a bias in favor of stories about polls and money—the horse race kinds of coverage that keep the focus on the contest itself and not on the proposals and policies of those who would be president. In 1972, two news organizations conducted a total of 3 election polls, but by 1988 eight news organizations conducted nearly 260 polls (Bauman & Herbst, 1994). Leading the pack in 1988 was the *New York Times*, which spent roughly $1.5 million on election polling and published the results of 31 polls (Lavrakas, 1991; Mann & Orren, 1992). In 1992, more than half of the network news coverage was about the horse race, while less than one fourth examined any kind of policy (Auletta, 1993). And in the 2000 election, polls and the horse race showed up in 71 percent of the stories on network news that ran between Labor Day and Election Day, while policy matters showed up in only 40 percent of the broadcast stories (Farnsworth & Lichter, 2003). The pattern also appears in print coverage, where an examination of a random sample of 871 stories about the 2004 election showed that polls and the horse race were played prominently in 21 percent of the stories. And in the stories that ran just before the election, horse race coverage was the focus of 31 percent of the stories in August 2004, 41 percent in September 2004, and 46 percent of the stories in October 2004. In those same months, issues were the focus of 5 percent of the August stories, 16 percent of the September stories, and 6 percent of the October stories. The 2000 and 2004 campaigns also saw a dramatic increase in the use of daily tracking polls, which use very small sample sizes and typically are limited only to assessing who's ahead.

Polls and strategy stories are more concrete, making them easier for reporters to write and making it less likely that their objectivity will be called into question. Assessing a candidate's plans for the economy or the environment can more readily open a journalist to charges that he or she is biased or simply doesn't understand the topic well enough. Stories about the numbers in a new poll and the behind-the-scenes campaign maneuvering are less likely to lend themselves to allegations of bias (Auletta, 1993; Kovach & Rosenstiel, 2001b). Polls also are new, and with the heavy use of the tracking poll in recent campaigns, there was at least some new news every day. And in a process that is often marked by tedium, polls and strategies are a way of injecting some drama into the race. Hanson (1996) said that the focus on Pat Buchanan's lead in New Hampshire in the 1996 Republican race was largely attributable to the "media's need for a strong challenger" (p. 3). The poll numbers and campaign strategists can provide that.

Journalists are divided on the usefulness of polls for their own coverage and the value of polls to the readers. *Washington Post* political reporter and columnist David Broder, in his book that takes an insider's look at news production, writes that news organizations are "saturated with polls" and that polls are given too much prominence and importance in political campaign coverage (1987, p. 295). Broder said in a speech at Colby College in 1990 that the only way to really gauge what the voters think is to get out and talk to them. The decision-making process that voters use can't easily be summed up in a few survey questions, so beating the streets and hanging out at coffee shops is still the best way to understand what the voters are thinking.

But the race itself often is the news, and that means that journalists covering campaigns have to know who's winning, and they have to report it. Cragg Hines of the *Houston Chronicle* falls in the same camp on this issue as Jack Germond (1999). While campaign coverage needs to provide a good mix of stories, including issue stories, the fact is "it is a horse race. Somebody is going to win and somebody is going to lose, and I think you cannot ignore that fact. It *is* an election," Hines said. Ed Chen of the *Los Angeles Times* said that while horse race stories can be superficial, "that's what it's all about. We have to write who's winning and who's losing and what the tactics are. That's news."

However, the criticism of horse race coverage is less concerned with the fact that polls and campaign strategies are considered stories but instead says that it's a question of volume. Dan Balz of the *Washington Post* said that even with newspapers making concerted efforts to reduce the amount of poll and horse race coverage, those stories still dominate the news and tend to "drown out" the policy stories and issue-oriented pieces. When more than half of the media's coverage of a race is on the mechanics of the race itself, then voters are not being given enough information to help them make informed electoral choices. *USA Today*'s Richard Benedetto said that while the public pays attention to the real votes that are cast, even during the primary season, voters have little interest in polls and campaign strategies.

The process—who's ahead, who's behind, who got one up on the other guy, who the new consultant is. You know, the average voter doesn't give a damn who your consultant is. To think that there's a story there that the average reader of a newspaper cares about is a joke.—Richard Benedetto, June 2001

If the horse race stories don't serve the voters, then what makes them newsworthy? One factor, again, is that there's often little else that's new coming from the campaign itself. Each campaign swing—generally a trip of three to five days—is designed to deliver a particular message. For the journalists on the press planes, then, the story after the first day has to be something else. And since members of the traveling press corps are shuttled from one staged event to another, with limited freedom to roam around and talk to real voters as David Broder advocates, they rely on the campaign for news. With nothing new coming from the candidates, they have to turn to whatever new information can catch up with them as they jet across the country. Most often that is the polls, which can be called up on the wires, and the strategies, since at least a few key members of the candidate's staff typically travel with the press. But there's another factor that drives the reliance on poll coverage—one attributable to the competitive nature of journalism.

The fact of the matter is that the horse race has become even more important because of the truncated campaign schedule. In this business, we all want to be first. We want to say, "We reported back in January that George Bush was going to win the Republican nomination. And it was just going to be Gore and Bush." We want to be first, and part of being first is to report some of the ups and downs of the campaign so we can look smart.—Ann Scales, July 1999

Scales, like Richard Benedetto, said that all of the nation's major newspapers place too much emphasis on "who's up, who's down, and who's raised the most money." But she qualified that by adding that those stories are important in the context of a political campaign, especially given the importance of money in running a successful national campaign. And some journalists, like Carl Leubsdorf of the *Dallas Morning News*, said that while polls are the focus of a lot of media criticism, they are only a small part of the election coverage of most major newspapers.

I think if you look at newspaper coverage—and I'm talking about papers like the *Los Angeles Times*, the *Wall Street Journal*, *USA Today*, the *New York Times*, the *Washington Post*, the *Dallas Morning News*, the *Chicago Tribune*, the [Boston] *Globe*—their coverage has been pretty good in the last couple of campaigns. It is not nearly as poll driven as smaller papers and as TV tend to be. *USA Today* does an enormous number of polls, but they do a lot of other stuff too. It's not as horseracy. I mean, you go through our coverage and you'll find relatively little about polls. And when we print something, we'll print a box unless it's our own poll. We'll run a poll this weekend. We did a poll comparing voters' attitudes in Texas and in the rest of the country on Bush, basically. But we're not as overwhelmed with that. And I think a lot of papers, too, they do serious profiles of these people. They do serious thematic pieces.—Carl Leubsdorf, July 1999

The problem, said both Carl Leubsdorf and Dan Balz, is that the poll coverage sticks out because it is more accessible and easier for readers to understand. Journalists, given their choice, would rather write in-depth issue pieces, but the reality is that voters ignore them in favor of the horse race precisely because they are more complex.

Toby Eckert of Copley News Service said that when he does talk to voters, or even to members of his own family, they complain about the lack of issue coverage. And often they ask him why an issue that's important to them—like Social Security or health care reform—hasn't been covered. "I'll point out that it has been, you just haven't read the newspaper. Their level of knowledge of candidates and the issues really seems to be very driven by what they see of the candidates' ads," Eckert said.

While reporters may think that voters want to read about the horse race, campaign consultants argue that the focus on polls and strategy results from what interests journalists. Mike McCurry, a senior adviser to the Kerry campaign, said that he believes voters do want issue coverage and they want it later in the campaign season, but "by the time the election rolls around, the reporters have ceased being interested in those issues. They're more interested in what's going on behind the curtain, and they miss the primary truth of campaign communication—that repetition is the key to informing people."

For Tracey Schmitt, the press secretary for the Republican National Committee and the Western states spokesperson for the Bush campaign in 2004, the abundance of horse race stories may not have a serious impact on the election. "Still, nobody wants to read that their campaign is losing two weeks before the election. It can depress not only morale, but most importantly voter turnout."

From the journalistic perspective, there is another side to the horse race in news coverage, according to Ed Chen of the *Los Angeles Times*. Polls also drive the decisions a news organization makes about where to invest its resources.

The polls clearly do play a role in influencing coverage, beginning with the first issue of all, which is do we cover a candidate? There are people from all over who run for president and most people you never hear of and we never, ever cover. We didn't cover Ralph Nader every single day, but we did travel with him from time to time. There you had a candidate who you think might cost another candidate a lot of votes. . . . But a lot of coverage is dictated by the polls, both with the candidates and with the issues as well. Candidates rely on them as well to decide what issues to emphasize. . . . It becomes sort of a circle.—Ed Chen, June 2001

Indeed, of the more than 200 people who filed to run for the presidency in the 2000 election, fewer than 20 received any coverage in the nation's major newspapers, and only a half dozen received a significant amount of coverage. Even as early as January 1999, the contest was quickly whittled down to the front-runners—George W. Bush and Al Gore—and the rest of the field. By the following fall, news coverage had narrowed even further to Bush and Gore and their top competition—John McCain in the Republican Party and Bill Bradley in the Democratic Party. In 2004, Bush was running for reelection, but there were other Republicans who filed for the presidency, according to Politics1.com. And when retired Gen. Wesley Clark entered the Democratic race in the fall of 2003, newspapers wrote about the Democratic field expanding to 10 candidates. In fact, there were more than 50 candidates in the Democratic race.

BALANCING THE NEWS

Jill Lawrence, a reporter for *USA Today*, was one of roughly 70 journalists flying to Clearwater, Florida, on Monday, September 25, 2000, aboard the press plane for the first day of Al Gore's three-day campaign swing through Florida, Michigan, and Iowa. She was thinking about what she might write for the first day of the trip. As reporters got on the plane at Andrews Air Force Base for the flight to Florida, they were given a stack of papers and a lengthy booklet outlining Gore's policy on Medicare and prescription drugs, which would be the focus of the campaign swing. Lawrence spent part of the plane ride sifting through the papers she'd just gotten. Trapped in the tightly scheduled campaign bubble, she didn't have an opportunity to call anyone on the Bush campaign, so she started scrolling through the hundreds of e-mail messages she had received from the Bush-Cheney campaign trying to find the right counterpoints to Gore's proposals. It was difficult to find any that really fit the bill. In the end, and with a deadline fast approaching, she filed the story focusing mostly on the Gore Medicare plan and noting for her editors that there was some response in some of the Bush-Cheney releases.

> When I finally took a look at some of the Bush-Cheney releases yesterday about Medicare, they were all over the map. I'm not sure what my paper did with them. I haven't had a chance to read the story yet. Bush's points don't really answer the ones that Gore is making, but you have to have something from the other side.—Jill Lawrence, September 2000

The idea of having an opponent's response, even if it doesn't directly mesh with the rest of the story, is important for journalists. For many of them, the idea of balance is summed up by providing space for response—essentially telling "both sides" of the story, whatever the story may be. Patty Reinert of the *Houston Chronicle* said that many times her job traveling with the Gore campaign involved getting a response from Gore or someone on his staff to something that was going on in the Bush campaign. "Sometimes the story of the day would have nothing to do with where the candidate was going or what they said there. It would be something that popped up on the other campaign that you needed a response to," Reinert said. And if there was something coming from the Gore campaign that needed a response from Bush, then Reinert would call the *Chronicle*'s reporter traveling with Bush or someone with the Bush campaign to get that balance in her story. Providing this kind of balance in a story—a quote or two from "the other side"—is one method reporters use to gain credibility for their stories and to help defend themselves against criticism that their news coverage is biased (Tuchman, 1978). As Shoemaker and Reese (1996) point out, this kind of balance is one of the tactics journalists rely on because the pressure of deadlines doesn't give them the time to verify the information they get from sources.

> Often, verifiable facts are not available, leading reporters to report the truth-claims of sources. Because they often lack time to verify such statements, reporters cannot claim they are factual. They can, however, report conflicting statements, which allows them to say both sides of the story have been told. Both statements may be false, getting the reporter no closer to the truth, yet the procedure helps fend off criticism. (p. 113)

While the practice may insulate journalists from criticism from their sources and perhaps even the courts, Kovach and Rosenstiel (2001a) argue that it does little to help establish credibility for the media since the routine of balance often means that opinions with little merit are given equal space. The "he said, she said" style of journalism, which merely pits one set of quotes against another, does little to help voters. But in trying to parse out the truth behind the quotes, journalists also get trapped. "Your instinct is that if we say bad things about one side, you have to say bad things about the other side. . . . You want to give equal scrutiny to both sides, but I don't think you should impose a false equivalence that doesn't exist," said Adam Nagourney, a *New York Times* reporter, in an interview with Howard Kurtz (2004, p. C1).

Steve Lovelady, managing editor of CampaignDesk.org, an online organization that was started in the 2004 campaign season to provide some analysis of campaign coverage and to fill in the gaps of daily journalism from the campaign trail, said the "he said, she said" formula really failed in news coverage of the Swift Boat Veterans for Truth ads that questioned John Kerry's service and injuries in the Vietnam War (D. Shaw, 2004b). Coverage of that story focused on what was being said by the Swift Boat Veterans and by people who supported Kerry's version of what occurred but failed to put any emphasis on military records that backed up Kerry's claims. Lovelady said that kind of journalism results from press fears of any charge of media bias. "The press is so sensitive now to charges of liberal bias that it bends over backwards to give the appearance of being evenhanded. . . . Reporters can and do argue that it's not their job to ascertain veracity. But that *is* their job, especially when the facts are so available," Lovelady told Shaw (2004b).

A form of bias that seems to concern journalists less is the bias that does, as Ed Chen noted, give more coverage to those who take the early lead in the polls or in campaign fundraising. And it's not an inconsequential matter. Candidates who get coverage early in the electoral season—often a year or more before the election year—can gain an early momentum. The tendency of most news organizations to give greater coverage to a frontrunner and his or her closest challenger means that candidates who are not faring as well in the polls or in fundraising have a difficult time getting any significant news coverage. Thus, journalists gauge balance early in the campaign season not by getting equal numbers of quotes from all of the candidates, but by providing similar coverage for front-runners and key challengers. Even before the race has started, then, the push to have balance within a story drives journalists to narrow down to two or three the field of viable candidates who are worthy of being included in a story. The balance, therefore, is among the powerful contenders in the race.

In the 2000 campaign, the determination of who was most powerful was made early on by most news organizations. Campaign financing and the candidates' poll standings were often the barometers that were used to assess viability. As early as the summer of 1999—more than a full year before the election—the *Dallas Morning News* and the *Houston Chronicle* were paying particular attention to George W. Bush, who was the governor of Texas at the time. As Texas governor, Bush was a "hometown" favorite. But he also was an early favorite in the Republican Party, and was generating a lot of support from influential backers. For the *Houston Chronicle*'s Cragg Hines, that meant that he had to be constantly aware of the volume and tone of coverage for Bush as compared to the other candidates in the field. "This is something we're sort of accustomed to, but in terms of considering fairness and whether there can be too much coverage, we have to kick in on coverage of the rest of the field to make sure we're being fair."

Carl Leubsdorf of the *Dallas Morning News* said he and his reporters also were already in high gear in 1999 "because with Bush running, of course, we recognized very early that that would drive our coverage to a considerable degree." The question that would arise, however, is how to balance coverage of Bush, who would get more ink in Texas because of his position as governor, with the other candidates.

> So, for example, we had a discussion fairly early of how do we handle the other candidates. We decided that the more important ones would get a page one story at the time they announced, but it wouldn't just be Lamar Alexander launched his second bid for the presidency saying, you know, I want to do blah. It would be a story telling the reader something about Lamar Alexander. . . . I knew that in order to maintain our reputation as a fair, balanced paper not only did we have to have balanced coverage of Bush, but we had to cover the others, which we've done to mixed success, I would say. Partly because we were short on people so we've missed some things we should have done, and we've tried, especially with the Democrats, with Gore, to do Gore stories. We've done relatively little on Bradley, I'm afraid to say.—Carl Leubsdorf, July 1999

The *Washington Post*'s Dan Balz said that the greater volume of coverage for Gore, and especially for Bush, throughout 1999 was driven by the consensus that they were the de facto nominees of their respective political parties—a consensus that was reached long before the first primary ballot was ever cast. With Bush this was particularly important, Balz said. Gore had a lot of national visibility as vice president, and while Bush had a lot of name recognition, voters outside of Texas didn't know much else about him. But by putting the spotlight on Bush so early in the campaign, some of his legitimate rivals were left out.

> You could not make an argument that there's been an equivalency of coverage between Bush and his Republican rivals in our newspaper. There has not been. But I think it's been for the reason that our belief is that if the Republican establishment and the Republican party in the process is pushing Bush ahead as rapidly as it has, we need to take stock of him in a way that we don't necessarily have to take stock of Lamar Alexander or Elizabeth Dole or John McCain, as legitimate and worthy as they may be to be genuine aspirants for the Republican nomination.— Dan Balz, July 1999

In the end, it is the media's perception of a candidate's legitimacy that determines whether he or she gets a significant amount of news coverage. The balance that campaign reporters seek in providing coverage is a balance between candidates who are likely to win—or who at least have a shot at providing a strong challenge to a front-runner—rather than a balance between all of the candidates for nomination. And their guide for determining a candidate's legitimate odds of winning in the year before the primaries, which is when many newspapers decide how to allocate their political reporters, comes down mostly to who has raised the most money, said Cragg Hines of the *Houston Chronicle*.

By putting the emphasis on front-runners and by coming to a consensus about who should be ahead in the election, journalists set up expectations that the candidates need to meet in order to be perceived as successful. A falter or misstep can be crucial to the way a story is framed, and the result can color voters' judgments of the viability of the candidates and help shape their electoral decisions. Howard Dean's loss in the Iowa caucuses in 2004—and the much debated "scream"—resulted in coverage that questioned his electability in a race against an incumbent president. In fact, in the news coverage leading up to the New Hampshire primary, electability became a buzzword for many television news commentators. In the 2000 primary season, George Bush's loss in New Hampshire to John McCain resulted in a spate of coverage about Bush's weakening hold on the Republican nomination. However, because he still led the pack in fundraising, Bush wasn't characterized as washed up. Coverage of Republican front-runner Bob Dole in 1996 was more critical. Although Dole won the February 12, 1996, Iowa caucuses, beating out Pat Buchanan and Lamar Alexander, the media focused on

> the narrowness of Dole's victory and his alleged feebleness. . . . Dole won, but really lost, Buchanan and Alexander lost but really won, his challengers are potent indeed. This is the consensus of the press corps, and the games have begun: every misstep by the front-runner must be treated as a potentially fatal fall, every little twitch must be covered like an earthquake. (Hanson, 1996, p. 3)

In part, campaign journalists have little else to cover but the twitches. Candidates who give the same stump speech day after day and who avoid much direct contact with reporters leave those reporters without very much new to write about. So they pay attention to the twitches and the nuances and, in an attempt to find something new for the next day's paper, they write about those missteps.

Reporters who cover political campaigns also see balance in news coverage as providing a good mix of story topics (Gans, 1979) and of being as tough on one candidate as on another. Although some scholars have found that news coverage of presidential campaigns has become increasingly candidate centered and focused primarily on the candidate's character (Sabato, 1991; Patterson, 1994; Cappella & Jamieson, 1997), journalists view character stories as an important part of the political news mix (Fiedler, 1992). Fiedler and others argue that it is more important for voters to understand a candidate's character than his or her issue positions, since it is the president's character that will be tested in a crisis. The *Houston Chronicle*'s Patty Reinert said that serving the readers means providing them with a range of stories—some that outline and compare the candidates on key election issues, some that size up the campaigns and how the candidates are doing, and some that try to gauge the timbre of the candidates and the advisers who are closest to them. Still, reporters like Bill Lambrecht of the *St. Louis Post-Dispatch* say that issue coverage can get overshadowed by other kinds of stories, especially the stories that focus on campaign strategies and the candidates' characters.

> I don't think there is too much focus on character. Sometimes it's off balance in the sense that there's not enough focus on substantive issues, but the answer there would be—in that equation—to say it's not one or the other. I think that the answer is trying to bring out more of the balance by covering more substantive issues and making people understand what can affect their lives and how it can do so.—Bill Lambrecht, July 1999

Just how much focus is put on a candidate's character is a function of the candidate's chances of being elected. Those who are long shots, as Carol Moseley Braun or Bob Graham were in 2004, won't get as much news coverage in general, and they certainly won't be put under the journalistic microscope. But front-runners and those who pose serious challenges to them become the focus of a lot of media scrutiny. As a rule of thumb, coverage of a candidate and his or her character will increase once he or she starts raising serious money or starts doing well in the preelection polls (Petrocik, 1995; Wolper & Mitchell, 2000), both indications that the candidate has a strong base of support and could get his or her party's nomination.

> The scrutiny of a candidate increases exponentially the closer they get to being a nominee. And so there may be rumors about four candidates who at some point think they might run for president. But there's a question of at what point do you sort of dig in on that, where do you put your resources. Just a lot of simple questions, as opposed to the larger question of what is legitimate.—Dan Balz, July 1999

As Balz notes, in the heat of the campaign, the questions about what to write are driven by the day-to-day concerns regarding resource allocation and what a reporter can write about, rather than from a larger perspective of what the newspaper wants to be covering. But even in the heat of the campaign, with news organizations targeting their reporting resources to the handful of candidates who are viewed as having a shot at winning the White House, campaign journalists try to reach some sort of balance in the tone of their news coverage. Stuart Rothenberg (2000) calls it part of the "ebb and flow" of campaign news coverage:

> First the media falls in love with one candidate, praising his assets and focusing on his opponent's faults. Then, afraid that they have been unfair or merely fatigued with one angle of the story, they seem to turn on the front-runner. Suddenly, his political warts seem a lot larger and his assets almost invisible. His opponent, who a week earlier was an idiot who couldn't do anything right, quickly is transformed into a genius who has quietly been doing everything right. (p. 1)

Journalists will sometimes change their tone of coverage of a candidate to even up the race out of a "semi-conscious urge" to create a horse race in an election, or simply out of a need to have a more dramatic narrative (Wolper & Mitchell, 2000, p. 19). Dan Balz of the *Washington Post* said that the lure of having a close race—or at least the appearance of one—is one element in the changing tone of candidate coverage. But reporters also listen to the complaints that come from readers, many of whom charge that election coverage is biased toward one candidate or another. As a result, the new paradigm for political reporters is to be equally hard on every candidate.

> Consumers of news kind of demand reciprocity in a way that they did not in the past. I mean the idea that you guys were tough on Clinton, you have to be tough on Dole. Or you were tough on the Republicans, you were tough on Newt, so why are you letting Hillary get away with something. I never used to get that kind of call in 1984 from people.— Dan Balz, July 1999

This is a stance that leads to still greater scrutiny of the candidates and makes the candidates and their press staffs, therefore, that much more wary of the journalists covering them.

AN EYE FOR THE UNEXPECTED

The crowd gathered at Penn State University in State College, Pennsylvania, on November 2 numbered about 1,200. They were there for a rally for Republican vice presidential nominee Dick Cheney. As Cheney started to talk, Penn State senior Alison Altman, the vice president of the university's College Democrats, reached into her book bag and pulled out a "Gore-Lieberman 2000" T-shirt. As she stood in the back of the room, a few feet in front of the press stand, Altman raised the T-shirt high over her head. She stood there, quietly holding the T-shirt, for several minutes.

Then a Penn State campus police officer walked up behind her and grabbed for the shirt. Altman resisted him and held the shirt high again. This time the officer reached over her head and, tugging down on the shirt, forced Altman's arms down and then wrapped the shirt around her arms, pinning them to her body. The members of the national press corps, who had barely been listening to Cheney before the Penn State officer first approached Altman, were now furiously taking notes and stepping forward to talk to Altman. A second officer walked up to the first officer, who still had Altman restrained by the Gore-Lieberman T-shirt, pointed to the press stand and spoke quietly into the first officer's ear. Seconds later, the first officer released Altman, leaving her with her T-shirt, and the two police officers walked away. For the next 20 minutes, reporters from national and local news organizations interviewed Altman about the incident, about her support for Al Gore, and about younger voters. In terms of media coverage, Cheney may as well have been speaking to the wind.

The appeal of Altman's story—both her support for Gore in the middle of a Cheney rally and her treatment by campus police—was newsworthy to the members of the national press corps because it was so unexpected and because of the quiet but highly visible clash between Altman and the first officer. The event deviated from the normal routine at political rallies, and journalists, hungry for anything different, latched onto Altman. For reporters on the campaign trail, then, their trained eye is looking for the element of surprise in any event or speech.

Earlier in the day, it had been Cheney's assertion in front of a crowd at a rally in Gallatin, Tennessee, that in a lot of communities schools simply weren't working the way they should that caught the ear of Associated Press reporter Karen Gullo. Gullo, who had been traveling with Cheney since the Republican Convention, jotted the mention down in her notes. And when the national press corps huddled—as they generally did—at the end of the rally to check on crowd estimates and see what was newsworthy, Gullo said that the reference to schools was the first time in more than a month that the vice presidential nominee had mentioned anything to do with education. Did it signal a shift in the campaign message, she wondered? Other reporters speculated that it might be the result of an attempt to appeal to Democratic voters, who were not responding as well to the Bush-Cheney messages about military strength and faith-based charities. At each stop, however, the reporters tried to catch even a whiff of something new—a different phrasing, an old issue being revisited in the final days, a person, like Altman, who was out of place.

Ann Scales of the *Boston Globe* said that the goal of any campaign reporter is to first find the element of the story or speech that is new or different. Other reporters said much the same thing.

When a candidate such as Al Gore gives a policy speech on education, you just know if it's something different, something you haven't heard before. You don't want to keep repeating the same thing to your readers. We want to say something different. We want the candidate to say something different so we can move the story along for the reader.— Ann Scales, July 1999

The thing is when you're out there you want to have something that looks a little fresh, or comes at the same story from a different angle.— Richard Benedetto, June 2001

Patty Reinert, a reporter for the *Houston Chronicle*, said that she spent her time at the rallies and speeches scanning the crowd for those who weren't the "rah-rah" supporters of the candidate. Someone wearing a Nader T-shirt or holding a "Democrats for Bush" sign would more likely be the focus of her attention since the speech typically was already too familiar. Ken Auletta, who followed the 1992 campaign, found the same pattern among members of the traveling press corps in that race. "News was what was new, and from the candidates they heard little that qualified as new" (Auletta, 1993, p. 71). Since the candidates weren't giving the media something new to cover each day, the press corps focused instead on the campaign advertising, candidate attacks, inside strategy, or an article from someone else that stirred a controversy (Auletta, 1993). Toby Eckert of Copley News Service said that was one reason the Swift Boat Veterans for Truth controversy generated a media firestorm.

The press overplayed that story, but I guess I would point the finger mostly at television and, to an extent, at the print media. One thing that especially television doesn't realize is that you're giving that ad more play, and much more of a reach than it would have had. You're kind of blowing up something that may not have been a big issue, and it sort of takes on a life of its own. Again, I think it's because campaigns are so scripted and so managed that when something unscripted happens, it becomes big news.—Toby Eckert, July 2006

David Lawsky, a reporter for Reuters, said the "RATS" story in the 2000 campaign was another example of a minicontroversy that got big play for two reasons—partly because it first ran in the *New York Times* and partly because there wasn't anything else coming from the campaigns that day to compete with the story. The story resulted from a Republican television ad about prescription drug benefits for the elderly that ran for two weeks in early September. In the ad the letters "RATS" flashed across the screen in large white type as the word "Bureaucrats" got larger and moved off-screen and an announcer said, "The Gore prescription plan: bureaucrats decide." Members of the Democratic Party said the ad was a cheap shot, while Republicans said it was an inadvertent slip. But for two days the story received good play in the nation's top newspapers and on the network news.

The journalists' eye for the unexpected not only explains why deviant events make news, but it also explains why well-planned events—even ones that are well attended by the press corps—are underplayed in the press itself. For example, despite the fact that more than 15,000 credentialed press members attended both the Republican and Democratic national conventions in 2004, the news coming out of the conventions received little attention. Instead the conventions became the political backdrop for stories generated by the media. In the 2000 campaign, *USA Today* held daily political roundtables with the top politicians and political party leaders at each of the conventions, and the roundtables—not the convention speeches—were considered more newsworthy. Most of the journalists covering the national political conventions derisively called them "coronations" and seemed to studiously avoid the main convention halls in favor of covering stories about celebrities at the conventions, campaign fundraising around the conventions, and campaign strategies for after the conventions. *USA Today*'s Richard Benedetto said that the conventions themselves don't draw as much media attention as the hoopla around them "because there's no conflict, there's no uncertainty about the outcome."

THE 2000 FLORIDA VOTE—AND OHIO IN 2004

The story of the presidential campaign process in the 2000 election is strikingly similar to the story of most recent campaigns. The campaign started earlier and lasted longer than campaigns of recent memory. Early money to the leading candidates translated into more media coverage and electoral success through the primaries. A front-loaded primary calendar got even more crunched, meaning that after March 7 the field of candidates had been whittled down to the two major party nominees—George W. Bush and Al Gore—and Ralph Nader, who continued his Green Party candidacy.

But the story of the 2000 election, as differentiated from the 2000 campaign, can be summed up in one word: Florida. Both George W. Bush and Al Gore knew that winning Florida would be important to winning the presidency. In the week before the election, their vice presidential nominees, Dick Cheney and Joe Lieberman, both spent time in the state stumping for votes. And on Election Day itself, Gore started out with a midnight rally in Miami and then headed to a hospital in Tampa for a 4 a.m. forum on cancer treatment before finally flying home to Tennessee to cast his own ballot in the election. But neither Bush nor Gore nor the phalanx of press corps members traveling with them were ready for what happened on election night. The race that had for weeks been too close to call finally was called about 7:45 p.m. Eastern Standard Time. The networks and the Associated Press—all using exit poll data and summaries provided by Voter News Service—predicted Gore would take the state. But the early returns from the state told a different story. At 10:13 p.m. VNS pulled Florida back from Gore's column, and the networks and the Associated Press followed suit.

Four hours later VNS—a consortium created by the networks and the Associated Press to help follow the state-by-state returns—reported that Gore was trailing by roughly 50,000 votes in Florida. Fox News went first, calling the state for Bush at 2:16 a.m. ABC, CBS, and NBC soon followed. The Associated Press, however, burned by the earlier mistaken call, did not give the state to Bush. Still, based on the network reports, Gore called Bush at 2:30 to concede the election and headed to the War Memorial Plaza in Nashville, Tennessee, to deliver his concession speech. He was within minutes of stepping up to the microphone when he was told that the state had once again become too close to call and that the margin of victory for Bush—now at less than one half of a percent—meant an automatic recount of all of Florida's ballots. So at 3:30 a.m. on Wednesday, November 8, Gore called Bush to retract the concession call he had placed only an hour earlier, and the story of Campaign 2000 became one about butterfly ballots and hanging chads and the media's role in an election night fiasco.

For the first day or two after the November 7 election, the story was a "what-a-story" (Tuchman, 1978, p. 60), characterized by a departure from normal newsgathering routines, which are quickly replaced by a new set of routines perhaps borrowed from a similar event. Reporters covering the 2000 presidential election scrambled in the first day or so after the election but quickly found a news routine that would guide their coverage for the next 36 days. Patty Reinert of the *Houston Chronicle* spent the final days of the campaign with Al Gore and ended up in Nashville on Election Day. But a few days later she was in Tallahassee, Florida, along with roughly 15,000 other journalists.

> Did I do my job differently? Well, yes. In Florida you no longer had a campaign taking you around or giving you daily updates or reports on what was going on. So Florida was kind of a scramble. It was kind of like starting over in a way. And then you became a courts reporter more than a political reporter or a campaign reporter. You're no longer covering the election at that point, you're just covering recounts and rallies and protests and how this moves through the courts.—Patty Reinert, June 2001

Thus, after a topsy-turvy day or two when the news coverage focused on the question of how something like this could happen, the journalists covering the election had found their ballast in the routines of the court system and the recasting of the election battle as a high-stakes court contest.

While the election outcome now had a familiar frame, the story of the Florida election also coalesced around the media's actions on election night. But interestingly, and despite the fact that many morning newspapers had a "Bush Wins" headline, the browbeating over the election night calls focused on the news networks and their use of results generated by Voter News Service.

> I think TV—justifiably—got the bad rap on this in that they kept jumping the gun because they wanted to be first on TV to declare the winner. On the other hand, it was a really close election and you can't dismiss that. I mean, in a way the mistake is sort of forgivable because it was very close. And there is a sense among Americans that we're going to know the winner tonight before we go to bed. And they tried to deliver that.—Patty Reinert, June 2001

Still, as 2 a.m. approached and then passed, many newspapers were beginning to feel the same kind of pressure to have a winner declared in their headlines for the morning edition. It was part of the normal election night ritual, and editors at many newspapers, who were monitoring the networks through the night, finally put a "Bush Wins" headline on their final editions. After all, television had already called the election for Bush. Richard Benedetto of *USA Today* said the editors at his newspaper were facing the same decision as the "drop dead point" to make any changes to the final edition approached.

> But even at two o'clock in the morning, when the networks started to call Bush the winner, we held back. We had a little time for the next edition and so we held back a while, and in the period that we held back, the call was rescinded, and so therefore our final, final edition never ended up calling the race. But some papers did call the race at that two o'clock point mainly because they were at a drop dead point. They had no further choice, and since the networks had all called the race, there were papers in the United States that declared Bush the winner and printed it. Each set of editors at a paper has to make their own calls on that. And no one wants to err on the side of caution. Caution would have been, "Well, let's wait. We'll wait." But they'll have to wait 24 hours. That's the other problem. So there's a pressure there.—Richard Benedetto, June 2001

For the next month, journalists converged on Florida and on the U.S. Supreme Court and watched as ballots were machine counted, then hand counted, then boxed up to await an appeal or the outcome of another court decision. The final blow to the Gore campaign came on Tuesday, December 12, 2000, when the U.S. Supreme Court voted 5 to 4 to overturn a lower court decision and to stop any hand counting of the Florida ballots. With the clock ticking for the state to name its electors to the Electoral College, the Supreme Court decision, handed out at 10 p.m., all but gave the presidency to Bush. As soon as the decision was handed down, the networks were on air and their correspondents were on camera. From one station to another, the picture on the television was the same—journalists were paging through the decision, with its concurring and dissenting opinions—trying to figure out what it all meant. One said the election was over. Another said Gore still had avenues of appeal. One actually asked the anchor to come back to him in three minutes so that he could read some of the decision before having to talk about it. For print reporters, who still had a few hours before their papers went to bed, the scene was very reminiscent of election night.

> Even though we were fresh off of the mistakes that were made in the election night calling of the election, they basically were making the same mistake again. In the need to get the story out within seconds of when they had the release put in their hands, many errors were made. . . . And I think it was CNN, but I'm not sure, but whoever was calling that had said this thing was not over—that was his first interpretation of it. And then I called my desk and they were kind of confused and then I went back to watching the TV and then I slowly started to see the story change around a little bit. But it took a good hour for everybody to kind of agree that the court had ruled that this is over. But many of the early reports were confusing, no question. And, as I say, instead of saying we'll read this and we'll get back to you in 10 minutes, the reporters ran right out on the steps and started yelling into the cameras. I mean, it was chaotic.—Richard Benedetto, June 2001

Benedetto said that looking back on his newspaper's coverage of the campaign left him with only one regret—that they would have spent more time covering Florida and talking about the pivotal role it might play in the final result. "But hindsight is 20-20. Everybody knew the state was going to be competitive, but nobody guessed that it would be the state that would decide the election," Benedetto said.

Four years later, the election outcome hinged on a state nearly 1,000 miles north of Florida—but coming off the 2000 election experience, journalists were vowing not to make a mistake by calling Ohio, or any other state, too early. Television journalists knew Ohio would be a critical state in 2004, but they were careful throughout the night, waiting until the polls closed in a state and waiting until enough votes were counted to make a reliable prediction. Stations held off on calling Florida for Bush until 11:45 p.m., and the first calls giving Ohio to Bush came at 12:45 a.m. on Wednesday, November 3, on NBC and Fox (Dawidziak, 2004). But early returns abounded on the Internet, especially at sites like the Drudge Report and on political blogs. Relying on early exit polls, which showed the race in many swing states going to Kerry, "the idea of holding back didn't pertain to 'new media' . . . which seemed almost overly eager to fill in the information gaps, even if it meant getting it wrong" ("Media," 2004, p. B12).

CHASING THE 'NET

At the national conventions in 2000, the Internet was the big story. Live webcasts from the Democratic and Republican conventions drew small crowds of mainstream journalists who wrote stories about how the Internet was impacting the political sphere, and the Internet denizens themselves were trying to figure how they fit into the scene. Some followed the lead of the national press, setting up interviews with spokespeople for the candidates and key convention delegates. Others, in a kind of odd symbiosis, interviewed reporters for mainstream media organizations who, in turn, were writing about the upstart Internet journalists. And some online journalists looked for the fun stories, including one who did a piece on a newly released "Convention Barbie."

Four years later, rather than being the focus of news stories simply because they were there, the Internet and bloggers were making and shaping news in some powerful ways. For better or worse, wrote Edward Wasserman,

> the Web stretched the universe of political news. The Internet has matured into a boisterous adolescence, with broad claims of diversity and public empowerment. We've entered what pioneer Matt Drudge once described as "an era vibrating with the din of small voices." Bloggers are more adept at verification than original reporting, and on the Internet it's not easy to know who's pulling the strings. But time and again the boundaries of coverage have expanded because of the persistence of Web-based reportage and commentary, which are now integral to any journalist's beat coverage. (Wasserman, 2004)

Sometimes the blogosphere simply added noise to the political debate, raising and debating questions about the boxy bulge in George W. Bush's suit during the presidential debates or rumors about the possibility of John McCain breaking with the Republican Party and becoming John Kerry's running mate. In other cases, though, Internet journalists and bloggers broke real news, particularly as they became watchdogs for the mainstream media outlets. It was bloggers who, almost as *60 Minutes* was airing its piece on Bush's National Guard service, started questioning the veracity of the documents—documents that CBS later admitted could not be proved to be real. And it was bloggers who provided the first links to Swiftvets.com, where people could find the anti-Kerry video produced by the group. But by putting the spotlight on these stories and keeping it there, the bloggers force the hand of mainstream journalists, who then have to report on what the Internet is reporting—and sometimes more quickly than they would like to.

> I do think that reporters are paying much more attention to blogs. They're much more likely to pay attention to what's on a blog and much more likely to credit a blog with being the first one to break a story. The blogs have, in a way, again shortened the news cycle. If you're a mainstream media practitioner working on a story and kind of taking your time to put all the pieces together, and all of a sudden before you're ready to write it you see a piece of it on a blog, you feel a pressure to get your story out there before you get beat even more. But I also think there may be some overreaction in the media to the blogs because I think here's some recognition that we were slow to recognize the impact of the Internet on the industry.—Toby Eckert, July 2006

But the threshold for making news on the Internet is much lower, say some journalists and even some campaign strategists. Bloggers, for instance, will report what they've heard, but often what they're reporting is mere rumor—and sometimes even rumors planted by "critics, cranks and the 'dark arts crowd' in campaigns," said Mike McCurry, a senior adviser to the Kerry campaign. "The barrier for questionable information to circulate is much lower. And the mainstream press has not decided how and when to confront and debunk 'rumor' in the zeitgeist." But the public pays attention, he said, because "they're writing from an antiestablishment perspective. That's what gives them authenticity—a voice." Campaigns also are paying attention to blogs, said Patrick Ruffini, the eCampaign director for the Republican National Committee, and "they also wield influence on Capitol Hill, with their voice being heard in the legislative process."

For reporters like *USA Today*'s Richard Benedetto, who end up having to chase the rumors that fly on the Internet, the frustration is that "editors wonder why can't your news stories be like blogs, be sexy and jazzy. But it's no substitute for real reporting. It's one more aspect of information out there, but it's not a substitute for the good, solid reporting that needs to be done."

And some argue that the volume of information on the Internet—even though it is having greater impact on mainstream reporting and on campaign politics—isn't serving voters any better. Blogs more typically provide links to mainstream media sites rather than other blogs or other sources of information (Adamic & Glance, 2005), and a study of blogs in the 2004 election showed that "they are conspicuously similar to the mainstream press in what they covered, the tone of that coverage and even in the angle writers took" (Project for Excellence in Journalism, 2004b, p. 1). The Internet and weblogs often report the same information as the mainstream media, but they more often do it through the lens of a political point of view. And rather than serving as an open forum for broad-ranging discussions, the Internet may have further polarized voters in 2004, argues Sam Smith.

> Consumers strapped on their blinders, hit the entrance at a dead spring, hung a fast left or right, and ran like hell for the section dedicated to their political dogmas and preconceptions. . . . In this election, the Internet did far less actual informing than it did providing ammunition for people whose minds were already made up.
>
> Therein lies the Great Lesson of 2004: Technologies can mostly be counted on not to change us or improve us but to serve that which we already are. (Smith, 2004).

Despite the sometimes dubious quality of political information on the Internet, it is growing in its reach. Research conducted by the Pew Internet & American Life Project shows that 32 million Americans read weblogs and that people are using the Internet in greater numbers to stay informed about politics—30 million went online in March 2000 for political information compared to 63 million in mid-2004 (as cited in Adamic & Glance, 2005). DailyKos.com, ranked fifth among the most popular blog sites and the most popular political blog, records roughly 600,000 visitors a day (Bai, 2006). Patrick Ruffini said that because people are going online more for their news, it changes the ability of a political campaign to respond quickly and effectively to campaign events. And blogs that come from the political right—Red State, Power Line, Hugh Hewitt, and Right Wing News—are no longer viewed as "toothless tigers." Both Ruffini and McCurry say that bloggers and the Internet are adding to the range of political debate, but they are not replacing the mainstream media as a primary focus of campaign communication.

8

A Prescription for Improving Campaign Coverage

The day after the second debate in St. Louis, Missouri, John Kerry, his campaign staff, and his entourage of traveling press were heading to Ohio for a rally, then to Florida for a town hall meeting. The roughly 75 reporters who made up the traveling press that day had to have their luggage in the Landmark Room at the Westin Hotel by 6 a.m. so it could be checked by the Secret Service before it got loaded on the plane. The reporters themselves had to meet in the hotel's lobby by 7:10 a.m. so they could be swept by security before boarding the press buses at 7:15 to head to the St. Louis airport. But the campaign was running late, and at 8:35 a.m. the reporters were still waiting for the Kerry campaign to get going. It wasn't unusual, they said. Kerry often ran late. One reporter said the traveling press once waited six hours for Kerry to show up. Waiting, they said, is just part of the job. Unless you're traveling with George W. Bush, one said; he's meticulous about keeping his schedule.

As they waited for press buses to roll out that morning, they started comparing campaigns and sharing war stories from other trips on the campaign trail. Scott Shepard of Cox Newspapers talked about the access that he had to candidates like Hubert Humphrey, who, when he ran for the presidency in 1968, was known to invite reporters out to dinner with him. Toby Eckert of Copley News Service and David Jackson of the *Dallas Morning News* lamented that they barely got to talk to Al Gore during the 2000 campaign—but on some level they understood the reasons for keeping the press at bay. Jackson said that once when Gore did talk to the press, off the record, of course, he was being peppered with questions about the tightness of the race and his campaign strategy. Jackson said he asked a softball question "just to lighten the mood" and to get the candidate to relax a little. He hoped that some of the other reporters would follow suit, but the next question came from Ceci Connolly, a *Washington Post* reporter and one of the "Spice Girls," a less-than-flattering nickname given to three women journalists covering Gore and known for asking tough questions (Mnookin, 2000b). Connolly, he said, tried to nail Gore down on when he would hold an on-the-record press availability.

Shepard shook his head knowingly. "They took it beyond adversarial," he said. He told his own Connolly story—that on a riverboat trip on the Mississippi River after the Democratic Convention, Chris Lehane, Gore's press secretary, came to the press level of the boat to say that Gore would come down for an off-the-record chat. "Connolly wasn't going for it," Shepard said. In the end, Lehane offered to let reporters who would agree to the off-the-record condition go upstairs to chat with Gore. Most did, but Connolly and a reporter from Reuters stayed behind.

As the buses headed out for the St. Louis airport, Eckert, Jackson, and Shepard talked about the value of traveling with the candidate. The lack of access, they said, was frustrating, but they could glean something from the few times they did get to talk to Kerry. And it was useful to get to different parts of the country to see how the candidates were being received, even if there really wasn't much time to talk to people at the rallies and even less time to talk to the people in those towns who didn't turn out to hear Kerry speak. But the schedule could be demanding, especially as Election Day approached, and the cost, which ran $1,000 a day or more, said Eckert, was getting prohibitive. While some of the larger—and more well-funded news organizations—could still commit to having journalists on the campaign planes, "Copley's not going out as much this year. It's just too expensive," Eckert said.

THE PROBLEM OF PRESIDENTIAL CAMPAIGN COVERAGE

For the journalist trapped "in the bubble" of a presidential campaign, the combination of tight schedules, limited access to the candidate, and pressure from the home office to file means that stories often turn to the game. Reporters on the road do have access to the campaign strategists—who often want to talk about strategy. And they have access to new poll numbers. The result, as scholars have noted in studies of news content, is a focus that makes the election seem more like a game to be watched than a process that requires citizen participation (Patterson, 1994; Project for Excellence in Journalism, 2004a, 2004b).

But even reporters who aren't "in the bubble" are biased, says Eric Burns of Fox News, "toward simplicity—stripping a story of its necessary nuance—and toward sensationalism, making a story that really isn't that important seem as if it is" (Steigerwald, 2006). Richard Benedetto of *USA Today* said reporters and editors need to remember that they're in the information business. Their job is to give readers and viewers information about the candidates so that they can figure out what it means and what matters to them. "Instead, we overemphasize the conflicts and we overemphasize the strategy, and we don't tell them enough about where the candidates stand and why."

In her critique of campaign journalism, former Poynter Institute columnist Geneva Overholser—citing an interview with Washington journalist Elizabeth Drew—identifies several key problems with the way candidates and elections are covered. The news coverage lacks substance, favoring Hollywood entertainment standards over standards that are relevant to governing a nation; it lacks fairness, focusing on the gaffe or the odd moment (the Dean "scream"); it lacks an evenhandedness, favoring some candidates over others, or at least not treating them as skeptically; and it lacks balance, putting greater emphasis on the horse race and on electability even early on in the election season (Overholser, 2004). Toby Eckert of Copley News Service recognizes the flaw in focusing on poll numbers and electability.

> It's sort of like writing about the science of a pharmaceutical drug rather than what the drug does itself. I think that's probably what people perceive about it. I think it is important to discuss some of the horse race aspects, particularly who's advising a candidate and how they're devising their strategies. That kind of gives people a sense of who these people are and what's driving them. But I think we tend to focus on that too much to the detriment of covering serious issues. But it's hard to tell whether people would really read these very lengthy articles on health care or on prescription drugs. I think you have to balance the two as much as possible and bring the issue coverage down to a simple, straightforward level.—Toby Eckert, July 2006

But the lack of balance that currently exists leads, inevitably, to a kind of political reporting that no longer explains politics. Instead, say Bill Kovach and Tom Rosenstiel, today's political reporting has morphed into something much narrower—campaign reporting—which "gives us a better understanding of large-scale campaign mechanics, but a weaker grasp of how voters are actually reacting" (2001b, p. 2).

Since the media are "virtually the only source of campaign information" (Ramsden, 1996, p. 6) for the public, the narrow range of information that is given prominence in the press makes it difficult for voters to make rational decisions. Instead, faced with coverage that is primarily strategic, voters behave strategically and make choices based on who's likely to win the election rather than whom they prefer (Ramsden, 1996). Journalists assume that when they report what is newsworthy—and that includes issue coverage and political polls and strategy—citizens will sift through it all and find the information they need to make choices (Gans, 1998). But the fact that the horse race and strategy coverage predominates, especially later in the election season when more undecided voters are finally paying attention, and the fact that people tend to look for informational shortcuts for decision making (Ryfe, 2005), leaves little room to believe that undecided voters are doing much sifting.

MAKING NEWS RELEVANT

The task for journalists covering campaigns, then, is to find ways to report on electoral politics that give readers—and presumably voters—information that will help them make choices, and to give it to them in a way that's useful and user-friendly. Adam Clymer of the *New York Times* writes that journalists have an obligation to make sense of the issue proposals that the candidates make, and to thoroughly explore and explain the candidates' records and background experience (Clymer, 2001). "Combined, they give voters a chance to know what to expect if a candidate is elected," he writes (Clymer, 2001, p. 781). At a very basic level, that means more charts and boxes. It means more grids that compare candidates on their stances on key issues in the election. It means more photos and graphics to draw readers to the stories. But it also means rethinking the notion of news, at least when it comes to campaign reporting, said Tracey Schmitt, the press secretary for the Republican National Committee and the Western states spokesperson for the Bush campaign in 2004.

> Ultimately, most candidates want to be viewed through a policy prism, where they stand on the issues and why this is a superior position to their opponent. It makes sense that the media is going to spend 80 to 90 percent of their time covering the news of the day, and breaking down candidate positions on lesser known issues is going to be secondary. It's not ideal, but it is what it is.—Tracey Schmitt, September 2006

Mike McCurry, a senior adviser to the Kerry campaign in 2004, said that even though a speech or policy statement may be old news to a reporter who has been on the campaign trail for months, it may be quite new to the voter who, in September or October of the election year, is just tuning in.

> I think the primary problem here is the whole definition of the business we're in. The journalist wants to report "new" news, and the candidate must find some way to make that stump speech newsworthy. What I'm

arguing here is that there needs to be a deeper examination of the journalistic function. There has to be a new approach to how you cover a campaign. I think you have to keep coming back to the same central story line so that you remind the voter about what's really important. And yes, that's advocacy journalism, and there's a real deep reluctance among journalists to inject themselves in the debate. But what clearly is the premium is finding the way to make important information interesting to the public. We have to be much more creative in how we engage people.—Mike McCurry, August 2006

Reporters, while recognizing the problems in their news coverage, also note that the picture is not as grim as the one painted by scholars and strategists. Martin Kasindorf of *USA Today* said that reporters do cover issues, and in some depth, when candidates actually talk about them and say something new. Campaigns have to realize that the stump speech quickly loses its news value, he said.

But I know every time Kerry talked about Iraq or health care, we covered it. Certainly we wrote about stem cell research and the science that he tried to make an issue of. We were there on the plane to tell readers what the candidate was trying to do. So when Kerry raised science and the administration and the religious focus on science, we wrote about that. In my opinion, we were frequently writing about issues and we had to steep ourselves in them and write a lot about them.—Martin Kasindorf, July 2006

But the contest—who was ahead and what was going on in the swing states—certainly took up most of the limited space in newspapers and the limited time on television. Toby Eckert of Copley News Service said that the Internet, with its ability to hold archives of news coverage, "offers a great opportunity not only for the media, but for the public to educate themselves about the candidates." But Mike McCurry said that's not enough. The Internet is a great resource, but it takes a more motivated voter to seek out information in a news organization's archives. If the goal of political communication is to serve voters, he argues, then repetition is the key. People need to hear a message several times in order to process it and have it become part of their decision-making model. News simply doesn't allow for that, he said, and while the Internet can help, it's not the sole solution.

I think it wouldn't hurt for the nightly news to say, as a reminder, that you can find a compendium of our campaign coverage on NBC.com, for instance. But they also need to provide a brief capsule of their earlier coverage, bringing people up to date on the issues. Obviously, no network producer is going to give up any of the 21 precious minutes he has in a newscast to do that. Newspapers can do it more than television, but they're limited too. But with the Internet and other technologies, the competition model in journalism will move away from speed and will move toward substance and thoroughness.—Mike McCurry, August 2006

Accomplishing that, say some reporters, will take some work on the part of campaigns as well. The current formula, which keeps candidates almost relentlessly on message, doesn't help reporters do a better job of informing the public. But the campaigns have to view reporters as more than simply stenographers. They have to be willing to make the candidate available for more questions if they want better coverage, and they have to be willing to risk that a reporter might ask a question that could pull the candidate off message.

> They have to give you substance to talk about. But they hate risk, and they hate surprise, and they don't want any distraction. So you try to break through the theater and the spin. We kind of try to dig a little deeper, hopefully without alienating them too much. But yeah, you try to ask a tougher question when you can.—Martin Kasindorf, July 2006

Gans (1998) said that the even-centered nature of political news makes it more difficult to provide meaningful coverage. He suggests that longer stories and more topic-oriented stories would serve readers better, although journalists like Bill Lambrecht of the *St. Louis Post-Dispatch* and Toby Eckert of Copley News Service question whether voters are willing to wade through the longer stories. But Gans argues that the current coverage model, which seems to focus on "partisan squabbling," leaves readers with "the impression that politicians are not very interested in their problems and that there is little reason to become informed" (1998, p. 9). Ramsden suggests that political reporters put the emphasis back on the voters by understanding how voters react to news coverage.

> The relative allocation of issue coverage matters, because readers remember what the media emphasize, and they use that information as a basis to assess the candidates. With this in mind, I argue that the media should rank their coverage in terms of policies and issues first, character issues second, horse race stories third, and events stories last. Furthermore, I argue that early on in political campaigns, all candidates deserve to be treated equally; as the race progresses, the media should then look to the process for clues about how to allocate coverage. (Ramsden, 1996, p. 70)

Ramsden's model makes room for the horse race coverage, since that information can help voters narrow the range of candidates they have to pay attention to. Of course, that argument favors the well funded, who tend to get the early news coverage and, as a result, tend to do better in the polls. But news coverage clearly can't provide equal attention to all of the candidates who file for the presidency. In the 2004 race, doing so would have meant covering more than 150 people, including 29 Republicans and 55 Democrats (Skewes & Plaisance, 2005). Still, to artificially narrow the race based on poll numbers, especially early in the electoral season, also has the effect of narrowing the range of political debate since some of the candidates with lower poll ratings—or no poll ratings—are candidates who are running to bring a fresh voice to the discussion of the issues of the day. Later in the election—once the major party nominees have been determined—focusing on the more viable candidates makes sense. And certainly for voters, the horse race matters. But even horse race stories can be about more than just the numbers. Adam Clymer of the *New York Times* writes that the same polls that generate the horse race stories typically turn up other information about how voters feel about the candidates. So a story that leads with that type of information—showing whether Americans feel the candidates are genuinely different, or how they rate on perceived leadership ability, or what issues seem to be driving voter decisions—can be very useful (Clymer, 2001).

It's also important to let the candidates talk more, said *USA Today*'s Richard Benedetto, even if they're not talking to the press directly. What they say in their speeches and at rallies is news, he argues, even if it seems repetitive to the reporter on the plane. The idea that the public should hear or read more of the candidate's words isn't new. Scholars have noted the shrinking sound bite, which went from an average of 42.3 seconds in 1968 down to 7.8 seconds in 2004 (Wayne, 2000; Farnsworth & Lichter, 2007). And despite pledges from television stations to provide more "candidate-centered discourse" in the 2000 election cycle, a study of news coverage prior to the Super Tuesday primary election and the November general election found little improvement (Falk & Aday, 2000). In election coverage leading up to the general election, the average sound bite was just nine seconds (Falk & Aday, 2000).

Most calls for improving campaign reporting also call for more analysis, once again moving away from events and away from the "he said, she said" kind of reporting that often passes for balance and neutrality. In an article for *The American Prospect*, Eric Alterman and Michael Tomasky identified five changes that could make campaign coverage more meaningful, and top among those was bypassing the neutral voice to "tell us what you believe to be true and important about a story" (2004, p. 2). They also argue for more investigative reporting, which is hampered by a 24-hour news cycle, by shrinking newsroom resources, and by media fears of charges of bias.

Speaking at Harvard University last spring, *Washington Post* Executive Editor Len Downie said the following: "So if you do tough investigative reporting about Democrats or about issues that are important to the left, you'll get strong backlash from the left. Similarly, if you do tough investigative reporting of the Republicans or people on the right, you'll get a strong backlash from them. And I think this is also having an impact on the media. It's scaring people." (Alterman & Tomasky, 2004, p. 2).

Additionally, Alterman and Tomasky call for journalists to be more proportional in covering campaign controversies, to be less willing to accept all of the ground rules that the campaigns want to enforce when it comes to news coverage, and to stop letting "non-news organs drive the news cycle" (Alterman & Tomasky, 2004, p. 3). In this last point, the authors are trying to encourage journalists to follow their own instincts and to avoid the rush to publish or air a story that serves a partisan purpose. Journalists now have to spend time chasing down these stories—whether they break on a partisan website, in a tabloid newspaper (like the Gennifer Flowers story did), or someplace else. And, as Dan Balz of the *Washington Post* noted, the fact that a reporter spends time trying to track down the truth behind these stories starts to create some pressure to publish something about them—otherwise the hours spent on the goose chase are wasted.

CHANGING THE PERSPECTIVE

One recurring theme that shows up in the recommendations for making campaign coverage better is to simply step off the press plane or bus. It's risky, because no major news organization wants to rely on the wire services if a "what-a-story" like the George Wallace assassination attempt occurs. But those stories are rare. In fact, D. D. Guttenplan argues that the last "pivotal" story that was filed from the campaign trail was a piece that ran on May 3, 1987, in which Democratic front-runner Gary Hart denied rumors that he was a womanizer and challenged the press by saying, "Follow me around. I don't care. I'm serious. If anyone wants to put a tail on me, go ahead. They'd be very bored" (Guttenplan, 1992a, p. 2). Guttenplan notes that the Hart story ran on the same day the *Miami Herald* broke the story about Hart's affair with Donna Rice, complete with a photo of the two on a boat called *Monkey Business*. Still, given the highly scripted nature of today's campaign politics, the best place to be may be where the candidate isn't. Rick Lyman, the *New York Times* reporter who was denied a seat on Dick Cheney's plane in the 2004 election, described his view from outside the campaign bubble as "a weird kind of gift" (Lyman, 2004).

I may not spend a whole lot of time in the small towns and state fairs that the
vice president visits, but I spend a lot more than he does, or than members of
the press on the plane do. I talk to people everywhere, and not just the supporters who got tickets to sanctioned events. I listen to local radio stations,
get lost on local roads. (Lyman, 2004)

That kind of perspective on the campaign is one that has a better chance
of resonating with the electorate since it's their perspective. It requires
talking to voters, but it also involves listening to the nonvoters, who make
up nearly half of the country's eligible voters, and some of whom see non-
voting as a way of expressing their dissatisfaction with the system (Gans,
1998). Richard Benedetto of *USA Today* said that the best campaign coverage involves the voters—it listens to them about the issues that are important to them, lets them talk about those issues, and gives the candidates a chance to respond to their concerns and questions.

To assume that every voter in every district across the country cares
about stem cell research is probably a false assumption. But that's being
written about in terms of its political impact. We need to pay more attention to the issues that matter to voters. You've got to talk to people,
too, to hear what's on their minds. You've got to be talking to people
continuously—not just the people who are involved or the political
operatives—but the people who are out there just living their lives.—
Richard Benedetto, July 2006

And finding out about those issues requires the kind of on-the-ground reporting that Lyman was able to do when he was left off the Cheney press
plane. Being on the ground has another huge advantage for a political reporter, Benedetto said. In the rarified air of the campaign press plane, reporters can lose perspective on the race. Kovach and Rosenstiel (2001b)
recommend that journalists do "bottom-up" reporting by going to civic
clubs, union halls, coffee shops, and churches—anywhere in a community
where the conversation might turn to politics. "Regular reporting that
sweeps through these venues during an election year could provide a
wealth of information about the mood and the interests of the voters" (Kovach & Rosenstiel, 2001b, p. 9). It also can serve as a reality check for journalists. In 1972, the reporters covering George McGovern thought he had
a chance of unseating incumbent President Richard Nixon—even in the final weeks of the campaign in an election that Nixon won with 61 percent
of the popular vote and 520 electoral votes to McGovern's 17 electoral
votes (Crouse, 1973). With a little more reporting on the ground, the Mc-
Govern press corps might have seen the landslide coming. And reporters
covering Dean in 2004 were surprised when he came in third behind John
Kerry and John Edwards in the Iowa caucuses precisely because they were

spending too much time on Dean and not enough time on the voters, Benedetto said.

> If they had been covering Iowa the way it should have been covered, they would have seen it coming. You've got to step out of the bubble. Go out on your own to Waterloo, Iowa, or Davenport. That's how you find out whether or not the guy is catching on. The polls showed Dean was slipping in the final days, but the reporters with him didn't want to cover that. But if you're out in the state talking to people, you can see it coming. The same in New Hampshire in 2000. I could see a [John] McCain victory coming. Ground reporting is so important in any campaign. . . . But it's hard to break away from the pack, and maybe your editors don't want you to, especially if you're the only person they've got out there.—Richard Benedetto, July 2006

Toby Eckert of Copley News Service said editors are reluctant to have their reporter break away to do the unique stories from the road. They want those stories, "but then they say that everyone else is doing this, so we need that story, too." The impact of intermedia agenda setting is too strong a pull, and few news organizations would commit to having a second reporter on the plane who could break away for the voter impact stories. Guttenplan (1992a) suggests that news organizations themselves create press pools to travel with the candidates, and that they rely on local news organizations for the event-driven coverage in each state. That would free up valuable resources—in terms of both money and a reporter's time—to provide the kind of issue-driven, analytic news that could truly inform the public.

For news organizations that worry about missing the big story that could happen on the campaign trail—or for those that don't want to rely on the wire services for news coverage—Mike McCurry suggests rotating reporters off the plane, which some news organizations already do, and having reporters from nonpolitical beats rotate onto the press plane occasionally just to bring some fresh perspectives to the process. Political beat reporters quickly come to view the campaign through the lens of political strategy because that interests them. A reporter from a lifestyles beat or an education beat "would hear nuances and subtle differences in discussions of social issues that political beat reporters might miss," McCurry said. Another way of adding fresh perspectives is to broaden the range of sources used in political reporting (Stepp, 1992). In addition to the official sources—the candidates, the campaign managers, the issue advocates— Stepp, quoting New York University professor Neil Postman, suggests thinking outside the box to include artists, philosophers, and others in the mix since politics affects a broad range of people.

Journalists also can demand more from campaigns. It won't be an easy thing to do because the press typically doesn't act collectively, Toby Eckert said.

> But I think that what would have to happen for campaigns to change would be for the media to stop covering some of the dog-and-pony elements of this. They'd have to stop feeling compelled to file the story that says here's what happened on the campaign trail today and it's not much different than yesterday. And you'd have to get the people in the local media market to do the same thing. The whole media would have to change its approach to campaign coverage, and I don't think that's going to happen. But if they all kind of demanded, day after day, to talk about substantive issues and to have access to the candidates, it might cause that to happen. But there isn't enough commonality of interest to have that happen.—Toby Eckert, July 2006

Mike McCurry, a senior adviser to John Kerry, said the press actually could wield more clout than it does when it comes to access, but that the reluctance of journalists to make themselves part of the story works against any collective action. Still, he said, if reporters for the *New York Times* and other major news organizations wrote that their questions to the candidates had gone unanswered and that the stump speeches were identical, it would have some impact. And if they relegated a candidate's coverage to an inside page day after day as a result, the campaigns might make the candidates more available, even though they'd still try to set ground rules to insulate the candidate from potential missteps.

Journalists also should do more truth telling, McCurry said. One of the better journalistic innovations in recent election cycles has been the use of the "ad watch," he said. Campaign advertising has a significant impact on the public, since many voters rely on advertising for political information. And the increasing reliance on negative campaign advertising is having particularly insidious effects, driving down voter turnout and contributing to an increasingly polarized electorate (Ansolabehere & Iyengar, 1995). But the ad watch can remedy some of that by parsing out the statements in a political ad and separating fact from fiction. McCurry said the introduction of ad watches "was a real step forward" in terms of campaign coverage. But it made reporters a little nervous because it means they become part of the story. And the real problem with ad watches, he said, is the problem with most campaign journalism—it's too ephemeral for the average citizen.

> The problem is they run the ad watch box once. But you need to run it every day to remind the audience that the ad is not true, because the ad is still running. By doing that, though, you've crossed over into the

advocacy role, which journalists don't like to do. But that's what it's going to take—forcing the debate back to certain central premises. If a major news organization took on that role, it would be very interesting.—
Mike McCurry, August 2006

Some people suggest that a more partisan media, with news organizations that clearly project their political preferences and ideologies, might
invigorate the public debate. Certainly the Web and bloggers are doing
that, and Toby Eckert predicts that the 2008 election could be "a blogosphere free-for-all, especially if the feelings that were kind of raw in 2004
in terms of partisanship are as prevalent in 2008." But Eckert said he
doesn't want to see the traditional mainstream press change its role to a
more partisan one. "That may be a model that's worth exploring, but I
wouldn't want to be a part of a media that doesn't try to present both
sides of the story," he said.

Mike McCurry said newspapers already are rethinking the volume of
coverage they give to presidential campaigns. In recent elections, newspapers have been getting out early, often more than a year before Election
Day, with long candidate profiles and stories that explore the issues. But
those stories, coming out when they do, aren't read by a wide audience.
The *Washington Post*, McCurry said, planned to hold off on any 2008 campaign coverage until well into 2007, and the coverage they did plan would
be "more personalized. The journalists there, especially Dan Balz and
David Broder, understand that our system is seriously broken, and they
think that they have an obligation to do more than report the same old
stuff," he said. "It starts with experimentation, with trying new things."

SUMMING UP

Most journalists who cover presidential campaigns end up spending
much of their time among the "enemy." Their closest colleagues on the
press planes are the people who would be their competition under other
circumstances. The members of the traveling press corps have to rely on
the candidate's staff for travel, food, and lodging arrangements, in addition to information about the campaign and the candidate. The close
quarters of the campaign trail breed some familiarity. Journalists talk
about their stories and they sometimes even talk about what they're planning to file for the next edition. While campaign reporters typically have
an eye out for a scoop, they also turn to each other to verify crowd estimates and get a consensus about whether there was any new twist or nuance in the candidate's speech. And off the job, but still on the trail, journalists and campaign staff members are cordial—sometimes stopping for

a drink at the end of a long day or pausing to play a quick game of touch football in a parking lot while they wait for the motorcade to start moving to the next stop.

But the confines of the campaign trail also breed some measure of contempt, particularly among the journalists, who are trying to cover the candidate, and the campaign staff members, who are trying to protect the candidate from any adverse news coverage. Candidates are largely inaccessible to the national press corps—even when they are traveling on the same plane together. On the few occasions that candidates are made accessible, they are kept on message by their strategists and press secretaries. Meanwhile the members of the national press corps, wary of being used by the campaigns, struggle to pull the candidates off message so that they can control what goes in their news columns.

All of this factors into the content of campaign coverage in subtle ways. The focus on an Al Gore supporter at a Penn State University rally for Republican vice presidential nominee Dick Cheney in 2000 was motivated in part by the deviance of the occurrence—particularly since the young woman was harassed by campus police. But the members of the national press corps also saw her as the story for other reasons. For instance, after four days of hearing Cheney talk about the readiness of the U.S. military, they were hearing nothing new in what Cheney was saying to the Penn State crowd. And they were frustrated that Cheney, who had talked to them only once—and off the record—during the trip, was not accessible to them on the flight to State College when they needed a quote for a breaking news story about George W. Bush's driving under the influence arrest in Maine in the early 1970s. They also were tired. After a day that had started roughly 14 hours earlier in Nashville, Tennessee, most of the reporters in the press corps were looking forward to getting to a hotel for the night, checking in with editors at home, and hopefully getting a few hours of sleep. They knew that nothing Cheney said at 9 p.m. would make news, but they were captive to the logistics of the campaign and the press plane. So tired, and maybe even a little grumpy, the journalists at Cheney's rally turned their attention to the person in the crowd who was visibly opposed to Bush and Cheney.

The rigors and culture of the campaign trail have to influence what becomes news. Reporters on the press planes see little else, so just as voters' views of the candidates are shaped by the media's coverage of the campaigns, journalists' views of the candidates are shaped by what they see and hear on the press planes. And while they recognize that life "in the bubble" is not reality for the average reader, it is reality for the traveling press corps. So their news coverage is viewed through the prism of stump speeches and campaign strategies, and it is colored by the cordial but also adversarial role that develops with the candidates and their staffs. And what about the best laid plans to provide meaningful news coverage that focuses on issues and provides voters with information to help them make electoral choices? By the campaign's end, most of that has been left behind, only to be picked up as the battle cry for covering the next presidential election.

Appendix: Sources

INTERVIEWS

Subject Name	Affiliation	Interview Dates
Balz, Dan	*Washington Post*	July 1999, February 2000
Benedetto, Richard	*USA Today*	July 1999, June 2001, July 2006
Boucher, Geoff	*Los Angeles Times*	October 2000
Burka, Paul	*Texas Monthly*	August 2005 (panel)
Chen, Edwin (Ed)	*Los Angeles Times*	June 2001
Douglas, Bill	McClatchey Newspapers	August 2005 (panel)
Eckert, Toby	Copley News Service	September 2000, October 2004, July 2006
Frederick, Don	*Los Angeles Times*	July 1999
Gerstenzang, James	*Los Angeles Times*	September 2000
Hines, Cragg	*Houston Chronicle*	July 1999
Kasindorf, Martin	*USA Today*	July 2006
Lambrecht, Bill	*St. Louis Post-Dispatch*	July 1999
Lawrence, Jill	*USA Today*	September 2000
Lewis, Charles	Hearst Newspapers	July 1999
Leubsdorf, Carl	*Dallas Morning News*	July 1999
Lightman, David	*Hartford Courant*	September 2000
Mason, Julie	*Houston Chronicle*	August 2005 (panel)
Reinhert, Patty	*Houston Chronicle*	September 2000, June 2001
Scales, Ann	*Boston Globe*	July 1999
Shepard, Scott	Cox Newspapers	October 2004
Anonymous	East Coast daily reporter	October 2000
Anonymous	Wire reporter	October 2000

(continued)

Subject Name	Affiliation	Interview Dates
McCurry, Mike	Kerry Campaign	October 2004, August 2006
Pfeiffer, Dan	Gore Campaign	October 2000
Ruffini, Patrick	Republican National Committee	September 2006
Schmitt, Tracey	Republican National Committee	September 2006

FIELD RESEARCH

Event	Dates
New Hampshire Primary Concord, New Hampshire Manchester, New Hampshire Raymond, New Hampshire Windham, New Hampshire Derry, New Hampshire Peterborough, New Hampshire Nashua, New Hampshire Keene, New Hampshire Somersworth, New Hampshire Tilton, New Hampshire	January 26 to February 1, 2000
2000 Republican National Convention Philadelphia, Pennsylvania	July 31 to August 4, 2000
2000 Democratic National Convention Los Angeles, California	August 14 to August 17, 2000
Gore campaign press plane Washington, D.C. Clearwater, Florida Ann Arbor, Michigan Altoona, Iowa Des Moines, Iowa Washington, D.C.	September 25 to September 27, 2000
Cheney campaign press plane Dulles, Virginia Rochester, Minnesota Dubuque, Iowa Peoria, Illinois Kansas City, Missouri Hot Springs, Arkansas New Orleans, Louisiana West Palm Beach, Florida Port St. Lucie, Florida Punta Gorda, Florida Brooksville, Florida	October 30 to November 2, 2000

Event	Dates
Nashville, Tennessee Gallatin, Tennessee Chicago, Illinois State College, Pennsylvania Harrisburg, Pennsylvania	
2004 Democratic National Convention Boston, Massachusetts, including Colorado delegation meetings	July 26 to July 29, 2004
2004 Republican National Convention New York City, New York	August 30 to September 2, 2004
Kerry campaign press plane Englewood, Colorado St. Louis, Missouri Cleveland, Ohio Elyria, Ohio Ft. Lauderdale, Florida Davie, Florida Miami, Florida Albuquerque, New Mexico Santa Fe, New Mexico Tempe, Arizona	October 7 to October 13, 2004

2004 PRESS POOL REPORTS

Date/Time	Filed By
October 12, 4:09 p.m.	Scott Shepard, Cox Newspapers
October 13, 12:46 p.m.	David Jackson, *Dallas Morning News*
October 13, 7:10 p.m.	David Jackson, *Dallas Morning News*
October 13, 8:19 p.m.	David Jackson, *Dallas Morning News*
October 14, 3:38 p.m.	Jim Kuhnhenn, Knight Ridder
October 14, 7:03 p.m.	Jim Kuhnhenn, Knight Ridder
October 15, 12:29 p.m.	Matea Gold, *Los Angeles Times*
October 16, 1:21 p.m.	David Halbfinger, *New York Times* and Jake Schlesinger, *Wall Street Journal*
October 17, 10:58 a.m.	Tom Frank, *Newsday*
October 17, 2:34 p.m.	Tom Frank, *Newsday*
October 19, 11:42 a.m.	Martin Kasindorf, *USA Today*
October 19, 1:34 p.m.	Martin Kasindorf, *USA Today*
October 20, 4:32 p.m.	Shailagh Murray, *Wall Street Journal*
October 20, 7:43 p.m.	Becky Diamond, NBC
October 20, 7:47 p.m.	Charlie Hurt, *Washington Times*
October 22, 10:36 p.m.	Lois Romano, *Washington Post*

References

Adamic, L., & Glance, N. (2005, March 4). *The political blogosphere and the 2004 U.S. election: Divided they blog.* Retrieved April 14, 2006, from http://www .blogpulse.com/papers/2005/AdamicGlanceBlogWWW.pdf.

Alterman, E., & Tomasky, M. (2004, March 1). Wake-up time. *The American Prospect, 15* (3). Retrieved February 16, 2004, from http://www.prospect.org/ print-friendly/print/V15/3/alterman-e.html.

Althaus, S. L. (2005). How exceptional was turnout in 2004? *Political Communication Report, 15* (1), 1–5. Retrieved January 20, 2005, from http://www.ou.edu/ policom/1501_2005_winter/commentary.htm.

Ansolabehere, S., & Iyengar, S. (1995). *Going negative: How political advertisements shrink and polarize the electorate.* New York: The Free Press.

Atwater, T., Fico, F., & Pizante, G. (1987). Reporting on the state legislature: A case of inter-media agenda setting. *Newspaper Research Journal, 8,* 52–61.

Auletta, K. (1993). On and off the bus: Lessons from campaign '92. In *1-800-President: The report of the Twentieth Century Fund Task Force on television and the campaign of 1992* (pp. 63–89). New York: The Twentieth Century Fund Press.

Auletta, K. (2004, January 19). Fortress Bush: How the White House keeps the press under control. *The New Yorker,* 52–65.

Bagdikian, B. H. (1997). *The media monopoly* (5th ed.). Boston: Beacon Press.

Bai, M. (2006, May 28). The way we live now: Can bloggers get real? *The New York Times Magazine.* Retrieved June 12, 2006, from http://select.nytimes.com/ search/restricted/article?res=F70711FC3B5A0C7B8EDDAC0894DE404482.

Bantz, C. R. (1997). News organizations: Conflict as a crafted cultural norm. In D. Berkowitz (Ed.), *Social meanings of news: A text-reader* (pp. 123–137). Thousand Oaks, CA: Sage.

Baran, S. J., & Davis, D. K. (1995). *Mass communication theory: Foundations, ferment and future.* Belmont, CA: Wadsworth.

Bauman, S., & Herbst, S. (1994). Managing perceptions of public opinion: Candidates' and journalists' reactions to the 1992 polls. *Political Communication, 11,* 133–144.

Becker, L. B., & Whitney, D. C. (1980). Effects of media dependencies: Audience assessments of government. *Communication Research, 7,* 95–120.

Berkowitz, D. (1990). Refining the gatekeeper metaphor for local television news. *Journal of Broadcasting & Electronic Media, 34* (1), 55–68.

Blendon, R. J., Young, J. T., Brodie, M., Morin, R., Altman, D. E., & Brossard, M. (1998). Did the media leave the voters uninformed in the 1996 election? *Harvard International Journal of Press/Politics, 3* (2), 121–130.

Bleske, G. L. (1991). Ms. Gates takes over: An updated version of a 1949 case study. *Newspaper Research Journal, 12* (4), 88–97.

Breed, W. (1955). Social control in the newsroom: A functional analysis. *Social Forces, 33,* 326–355. Reprinted in D. Berkowitz (Ed.), *Social meanings of news: A text-reader* (pp. 107–122). Thousand Oaks, CA: Sage.

Broder, D. (1990). Convocation address. Retrieved February 13, 2007, from http://www.colby.edu/academics_cs/goldfarb/lovejoy/recipients/david-broder.cfm.

Broder, D. S. (1987). *Behind the front page: A candid look at how the news is made.* New York: Simon & Schuster.

Buell, E. H. (2000). The changing face of the New Hampshire primary. In W. G. Mayer (Ed.), *In pursuit of the White House 2000: How we choose our presidential nominees* (pp. 87–144). New York: Seven Bridges Press.

Bumiller, E., & Halbfinger, D. M. (2004, October 14). Bush and Kerry, feeling like winners, go to Las Vegas. *The New York Times,* p. A21. Retrieved July 7, 2006, from Lexis-Nexis.

Busch, A. E. (2000). New features of the 2000 presidential nominating process: Republican reforms, front-loading's second wind, and early voting. In W. G. Mayer (Ed.), *In pursuit of the White House 2000: How we choose our presidential nominees* (pp. 57–86). New York: Seven Bridges Press.

Cappella, J. N., & Jamieson, K. H. (1997). *Spiral of cynicism: The press and the public good.* New York: Oxford University Press.

Chaffee, S. H., Zhao, X., & Leshner, G. (1994). Political knowledge and the campaign media of 1992. *Communication Research, 21,* 305–325.

Charting the Campaign (2004, November 1). *The Washington Post.* Retrieved July 24, 2006, from http://www.washingtonpost.com/wp-srv/politics/elections/2004/charting.html.

Clarke, P., & Fredin, E. (1978). Newspapers, television and political reasoning. *Public Opinion Quarterly, 42,* 143–160.

Clymer, A. (2001, December). Better campaign reporting: A view from the major leagues. *PS: Political Science and Politics, 34,* 779–784.

Cohen, B. C. (1963). *The press and foreign policy.* Princeton, NJ: Princeton University Press.

Commission on Presidential Debates. (1976, October 6). *The second Carter-Ford presidential debate.* Retrieved August 5, 2006, from http://www.debates.org/pages/trans76b.html.

Committee of Concerned Journalists. (2004). *Journalists not satisfied with their performance in the campaign: A survey of members of the Committee of Concerned Journalists.* Washington, DC: Author.

Comstock, G., & Scharrer, E. (1999). *Television: What's on, who's watching, and what it means.* San Diego, CA: Academic Press.

Cornfeld, M. (2006). Going broadband, getting netwise: The cyber-education of John Kerry and other political actors. In L. J. Sabato (Ed.), *Divided states of America: The slash and burn politics of the 2004 presidential election* (pp. 207–220). New York: Pearson Education.

Cornfeld, M., & Seiger, J. (2004). The net and the nomination. In W. G. Mayer (Ed.), *The making of the presidential candidates 2004* (pp. 199–228). Lanham, MD: Rowman & Littlefield.

Covington, C. R., Kroeger, K., Richardson, G., & Woodard, J. D. (1993). Shaping a candidate's image in the press: Ronald Reagan and the 1980 presidential election. *Political Research Quarterly, 46,* 783–798.

Cronkite, W. (1998). Reporting presidential campaigns: A journalist's view. In D. Graber, D. McQuail, & P. Norris (Eds.), *The politics of news: The news of politics* (pp. 57–69). Washington, DC: Congressional Quarterly Press.

Crossen, C. (2004, October 19). "The Boys on the Bus": A pioneering look at political journalism retains its appeal seven elections on. *The Wall Street Journal Online.* Retrieved October 19, 2004, from http://online.wsj.com/article_email/article_print/0,,SB109811706450248109-IhjeoNhalah3npyobX mHba6Em4,00 .html.

Crouse, T. (1973). *The boys on the bus: Riding with the campaign press corps.* New York: Random House.

Culbertson, H. M. (1983). Three perspectives on American journalism. *Journalism Monographs, 83.*

Dautrich, K., & Hartley, T. H. (1999). *How the news media fail American voters: Causes, consequences, and remedies.* New York: Columbia University Press.

Davis, R. (1992). *The press and American politics: The new mediator.* White Plains, NY: Longman.

Dawidziak, M. (2004, November 4). TV networks resist urge to call races before they're over. *Cleveland Plain Dealer,* p. A13. Retrieved August 7, 2006, from LexisNexis.

Didion, J. (1988, October 27). Insider baseball. *New York Review of Books,* 19.

Doppelt, J. C., & Shearer, E. (1999). *Nonvoters: America's no-shows.* Thousand Oaks, CA: Sage.

Edsall, T. B., & Cohen, S. (2004, January 30). $31 million spent on Bush's campaign; President outspends Democrats, raised record $131 million. *The Washington Post,* p. A6. Retrieved August 2, 2006, from LexisNexis.

Entman, R. (1993). Framing toward a clarification of a fractured paradigm. *Journal of Communication, 43* (4), 51–58.

Eskenazi, M. (2000). A primer on the primaries. *Time.com.* Retrieved February 2, 2000, from www.time.com/time/daily/special/look/0,2633,37744,00.html.

Falk, E., & Aday, S. (2000, December 20). *Are voluntary standards working? Candidate discourse on network evening news programs.* The Annenberg Public Policy

Center. Retrieved July 30, 2003, from http://www.appcpenn.org/political/freetime/2000-general-report-final.htm.

Farhi, P. (2004, September 16). For media on campaign trail, little access to candidates. *The Washington Post*, p. A9. Retrieved September 16, 2004, from http://www.washingtonpost.com/ac2/wp-dyn/A24541-2004Sep15.

Farnsworth, S. J., and Lichter, S. R. (2003). *The nightly news nightmare: Network television's coverage of U.S. presidential elections, 1988–2000*. Lanham, MD: Rowman & Littlefield.

Farnsworth, S. J., & Lichter, S. R. (2007). *The nightly news nightmare: Television's coverage of U.S. presidential elections, 1988–2004*. Lanham, MD: Rowman & Littlefield.

Fiedler, T. (1992). The character issue: A political writer's perspective. *Political Psychology, 13*, 553–563.

Fishman, M. (1997). News and nonevents: Making the visible invisible. In D. Berkowitz (Ed.), *Social meaning of news: A text-reader* (pp. 210–229). Thousand Oaks, CA: Sage.

Frankovic, K. A., and McDermott, M. L. (2001). Public opinion in the 2000 election: The ambivalent electorate. In G. M. Pomper (Ed.), *The election of 2000* (pp. 73–91). New York: Chatham House/Seven Bridges Press.

Funkhouser, G. R. (1973). The issues of the sixties: An exploratory study in the dynamics of public opinion. *Public Opinion Quarterly, 37*, 62–75.

Gans, H. J. (1979). *Deciding what's news: A study of CBS Evening News, NBC Nightly News, Newsweek and Time*. New York: Vintage.

Gans, H. J. (1998). What can journalists actually do for American democracy? *Harvard International Journal of Press/Politics, 3* (4), 6–12.

Germond, J. W. (1999). *Fat man in a middle seat: Forty years of covering politics*. New York: Random House.

Gilberg, S., Eyal, C., McCombs, M., & Nicholas, D. (1980). The State of the Union address and the press agenda. *Journalism Quarterly, 57*, 584–588.

Gilbert, R. B. (1986). Press libertarianism's toll on democracy. *Journal of Social, Political and Economic Studies, 11*, 174–188.

Gitlin, T. (1980). *The whole world is watching: Mass media in the making and unmaking of the new left*. Berkeley: University of California Press.

Glasser, T. L. (1999). The idea of public journalism. In T. L. Glasser (Ed.), *The idea of public journalism* (pp. 3–18). New York: Guilford Press.

Glionna, J. M. (2004, January 24). Primaries bring big-name news to small paper. *Los Angeles Times*. Retrieved January 26, 2004, from http://www.latimes.com/news/custom/showcase/la-na-monitor24jan24.story.

Graber, D. A. (1988). *Processing the news: How people tame the information tide* (2nd ed.). New York: Longman.

Grossman, M. B., & Kumar, M. J. (1979). The White House and the news media: The phases of their relationship. *Political Science Quarterly, 94* (1), 37–53.

Guttenplan, D. D. (1992a, July/August). Campaign coverage: Out of it. *Columbia Journalism Review*. Retrieved April 17, 2006, from http://archives.cjr.org/year/92/4/perot.asp.

Guttenplan, D. D. (1992b, November/December). Covering a runaway campaign. *Columbia Journalism Review*. Retrieved May 5, 2000, from www.cjr.org/year/92/6/election.asp.

Hagen, M. G., & Mayer, W. G. (2000). The modern politics of presidential selection: How changing the rules really did change the game. In W. G. Mayer (Ed.), *In pursuit of the White House 2000: How we choose our presidential nominees* (pp. 1–55). New York: Seven Bridges Press.

Hanson, C. (1996, May/June). Lost in Never-Never Land. *Columbia Journalism Review*. Retrieved May 12, 2001, from http://www.cjr.org/year/96/3/primary.asp.

Hart, R. P. (2000). The unheralded functions of campaign news. In S. Chambers & A. Costain (Eds.), *Deliberation, democracy, and the media* (pp. 85–105). Lanham, MD: Rowman & Littlefield.

Herman, E. S., & Chomsky, N. (1988). *Manufacturing consent: The political economy of the mass media*. New York: Pantheon Books.

Institute of Politics, John F. Kennedy School of Government, Harvard University (Eds.) 2006. *Campaign for president: The managers look at 2004*. Lanham, MD: Rowman & Littlefield.

Iyengar, S. (2005). Speaking of values: The framing of American politics. *The Forum, 3* (3), Article 7. Retrieved July 8, 2006, from http://pcl.stanford.edu/common/docs/research/iyengar/2005/speaking.pdf.

Jamieson, K. H. (1993). The subversive effects of a focus on strategy in news coverage of presidential campaigns. In *1-800-President: The report of the Twentieth Century Fund Task Force on television and the campaign of 1992* (pp. 35–61). New York: The Twentieth Century Fund Press.

Jamieson, K. H., & Campbell, K. K. (1992). *The interplay of influence: News, advertising, politics, and the mass media* (3rd ed.). Belmont, CA: Wadsworth.

Janowitz, M. (1975). Professional models in journalism: The gatekeeper and the advocate. *Journalism Quarterly, 52,* 618–626, 662.

Johnstone, J., Slawski, E. J., & Bowman, W. W. (1972). The professional values of American newsmen. *Public Opinion Quarterly, 36,* pp. 522–540.

Johnstone, J. W. C., Slawski, E. J., & Bowman, W. W. (1976). *The news people: A sociological portrait of American journalists and their work*. Urbana: University of Illinois Press.

Just, M. R., Crigler, A. N., Alger, D. E., Cook, T. E., Kern, M., & West, D. M. (1996). *Crosstalk: Citizens, candidates and the media in a presidential campaign*. Chicago: University of Chicago Press.

King, A. (2001a, May 23). Why poor turn-out points to a healthy democracy. *Gallup Poll News Service*. Retrieved June 16, 2001, from www.gallup.com/poll/releases/pr010523b.asp.

King, A. (2001b, May 24). Election analysis. *Gallup Poll News Service*. Retrieved June 16, 2001, from www. gallup.com/poll/releases/pr010524d.asp.

King, P. (1997). The press, candidate images, and voter perceptions. In M. McCombs, D. Shaw, & D. Weaver (Eds.), *Communication and democracy: Exploring the intellectual frontiers in agenda-setting theory* (pp. 29–40). Mahwah, NJ: Lawrence Erlbaum Associates.

Klein, J. (2006, April 17). Pssst! Who's behind the decline of politics? [Consultants.] *Time,* 64–66, 69.

Kohut, A. (1999, November/December). Why voters avoid the story. *Columbia Journalism Review*. Retrieved March 24, 2001, from www.cjr.org/year/99/6/kohut/asp.

Kovach, B., & Rosenstiel, T. (2001a). *The elements of journalism: What newspeople should know and the public should expect.* New York: Crown Publishers.

Kovach, B., & Rosenstiel, T. (2001b, January/February). Campaign lite: Why reporters won't tell us what we need to know. *The Washington Monthly Online.* Retrieved January 29, 2002, from www.washingtonmonthly.com/features/2001/0101.kovach.rosenstiel.html.

Kurtz, H. (2004, October 18). "Balance" in a spinning world. *The Washington Post,* p. C1. Retrieved October 18, 2004, from http://www.washingtonpost.com/ac2/wp-dyn/A40668-2004Oct17.

Kurtz, H. (2005, October 16). Sparring between McClellan and reporters escalates. *The Washington Post,* p. A6. Retrieved May 13, 2006, from http://pqasb.pqarchiver.com/washingtonpost/access/911974731.html.

Lavrakas, P. J. (1991). Introduction. In P. J. Lavrakas & J. K. Holley (Eds.), *Polling and presidential election coverage* (pp. 9–18). Newbury Park, CA: Sage.

Lewis, M. (1997). *Trail fever: Spin doctors, rented strangers and thumb wrestlers on the road to the White House.* New York: Vintage.

Lichter, S. R., & Lichter, L. S. (2000). Campaign 2000 final: How TV news covered the general election campaign. *Media Monitor, 14* (6). Retrieved February 23, 2001, from www.cmpa.com/mediaMonitor/MediaMonitorArchive.htm.

Lightman, D., & Halloran, L. (2000, November 2). The Florida squeeze: "Nice guys" Lieberman, Cheney take up traditional VP attack roles. *The Hartford Courant,* p. A1. Retrieved August 6, 2006, from http://www.courant.com.

Lippmann, W. (1997). *Public opinion.* New York: Free Press Paperbacks. (Original work published 1922.)

Lopez-Escobar, E., Llamas, J. P., McCombs, M., & Lennon, F. R. (1998). Two levels of agenda setting among advertising and news in the 1995 Spanish elections. *Political Communication, 15,* 225–238.

Lowery, S. A., & DeFleur, M. L. (1995). *Milestones in mass communication research: Media effects* (3rd ed.). White Plains, NY: Longman.

Lyman, R. (2004, September 19). Desperately seeking Dick Cheney. *The New York Times.* Retrieved September 21, 2004, from http://www.nytimes.com.

Mann, T. E. , & Orren, G. R. (1992). To poll or not to poll . . . and other questions. In T. E. Mann & G. R. Orren (Eds.), *Media polls in American politics* (pp. 1–18). Washington, DC: Brookings Institution.

McChesney, R. W. (2004). *The problem of the media: U.S. communication politics in the 21st century.* New York: Monthly Review Press.

McCombs, M. (1994). News influence on our pictures of the world. In J. Bryant & D. Zillman (Eds.). *Media effects: Advances in theory and research.* Hillsdale, NJ: Lawrence Erlbaum Associates.

McCombs, M., & Bell, T. (1996). The agenda-setting role of mass communication. In M. Salwen & D. Stacks (Eds.), *An integrated approach to communication theory and research* (pp. 93–110). Mahway, NJ: Lawrence Erlbaum Associates.

McCombs, M. E., & Shaw, D. L. (1972). The agenda-setting function of the mass media. *Public Opinion Quarterly, 36,* 176–187.

McLeod, J. M., Glynn, C. J., & McDonald, D. G. (1983). Issues and images: The influence of media reliance in voting decisions. *Communication Research, 12,* 3–34.

Media get it (mostly) right. (2004, November 4). *San Francisco Chronicle*, p. B12. Retrieved August 7, 2006, from LexisNexis.

Mencher, M. (1997). *News reporting and writing.* (7th ed.). Madison, WI: Brown & Benchmark.

Mnookin, S. (2000a, September). The charm offensive. *Brill's Content, 3* (7), 76–81, 128.

Mnookin, S. (2000b, October). In the crowd: Spice Girls on the bus. *Brill's Content, 3* (8), 33.

Moore, D. W. (2000, November 7). Major turning points in the 2000 election: Primary season, party conventions, and debates. *The Gallup Organization poll analyses.* Retrieved December 5, 2000, from www.gallup.com/poll/releases/pr001107c.asp.

Moscovici, S. (1991). Silent majorities and loud minorities. In J. A. Anderson (Ed.), *Communication Yearbook/14* (pp. 298–308). Newbury Park, CA: Sage.

Neal, T. (1999, November 5). Bush falters in foreign policy quiz; Asked by TV reporter to name leaders, candidate connects on 1 of 4. *The Washington Post.* Retrieved July 3, 2006, from LexisNexis database.

Neuman, W. R., Just, M. R., & Crigler, A. N. (1992). *Common knowledge.* Chicago: University of Chicago Press.

Newport, F. (2000, January 13). Bush and Gore maintain leads for their party's nomination. *The Gallup Organization poll analyses.* Retrieved January 15, 2000, from www.gallup.com/poll/releases/pr/000113.asp.

Norris, P., Curtice, J., Sanders, D., Scammell, M., & Semetko, H. A. (1999). *On message: Communicating the campaign.* London: Sage.

Overholser, G. (2004, June 24). Press criticism: Left, right and within. *Journalism Junction.* Retrieved June 25, 2004, from http://www.poynter.org.

Patterson, T. E. (1993). Let the press be the press: Principles of campaign reform. In *1-800-President: The report of the Twentieth Century Fund Task Force on television and the campaign of 1992* (pp. 91–109). New York: The Twentieth Century Fund Press.

Patterson, T. E. (1994). *Out of order.* New York: Vintage Books.

Patterson, T. E., & McClure, R. D. (1976). *The unseeing eye: The myth of television power in national elections.* New York: G. P. Putnam's Sons.

Perlmutter, D. D. (2006, May 26). Political blogs: The new Iowa? *The Chronicle of Higher Education*, B6–B8.

Petrocik, J. R. (1995). Reporting campaigns: Reforming the press. In J. A. Thurber and C. J. Nelson (Eds.), *Campaigns and elections American style* (pp. 126–137). Boulder, CO: Westview Press.

Petty, R. E., Priester, J. R., & Briñol, P. (2002). Mass media attitude change: Implications of the elaboration likelihood model of persuasion. In J. Bryant and D. Zillman (Eds.), *Media effects: Advances in theory and research* (2nd ed.) (pp. 155–198). Mahwah, NJ: Lawrence Erlbaum Associates.

Pinkleton, B. E., Austin, E. W., & Fortman, K. K. J. (1998). Relationships of media use and political disaffection to political efficacy and voting behavior. *Journal of Broadcasting & Electronic Media, 42*, 34–49.

Project for Excellence in Journalism. (2000). *In the public interest? A content study of early press coverage of the 2000 presidential campaign.* Retrieved December 5, 2001, from www.journalism.org/pej/publ_research/election1.html.

Project for Excellence in Journalism. (2004a, July 12). *Character and the campaign: What are the master narratives about the candidates in 2004 and how is the public reacting to them?* Retrieved December 2, 2004, from http://www.journalism.org/pej/node/168.

Project for Excellence in Journalism. (2004b, October 27). *The debate effect: How the press covered the pivotal period of the 2004 presidential campaign.* Retrieved December 2, 2004, from http://www.journalism.org/pej/node/163.

Ramsden, G. P. (1996). Media coverage of issues and candidates: What balance is appropriate in a democracy? *Political Science Quarterly, 111* (1), 65–81.

Rasmussen Reports. (2004, October 24). *Week-by-Week Numbers.* Retrieved August 2, 2006, from http://www.rasmussenreports.com/Weekly_Tracking_Updates.htm.

Reese, S. D., & Danielian, L. H. (1991). Intermedia influence and the drug issue: Converging on cocaine. In D. L. Protess & M. McCombs (Eds.), *Agenda setting: Readings on media, public opinion, and policy making* (pp. 237–249). Hillsdale, NJ: Lawrence Erlbaum Associates.

Reynolds, M., & Chen, E. (2004, October 15). Bush camp's friendly overtures may belie case of jitters. *Los Angeles Times.* Retrieved October 18, 2004, from http://www.latimes.com/news/custom/showcase/la-na-fear15oct15,0,6241278.

Rich, C. (2000). *Writing and reporting news: A coaching method* (3rd ed.). Belmont, CA: Wadsworth.

Rieder, R. (1996, April). No wonder they're cynical. *American Journalism Review.* Retrieved April 17, 2006, from http://www.ajr.org/article_printable.asp?id=40.

Rivlin, A. (1999, September 11). First, kill all the pollsters. *The National Journal, 31* (37), 2572. Retrieved February 23, 2001, from http://web.lexis-nexis.com.

Robinson, M. J. (1974). The impact of the televised Watergate hearings. *Journal of Communication, 24,* 17–30.

Robinson, M. J. (1981). A statesman is a dead politician: Candidate images on network news. In E. Abel (Ed.), *What's news: The media in American society* (pp. 159–186). San Francisco: Institute for Contemporary Studies.

Robinson, M. J., & Sheehan, M. A. (1983). *Over the wire and on TV: CBS and UPI in campaign '80.* New York: Russell Sage Foundation.

Rogers, E. M., Dearing, J. W., & Chang, S. (1991). AIDS in the 1980s: The agenda-setting process for a public issue. *Journalism Monographs, 126.*

Rosen, J. (1999). *What are journalists for?* New Haven, CT: Yale University Press.

Rosenstiel, T. (1994). *Strange bedfellows: How television and the presidential candidates changed American politics, 1992.* New York: Hyperion.

Roth, A. L. (2005). "Pop quizzes" on the campaign trail: Journalists, candidates, and the limits of questioning. *Harvard International Journal of Press/Politics, 10* (2), 28–46.

Rothenberg, S. (2000, June 21). Are reporters ready to even up the presidential race? CNN.com. Retrieved July 16, 2000, from www.cnn.com/2000/ALLPOLITICS/stories/06/21/rothenberg.column/index.html.

Ryfe, D. M. (2005, Winter). Deliberation and the 2004 presidential election. *Political Communication Report, 15* (1). Retrieved January 20, 2005, from http://www.ou.edu/policom/1501_2005_winter/roundtable_ryfe.htm.

Sabato, L. J. (1991). *Feeding frenzy: How attack journalism has transformed American politics.* New York: The Free Press.

Schattschneider, E. E. (1975). *The semisovereign people: A realist's view of democracy in America.* Fort Worth, TX: Harcourt Brace Jovanovich College Publishers. (Reissued edition; original work published in 1960.)

Sella, M. (2000, September 24). The stiff guy vs. the dumb guy. *The New York Times Magazine,* 72–80, 102.

Shaw, D. (2004a, February 14). Administration adept at keeping journalists at bay. *Los Angeles Times.* Retrieved February 16, 2004, from http://www.latimes.com/news/custom/showcase/cl-ca-shaw15feb15,0,1391601.

Shaw, D. (2004b, September 5). Campaign coverage needs to read between the lines. *Los Angeles Times.* Retrieved September 8, 2004, from http://www.latimes.com/news/custom/showcase/cl-ca-shaw5sep05.column.

Shaw, D. L., & McCombs, M. E. (1977). *The emergency of American political issues: The agenda-setting function of the press.* St. Paul, MN: West Publishing.

Shaw, D. R. (2001). Communicating and electing. In R. P. Hart & D. R. Shaw (Eds.), *Communication in U.S. elections: New agendas* (pp. 1–17). Lanham, MD: Rowman & Littlefield.

Sherman, M. (2000, October 1). Cheney: Uncomfortable on the campaign trail. *The Atlanta Journal and Constitution,* p. 7G. Retrieved June 23, 2006, from LexisNexis .com.

Shoemaker, P. (1984). Media treatment of deviant political groups. *Journalism Quarterly, 61,* 66–75, 82.

Shoemaker, P. J. (1991). *Gatekeeping.* Newbury Park, CA: Sage.

Shoemaker, P. J. (1997). A new gatekeeping model. In D. Berkowitz (Ed.), *Social meanings of news: A text-reader* (pp. 57–62). Thousand Oaks, CA: Sage.

Shoemaker, P., Chang, T. K., & Brendlinger, N. (1987). Deviance as a predictor of newsworthiness: Coverage of international events in the U.S. media. In M. McLaughlin (Ed.), *Communication yearbook, 10* (pp. 348–365). Newbury Park, CA: Sage.

Shoemaker, P. J., & Reese, S. D. (1996). *Mediating the message: Theories of influences on mass media content* (2nd ed.). New York: Longman.

Simon, J. (1996). Media use and voter turnout in a presidential election. *Newspaper Research Journal, 17* (1–2), 25–34.

Skewes, E. A., & Plaisance, P. L. (2005). Who's news? A new model for media coverage of campaigns. *Journal of Mass Media Ethics, 20,* 139–158.

Smith, S. (2004, November 15). Blogging USA: Thinkworld vs. shoutworld. *Editor & Publisher.* Retrieved November 15, 2004, from http://www.editorandpublisher.com/eandp/columns/shoptalk_display.jsp?vnu_content_id=1000719210.

Snider, P. B. (1967). "Mr. Gates" revisited: A 1966 version of the 1949 case study. *Journalism Quarterly, 44,* 419–427.

Soley, L. C. (1992). *The news shapers: The sources who explain the news.* New York: Praeger.

Soloski, J. (1989). News reporting and professionalism: Some constraints on the reporting of news. In D. Berkowitz (Ed.), *Social meanings of news: A text-reader* (pp. 138–154). Thousand Oaks, CA: Sage.

Stepp, C. S. (1992, March). Of the people, by the people, bore the people. *American Journalism Review*. Retrieved August 16, 2004, from http://www.ajr.org.

Steigerwald, B. (2006, September 12). Newsmaker interview: Eric Burns. *The Desert Sun*. Retrieved September 12, 2006, from http://www.thedesertsun.com/apps/pbcs.dll/article?Date=20060912&Category=OPINION&ArtNo=609120315&SectionCat=&Template=printart.

Stovall, J. G., & Solomon, J. H. (1984). The poll as a news event in the 1980 presidential campaign. *Public Opinion Quarterly, 48*, 615–623.

Sundquist, J. L. (1983). *Dynamics of the party system: Alignment and realignment of political parties in the United States*. Washington, DC: Brookings.

Templeton, F. (1966). Alienation and political participation: Some research findings. *Public Opinion Quarterly, 30*, 249–261.

Tuchman, G. (1973). Making news by doing work: Routinizing the unexpected. *American Journal of Sociology, 79* (1), 110–131.

Tuchman, G. (1978). *Making news: A study in the construction of reality*. New York: The Free Press.

Tumulty, B. (2004, September 15). New political group pokes fun at Kerry's football gaffes. *USA Today*. Retrieved February 12, 2007, from http://www.usatoday.com/news/politicselections/nation/president/2004-09-15-kerry-football_x.htm.

Turk, J. V. (1986). Public relations' influence on the news. *Newspaper Research Journal, 7* (4), 15–27.

Volgy, T. J., & Schwarz, J. E. (1984). Misreporting and vicarious political participation at the local level. *Public Opinion Quarterly, 48*, 757–765.

Voters find election a total turnoff. (2001, June 8). *Yahoo! Headlines*. Retrieved June 10, 2001, from uk.news.yahoo.com/010608/80/budf0.html.

Wasserman, E. (2004, November 1). Election 2004 will become a media milestone. *The Miami Herald*. Retrieved November 2, 2004, from http://www.miami.com/mld/miamiherald/news/columnists/edward_wasserman/10066651.htm.

Wayne, S. J. (2000). *The road to the White House 2000: The politics of presidential elections*. Boston: Bedford/St. Martin's.

Weaver, D. H., Beam, R. A., Brownlee, B. J., Voakes, P. S., & Wilhoit, G. C. (2007). *The American journalist in the 21st century: U.S. news people at the dawn of a new millennium*. Mahwah, NJ: Lawrence Erlbaum Associates.

Weaver, D. H., & Wilhoit, G. C. (1996). *The American journalist in the 1990s: U.S. news people at the end of an era*. Mahwah, NJ: Lawrence Erlbaum Associates.

White, D. M. (1950). The "gate keeper": A case study in the selection of news. *Journalism Quarterly, 27*, 383–390.

Whitney, D. C., & Becker, L. B. (1982). "Keeping the gates" for gatekeepers: The effects of wire news. *Journalism Quarterly, 59*, 60–65.

Witcover, J. (1977). *Marathon: The pursuit of the presidency, 1972–1976*. New York: Viking Press.

Wolper, A., & Mitchell, G. (2000, January 31). The haunting: Their past looked perfect, until reporters finally took another look. *Editor & Publisher*, 18–25.

Index

About the Author

Elizabeth A. Skewes is an assistant professor at the University of Colorado at Boulder, where she teaches courses in news writing, news editing, media ethics, media studies, political communication, and research methods. She is the coauthor of a chapter in *News Around the World* by Pamela J. Shoemaker and Akiba A. Cohen, and the author or coauthor of several journal articles. Before attending Syracuse University for her PhD, she was an alumni magazine editor at Dickinson College in Pennsylvania, and a newspaper reporter at the *Tampa Tribune* in Florida and the *Herald-Dispatch* in West Virginia.